I0138760

"This anthology reminds us that as restorative justice practitioners we are at once individual/community healers and social justice movement builders. Ours is a deep calling to decolonize typical systems of oppression and domination to *restor-ganize* in an arc towards justice. Much gratitude is expressed to the authors of this critically important work. The wisdom in their words brings us closer to the authentic indigenous roots of restorative justice."

—**Teiahsha Bankhead**, RJOY Oakland

"After decades of innovation, enthusiasm, and exploration, restorative justice has finally entered its maturity years often sitting side-by-side legislated and structured norms of justice. Only with age comes realization. This anthology dares to raise the mirror of responsibility and realization within the restorative justice movement in the hope that certain actions and reflections can take place for the benefit of next generations. A refreshing reading indeed."

—**Theo Gavrielides**, Founder and Director, Restorative Justice for All International Institute.

"This collection of essays is a timely and much needed look at the restorative justice field through the lens of social movements and social transformation. The accessible, and at times personal, essays raise key questions and lessons for future restorative justice practice in a variety of settings, while the introduction and epilogue offer a rich and comprehensive contextualization of the essayists' critical points within the bigger picture of restorative justice theory and practice. This anthology offers a vision for the future of restorative justice and its pivotal role in social change."

—**Barb Toews**, University of Washington Tacoma

Listening to the Movement

Listening to the Movement

Essays on New Growth and New Challenges in Restorative Justice

EDITED BY

Ted Lewis

AND

Carl Stauffer

FOREWORD BY

Fania E. Davis

CASCADE *Books* • Eugene, Oregon

LISTENING TO THE MOVEMENT
Essays on New Growth and New Challenges in Restorative Justice

Cascade Books
An Imprint of Wipf and Stock Publishers
199 W. 8th Ave., Suite 3
Eugene, OR 97401

www.wipfandstock.com

PAPERBACK ISBN: 978-1-5326-4741-3
HARDCOVER ISBN: 978-1-5326-4742-0
EBOOK ISBN: 978-1-5326-4743-7

Cataloguing-in-Publication data:

Names: Lewis, Ted, editor. | Stauffer, Carl, editor. | Davis, Fania E., foreword.

Title: Listening to the movement : essays on new growth and new challenges in restorative justice / edited by Ted Lewis and Carl Stauffer ; foreword by Fania E. Davis.

Description: Eugene, OR: Cascade Books, 2021. | Includes bibliographical references.

Identifiers: ISBN 978-1-5326-4741-3 (paperback). | ISBN 978-1-5326-4742-0 (hardcover). | ISBN 978-1-5326-4743-7 (ebook).

Subjects: LCSH: Restorative justice. | Reconciliation. | Social justice. | Conflict management.

Classification: HV8677 L25 2021 (print). | HV8677 (ebook).

02/15/21

Contents

Foreword

I AM HONORED AND thrilled to write this foreword to *Listening to the Movement: Essays on New Growth and New Challenges in Restorative Justice*, and in doing so to play a small role in this inaugural conversation about restorative justice as a social justice movement.

A new pattern has emerged: many now view restorative justice as an intervention to transform individuals *and* a movement to transform society. This emerging pattern of seeing ourselves as both social service providers and social movement participants was not imposed by a top-down directive. Self-organizing, it arose ground-up from internal interactions and transforming exchanges among diverse practitioners across varied locales and settings throughout the country.

Further, today, though we live in the Trump era and its xenophobia, misogyny, transphobia, homophobia, Islamophobia, anti-Semitism, racial terror, climate-change denial, militarism, and catastrophic global capitalism, we also live in a time of heightened activism. As in nature, where we find the poison, the antidote appears nearby. Growth and transformation within the restorative justice movement are spawned within an ecosystem of surging social justice activism, whether Black Lives Matter, indigenous rights, transformative justice, LGBTQ, Dreamers, #MeToo, anti-Islamaphobia, abolitionism, gun violence, or climate and environmental justice, food justice, electoral politics, economic justice, white anti-racism, truth-telling, reparations, anti-slavery and anti-lynching memorialization, and more. The groundswell of activism in these times is mind-boggling, without equal in history. Restorative justice is in the mix, transforming and being transformed.

Enormous and stunning body of literature amassed over nearly five decades notwithstanding, *Listening to the Movement* is the first book to explore the idea of restorative justice as a social justice movement. As co-editor Stauffer notes, though we have seen references in the literature since the 1990s to "the restorative justice movement," this is largely a quantitative signifier denoting the expansion of the restorative tent beyond traditional sites of justice and schools to enfold communities, workplaces, prisons, churches, and other settings.[1] This volume, however, signals qualitative change: the restorative justice community's emerging self-image as a *social justice* movement, a modality of both systemic and relational transformations.

Sullivan's and Tifft's *Healing the Foundations of Restorative Justice* (2001; 2005) is an exception; it was the only critical conversation I found in the early 2000s that challenged us to see ourselves as a movement that interrogates and transforms existing systems of domination. Much later, Wadhwa's *Restorative Justice in Urban Schools: Disrupting the School to Prison Pipeline* (2017) skillfully urges us to implement restorative justice as a means of interrupting racial inequity. I make the case in *The Little Book of Race and Restorative Justice: Black Lives, Healing and U.S. Social Transformation* (2019) that history is calling upon activists and restorative justice practitioners to be transformers of both systemic and interpersonal harm, not just one or the other.

The editors and contributors are well-equipped to co-create this book as their bios appearing elsewhere in this volume show. This collection emerged from an initiative where the Zehr Institute hosted two national convenings, and also traveled to six geographical regions in the U.S. and Canada to listen to and learn from 130 practitioners. Further, its twenty contributors all work at the intersections of restorative justice and other movements, whether prison-based, community, education, youth, environmental, gun violence, anti-racism, racial healing, international peacebuilding, and victims' rights.

I learned about restorative justice in the early 2000s, after four decades as a social justice activist, three as a civil rights trial lawyer, and after apprenticing with African indigenous healers. I was elated to discover its healing potential, springing from indigenous roots, as I saw it. Yet for nearly forty years the restorative justice community largely failed to address race, quite surprisingly, since it is people of color who overwhelmingly bear the brunt of the horrific inequities of U.S. hierarchies of power, past and present. This was actually not so surprising, I quickly realized, given the nation's white supremacist historical foundations, still intact and still defiling all aspects of life today. Restorative justice's whiteness was no different from other movements, whether women's, peace, environmental, victim's rights, or others.

However, in the Black Lives Matter era, this is shifting. At a 2011 restorative justice national conference, a small group gathered and resolved to take

1. Personal communication, May 22, 2019.

action to change the troubling whiteness of the movement. This resulted in an unprecedented national conference in 2013 (Toledo) whose express theme was the intersection of racial and restorative justice.

Today, less than a decade after that watershed conference, restorative justice interventions, convenings, research, publications, and curricula explicitly address equity. There are increasing numbers of school-based programs to reduce racial and gender disparities in school discipline and interrupt the school-to-prison pipeline. More and more conferencing programs to reduce disproportionate incarceration of boys and girls of color are emerging. Transformative justice and restorative justice initiatives are responding to intra-community harm with creative community accountability processes that do not rely on the carceral state. We also see increasing numbers of gatherings, research, and publications that explore the intersections of restorative justice with racial and social justice, including the Zehr Institute initiative that engendered this ground-breaking volume.

A dramatic visual embodiment of the transformation was the 2017 National Association of Community and Restorative Justice conference, co-hosted locally by Restorative Justice for Oakland Youth, the organization I co-founded and formerly directed. Being, at that time, the largest and most inclusive gathering in the history of the international restorative justice movement, the conference elevated indigeneity and centered historically marginalized voices based on race, gender, gender expression, age, class, religion, and incarcerated and immigration status. It is no coincidence that much of the transformative impulse originates from the restorative and transformative justice communities of Oakland, the birthplace of the Black Panther Party, an iconic racial and social justice organization founded in 1966.

Importantly, just as restorative justice embraces and advances a new paradigm of justice, it also instantiates a new paradigm of social justice movement.

As participants in the peace movement during the Vietnam War, we were present to one another in ways that were bellicose. Though zealous public proponents of equality, we perpetuated hierarchies of power within our freedom movements. Our male cisgendered leaders were sexist, too often relegating to the sidelines women who typically did the lion's share of the work. We uncritically espoused either/or, right/wrong, and good/bad binaries, reproducing punitive ways of being, and creating division within our ranks. While verbally affirming the importance of collectivity, in fact, we were ego-based and competitive in our interpersonal interactions, replicating the oppressive dynamics of the systems of domination we opposed.

Today's movements are interrogating these outdated patterns. During the 2014–2015 Ferguson protests, the press, frustrated because they could not identify a spokesperson, accused the activists of having a leaderless movement. The youth, predominantly queer black women, boldly responded that the movement was "leader-full," ticking off a long list of names of individuals as examples. This anecdote exemplifies the shift from the old vertical paradigm of movements headed by charismatic leaders to today's emerging horizontal paradigm of movements full of leaders.

This shift resonates with the group-centered leadership approach espoused by Ella Jo Baker, a relatively unsung civil rights luminary who played a key role in the most influential organizations of the freedom movement, particularly the youth-led Southern Negro Coordinating Committee. Baker objected to adult-centered, predominantly male, top-down leadership structures because this disempowered women, youth, and others.

Likewise, as Stauffer and Shah and other contributors to this volume affirm, shared leadership will nurture the restorative justice movement. Our problems are too complex to rely on a single charismatic leader; we need everyone's wisdom. The Circle process exemplifies the new shared leadership model: its communitarian ethos respects all voices and operates on consensus decision-making. Rhodes' pedagogy chapter explores the "radical act" of using circles in university classrooms as a counter-hegemonic process that, drawing out everyone's wisdom, is liberatory in the Freirean sense. Yet, as Stith's chapter about youth restorative justice organizing emphasizes, restorative justice is bigger than a Circle; it is a "social change strategy to . . . reshape society." Importantly, our intentionality in centering the voices and leadership of youth of diverse races and gender expressions and of those most directly impacted by systems of oppression will also nurture the movement as Stith's, ucker's, Elizondo's, and Ross's chapters urge. Another powerful expression of the shared leadership model are the hundreds of diverse and grassroots Peace Committees of Burundi, discussed by Juma.

Further, *Listening to the Movement* teaches that it is not enough to *have* a vision of a justice that heals; we must *be* that vision. Movements of today are asking the question, "Who do we need to *be* to bring forth the transformation we seek?" This augments the old movement paradigm query, "What do we need to *do*?" Several chapters in this volume exhort us to transform ourselves in ways we wish to transform our world. The Oakland-based Movement Strategy Center says by starting in this manner at the end of the story, social movements practice the art of time travel, "accelerating change by embodying and manifesting the values they seek in the world right here and now."[2] The future is now.

2. See Movement Strategy Center, *The Practices of Transformative Movements*, 2.

The vision we embody is of a world whose individuals, groups, norms, and structures no longer dominate, exploit, or harm. This is a communitarian, post-racial capitalist[3] world where everyone's needs are met, everyone lives out their purpose, everyone feels a sense of belonging, and where everyone joyously and humbly makes peace with one another and the Earth, healing both themselves and all their relationships.

Embodying the future means being strategic about creating laboratories within our movement that engender decolonizing structures and approaches that supplant existing systems of domination, particularly racial capitalism, white supremacy, punitive justice, heteropatriarchy, sexism, elitism, ageism, ableism, and—consonant with Serrel's chapter on restorative justice and the earth—human supremacy. Our movement will be immeasurably enhanced by a disciplined and intentional praxis of embodying the values of radical relationality and radical healing and creating "maroon spaces"[4] in schools, communities, prisons, families and other settings that, expanding geometrically in number, will reach a tipping point, break loose from being contained within small populations, and give way to new fractal patterns and new cultural norms.

Fittingly, *Listening to the Movement* features three chapters on race: a bold call to critically examine what it means to be white in America; a description of Coming to the Table's unparalleled work of transforming the historical harm of slavery; and examining restorative justice in education through a critical race theory lens. As the authors urge in the whiteness chapter, to be transformative, the restorative justice community must develop a complex awareness of the nuanced ways in which white individuals perpetuate structural and institutional racism. This chapter calls for nothing less than an identity transformation and renewal process that releases the "harmful, false and fractured ways of understanding ourselves as white people." The chapter on restorative justice in education delivers an excellent critical analysis of the prevailing use of the terms restorative "practices, approaches, or discipline" while inviting us to reclaim the language of "justice" to underscore the centrality of addressing issues of power and inequity in all restorative justice processes. Each chapter

3. Racial capitalism refers to a socioeconomic order in which all social institutions are inextricably bound up with the slave trade and slavery, indigenous land seizure, genocide, and colonization. "The history of capitalism . . . is a history of wages as well as whips, of factories as well as plantations, of whiteness as well as blackness, of 'freedom' as well as slavery" (Johnson and Kelley, "Race, Capitalism, Justice." Boston Review Forum 1, 21–22).

4. Runaway slaves in the Americas formed *maroon communities* where they developed their own culture, government, trade, etc., and sought to live as free people, beyond the control of the slavers and colonial officials.

expresses an unwavering commitment to eradicate the scourge of white supremacy on intrapersonal, interpersonal, intragroup, intergroup, and systems and intergenerational levels.

Ultimately, restorative justice is inspired by a vision of justice decolonized—one that pre-dates and challenges empire, the nation-state, the slave trade, genocide, and racial capitalism. Rooted in indigenous insights affirming humans' equal moral worth and dignity and inherent interrelationship, restorative justice's relational orientation evokes *ubuntu*: I am a person through my relationships. *Ubuntu* also affirms our reciprocal responsibility to one another and to the earth, flowing precisely from our connection. These ancient insights engender what Zehr identifies as the "three Rs of restorative justice:" respect, relationship, and responsibility, the lodestar values that guide and nurture the restorative justice movement.

To emphasize the indigenous ethos of restorative justice, however, is not to sanction cultural appropriation. If restorative justice facilitators wish to incorporate indigenous elements of another culture in their circle practice, for example, respect requires at minimum fully understanding and explaining the meaning of the cultural practice and identifying the individual who authorized its use. That said, *every* human being has indigenous roots, and non-indigenous practitioners might conduct ancestral research to unearth the healing and peacemaking ceremonies and practices of their own traditions.

The rapid spread of restorative justice into spaces, like schools and justice sites, that enact the dynamics of centuries-old systems of domination compels us to develop resilience strategies. One of the most powerful things we can do is hold fast to our values of a shared, visionary and futuristic leadership; embodying radical respect, relationality and responsibility; incarnating a deep anti-racist and anti-heteropatriarchal consciousness; infusing indigenous healing wisdom into our work and lives; and developing a radical critique of racial capitalism.

Listening to the Movement energizes us to continue and amplify its discourse to encompass restorative justice and sexual harm, restorative justice and heteropatriarchy, restorative justice and intersectional feminism, restorative justice and abolitionism, restorative justice and leadership of the formerly incarcerated, restorative justice and intergenerational trauma, restorative justice and food justice, restorative justice and socialism and restorative justice-based truth, racial healing and reparations processes for African-Americans, Native-Americans, Asian-Americans, and Latinx communities. This collection similarly inspires us to build upon the exciting conversation about systems thinking-based social movement theory that Stauffer launches in the Epilogue.

Finally, this book rouses us to build on Umbreit and Lewis's thought-provoking discussion about victims, perhaps querying whether the 1990s principle of victim centrality arises out of the paradigm of seeing restorative justice as a social service and perhaps exploring whether the emerging social movement paradigm prods us to broaden the meaning of "victim" to include historically marginalized persons. And, as Stauffer suggests, possibly even inquiring whether we wish to continue using the term? Further, do our deeper understandings about race today encourage critical thinking about the whiteness of the 1990s victims' rights movement, and how the term "victims" is socially encoded to signify whiteness, even though it is blacks in the United States who are disproportionately harmed by criminal wrongdoing?

Much rich and provocative discussion lies ahead.

As someone who has participated in successive waves of activism continuously since the 1950s, worked as a civil rights trial lawyer for almost three decades, and sat at the feet of African indigenous healers, I have been waiting for this conversation. I'm thrilled it has begun today with the publication of *Listening to the Movement.*

Fania E. Davis

March 2019
Oakland, California

Bibliography

Johnson, Walter, with Robin D. G. Kelley. "Race, Capitalism, Justice." *Boston Review*, Forum 1 (2017) 21–22.

Movement Strategy Center. *The Practices of Transformative Movements.* https://movementstrategy.org/b/wp-content/uploads/2016/07/MSC-Practices_of_Transformative_Movements-WEB.pdf.

Introduction

Restorative Justice

Taking the Pulse of a Movement

Carl Stauffer and Sonya Shah

At the opening of most restorative justice workshops people want to know in a sound bite, "What is restorative justice?" As practitioners, we know that it is impossible to communicate this paradigm shift in the first two minutes, in an hour, or even in a day-long workshop. We know that there is a gradual unfolding of what is learned and that this happens best when people *see it* in a restorative process. We take time together integrating restorative justice as a holistic way to address harm that is rooted in relationships and community. We understand that violence cannot be reduced to addressing isolated incidents. We seek to uncover a deeper root of violence that is connected to trauma, childhood, family, environment, history, and social location. All of this involves the discovery that healing and accountability are rooted in restoring balance to oneself, one's relationships, one's community, and even with nature.

The same must be done in a book. In 2020, we have to expand out of trying to tell a singular history of restorative justice, but articulate and honor the multiple, rich roots of this paradigm shift. We have to acknowledge that restorative justice has multiple histories, and various practices and strands as represented by the following: restorative justice, restorative justice practices, restorative practices, peacemaking, and indigenous concepts of justice that are holistic and reparative but do not use the wording of restorative justice. There is no one process to restorative justice either; different communities use different structures that at their best are birthed locally, be they highly urban and multicultural, or predominantly Maori, or perhaps rural Midwestern.

In our biggest hope for what it can be, restorative justice is an alternative paradigm to build community, address violence, and repair harm that is rooted in community solutions and relationships. It is a paradigm shift, not business-as-usual or simply a new program. It requires us to care deeply for each other; to work towards our intertwined liberation; to not outsource responding to harm to "the state"; to see that when one heals and is accountable, we all become freer; to understand that violence is simultaneously interpersonal and structural *all of the time,* and that every restorative practice and mindset should reflect this inter-relatedness.

This was not always the way restorative justice was defined, particularly in the United States where it is increasingly defined as moving from a *social service* to a *movement.* The term restorative justice was popularized by Howard Zehr[5] to give language to a growing sense that restorative justice was providing a framework for a paradigm shift (a new lens or worldview) in the way societies conceived of justice, especially in contrast to the dominant western justice system predicated on ideologies of punishment and retribution. However, parallel processes are happening across the world that are not called 'restorative justice' but still have its essence. To move towards the broadest inclusivity, we have to blow open any western conception of the word and adapt restorative justice to live into the biggest inclusive dream that includes practice iterations from New Zealand to the Yukon Territory, from the United Kingdom to South Africa. There are differences in our definitions, but there is a glue that holds it all together, namely a community-based practice to heal and repair harm.

Why This Anthology?

The authors of this anthology attempt to dispel the bifurcated way of seeing restorative justice. This book represents a range of people who have stepped into the movement in different ways to offer a variety of insights. They offer a widening of the restorative justice movement "tent" that rises above self-imposed, dichotomous thinking, and simultaneously embodies a transformative agenda where individual and systemic transformations are so well integrated as to become indistinguishable. This is a future vision for a transgenerational justice—a much needed corrective to a justice system that tends to singularly focus on the past (who is to blame) and the present (how do we administer pain). As an interdisciplinary movement, restorative justice offers a container

5. Zehr, *Changing Lenses.*

for trauma and memory-healing work, a vehicle for nonviolent social and structural change, a practice for building social networks (community activism, organizing and development), and the guiding values for restorative and indigenous approaches to transitional justice at national and international levels. The restorative justice movement provides hope for a form of justice that satisfies the demands of human 'well-being' (e.g. the respect and equity of all groups of people), and that has far reaching potential to impact multiple practices of justice from local to global levels.

The context for this anthology stems out of a three-year, grant-funded project conducted by the Zehr Institute for Restorative Justice, a program of Eastern Mennonite University. The express aim of this three-year project was to impact the field of restorative justice by channeling our energies into framing and influencing a social justice movement. To this end, the overall project goals were:

- To facilitate dialogue between and with diverse restorative justice communities and related social justice movements;
- To influence the evolution of the restorative justice field as a social justice movement;
- To give exposure to new, innovative restorative justice approaches, applications, and practices;
- To conduct a Listening Process to better understand the current landscape of the restorative justice movement.

Year One: In 2015, the Zehr Institute facilitated a consultation entitled, "RJ: The Next Generation," which was attended by 36 restorative justice thought leaders who were selected from the USA, Canada, UK, Pakistan, and the Democratic Republic of Congo. The consultation team designed a five-part process dealing with the history of restorative justice, identity, race and power issues, "best practices" of restorative justice, and finally, future scenario planning. The core outcome of the event was the utilization of a process called "Transformative Scenario Building"[6] where the group grappled with a matrix of four probable scenarios for the future trajectory of the restorative justice movement, describing the maximum/minimum coherence and the maximum/minimum impact of the restorative justice movement and its progression into the future.

Year Two: In 2016, the Zehr Institute hosted a public conference attended by 170 participants entitled, "RJ in Motion: Building a Movement." The conference expanded on the previous consultation and convened a

6. Kahane, *Transformative Scenario Planning.*

cross-section of practitioners, activists, organizers and academics to further reflect and deliberate on the process of describing, framing, and sustaining a restorative justice movement. The conference focused on the theme of building towards a restorative justice movement. Participants were provided opportunities to reflect on movement-making as well as to learn from colleagues in the restorative justice field. The conference was structured as a uniquely decentralized learning environment for the participants. With over fifty breakout sessions, the format provided space for people to congregate on issues of interest. The conference was preceded by a one-day "Theater of the Oppressed" event, which centered on issues of race, power, and privilege. Altogether, this year-two conference prioritized a diversity of ages, backgrounds, and voices, specifically elevating the youth voice in the process of movement building.

Year Three: In 2017, the Zehr Institute conducted an initiative titled, "Restorative Justice Listening Project"[7] which engaged five locations across the USA and one in Canada. The intention was to get a feel for "the state of the state" of restorative justice, that is, to take the pulse of where we are now as a movement, create a shared roadmap for the future, and offer recommendations to advocates and donors on how to resource and build the restorative justice movement. Also, in 2017–2018, the Zehr Institute engaged in a content creation (writing) process to get the message out about the restorative justice movement to a larger audience through the *publication of an anthology*. Hence, the product at hand.

What Did We Hear from the Listening Project?

As a result of the Listening Project, it is evident that we are now in the midst of a rising tide of interest and a swirl of applied practice around restorative justice writ large, and that many academics, practitioners, educators, community activists, and movement organizers across North America are engaging in restorative justice in some manner. However, as in all social movements, the depth of understanding and coherence of practice remains somewhat elusive. With this exceptional growth in restorative justice, a significant need has arisen to channel the movement with organic visioning and collective action for it to be fully impactful. The challenge is to form structures that have systemic influence at a national, regional and local level, reflective enough to remain true to restorative justice values, principles and practices, and centering a diversity of people

7. Shah, King, and Stauffer, "Restorative Justice Listening Project."

engaging in restorative justice, rather than asserting a top-down or power-over framework in movement-building itself.

The following seven themes emerged from the listening process and paint the general backdrop of issues to help position and frame this anthology.

1. Four Locations of Restorative Justice. It became clear that there are at least four distinct streams of restorative justice practitioners: those in indigenous and aboriginal settings, those in community-based organizations or activist settings, those in schools and educational environments, and those working with or in legal/criminal systems and institutions. Each of these restorative justice locations are distinct and driven by their historical context. Definitions and practices of restorative justice, language use, and strengths and challenges flow from there, which at times leads to confusion about how to define restorative justice. A more complex and inclusive understanding of restorative justice would include all of these streams of what are variously called restorative justice, restorative justice practices, restorative practices, peacemaking, and circles. In addition, there was a strong collective voice advocating for resources to support indigenous forms of peacemaking and restorative justice.

2. Naming Strengths and Being Honest about Barriers. In the work of justice and activism for social change, we tend to fall into two extremes: either to only talk about our successes and ignore our failures or to only focus on the barriers and obstacles we face and never take time to reflect on what is going well. In the listening sessions, we discovered that the restorative justice field has created the space for its practitioners to be reflective—to carefully assess both the strengths and challenges of our work with genuine honesty. These "reflective spaces" have allowed restorative justice to remain an adaptive-emergent social system according to the following four capacities: to name the need for theory and research development as a necessary corollary to good practice; to question the cooptation of the criminal legal system and its drive for standardization, accreditation, and ultimately a monetized justice process that finally benefits the elite of society; to think creatively and dream big visions of restorative justice being applied in all sectors of society; and to identify our racism, sexism, and classism and the hypocrisy of ascribing to the tenants of restorative justice while treating each other in the movement in harmful ways.

3. Living Our Values as Restorative Justice Practitioners and Organizations. Commonly referred to as 'walking our talk'— this theme emerged repeatedly. At an interpersonal level, this means that practitioners must connect to self, self-awareness, and self-healing as the starting points to link to others and to the work of restorative justice. At the community level, each organization must practice what they 'preach' and espouse restorative justice values within their organization. At a structural level, this means engaging with top-down reform and legislation with ethical integrity and organizing collaborative approaches to change things from the bottom-up.

4. Tensions in Scaling Up and Integrity of Practices. Considerable discussion was held around a number of issues: the co-optation of restorative justice into institutional systems (state, prison, judicial, school); concern about practitioners who are not well trained; pressure from system-based partners for restorative justice to be a quick fix rather than a paradigm shift; and how to scale up with integrity and without losing restorative justice values. The latter was discussed at great length at most of the listening sessions. A tension that captures this issue is the pressure from various stakeholders—systems partners, funders, and even those within the restorative justice community—to offer technical certification in restorative justice to meet the needs of scaling it up. However, this faces a strong resistance from many practitioners who see certification as a threat to authenticity of practice. This is largely because certification access to practice can become the domain of educated professional elites which excludes marginalized practitioners, directly-impacted people, and community wisdom. In other words, certification can be inherently oppressive. There was a strong recommendation to find ways to create strong practitioners without the need for formal accreditation. The positive side to this is to equally value community wisdom and the wisdom of directly-impacted people in relation to technical skills and formal education.

5. The Full Integration of Social Justice Values—Anti-oppression and Specifically Anti-racism—into the Restorative Justice Movement. The Western paradigm of restorative justice was not birthed out of inequity and oppression in the same manner that most social justice movements form and so this question arises in the movement about whether restorative justice is a social justice movement. Two factors have moved restorative justice partially in the direction of social justice: the increased recognition of the indigenous roots of peacemaking as a form of restorative justice and the adoption of restorative justice by practitioners who intersect with various social justice movements because of their identities as people of color or marginalized people. Most practitioners in the listening sessions were clear that the integration of social justice values into restorative justice must be centered by practitioners in the movement. Social justice values must become embedded at every level; the impact of oppression must be understood from every micro-interpersonal circle to the macro design of new restorative justice processes, to resourcing indigenous paradigms of peacemaking, addressing historical harms, and ensuring real diversity in national leadership structures, to name a few things.

6. Structures to Build the Movement: Partnerships, Coalitions, Regional Hubs, National Networks, and a National Fund. Conversations were had at all sites around effective partnership and coalition building. Sites reflected on failed attempts to establish better partnership and coalition structures, and also envisioned successful coalition structures. There is a strong desire to have a decentralized national network that can link the local and regional work and to develop a national fund that supports mid-sized and small regional and local community-based organizations. Most important was for local and regional coalitions and national networks to be characterized as having the following: the core values of collectivity and 'power-with' infused from the micro to macro levels; structures that redistribute power on a regular basis; and formations founded on mutual learning and growth among all stakeholders along the justice spectrum. Participants urged funders and all concerned to support the organic development (which is relationship-based and not institutionally mandated) of local, regional, and national coalitions and networks

7. Sustainable Funding. There was less enthusiasm among the sites to engage in this topic. This could have been due to many factors, one being that participants were interested in delving into content and movement issues since the Listening Project was framed as such. Building connections and networks between funders and organizations was a recommendation shared among all sites. Possible ideas included grassroots organizations working with funders to change the RFP process, better information flow and visibility between funders and grassroots organizations, and inclusivity of the funding community in restorative justice conversations. Many participants were concerned that as restorative justice practitioners, we have not effectively framed our public messaging, and that as a movement, restorative justice needs to tell a better story not just for garnering resources, but also to the end that people (the public) could better understand its scope.

Defining the Issues—Restorative Justice as Western and Indigenous

Even though many of the contributors to this anthology did not participate directly in the Listening Project of 2017, you will note how the seven themes listed above will all be echoed throughout the following chapters. One way to think of this collection is to see it as a window into the *growing pains* of movement that has a lot of new momentum. For this reason, we chose the wording of "new growth and new challenges" to be in the book's subtitle. We are at an interesting crossroads where the movement is undertaking a collective inventory of its mission and vision. One way to understand the currents of our present situation is to revisit the two primary roots of restorative justice and peacemaking, namely indigenous and western. Moving forward, it seems important for us to name and honor the multiple parallel histories of restorative justice. By examining the inter-connectivity of these two streams, we can better understand why the above seven themes are leading us to rethink every aspect of restorative justice in today's world.

The Indigenous Roots of "Restorative Justice"

Many indigenous communities do not use the term restorative justice, but have been doing their variation of it for centuries before the West created a term for it. Indigenous people have multi-varied circle practices of their own that should not be reduced and simplified as one process. As two non-indigenous western practitioners (writing this introduction), it is impossible and presumptuous for us to know or capture the history of "restorative justice" in the indigenous context. Below is a small and humble offering of what we learned in the listening session project.

In indigenous paradigms, justice is embedded in a holistic worldview. In a holistic worldview things are not separated; peacemaking and circle processes are embedded in a way of life, and the *outcome of justice is tied to healing and restoring balance* to oneself, one's relationships and to nature. The four aboriginal participants in British Columbia's listening session came with a strong message that their *justice outcome is holistic healing within an indigenous paradigm*—justice and healing are deeply linked. This was best highlighted by Faith Tait from the Nisga'a Nation of 7000 people who said, "We don't have a word for 'offender' in our language; the word we use means 'un-healed.'" A few participants in the closing circle said that this statement shifted their paradigm on restorative justice. Claire Whelan Sadike from the British Columbia Public Safety Ministry said, "This frame would change the way everyone thinks about that person (the person who has harmed). That is its ultimate overarching goal: to be about justice, repairing harm, and healing people versus punishing and destroying them."

This justice paradigm has to start with healing oneself and then moving outwards. Faith Tait continued, "We have to start with our own self-awareness, which then shapes our health and wellness. We have to understand our own layers of trauma and do our own work. If an unhealed person is facilitating, what are they passing on? You cannot reach out and be a connector if you are not in connection to yourself. Everything has to be reflected restoratively; the way I talk to people and relate to my environment has to show it. Otherwise people won't feel it."

To elaborate on the impact of healing to everyone else involved beyond the person who has caused the harm, Judge Carol Perry of the Navajo Nation described how it is when "you work to repair yourself and everyone is assisting you with that, whether it's the cook who is making fry bread with you or the person helping you to wash your car. Because by assisting you, they get better, too." She went on to explain how westerners stuck in the "good-bad" dichotomy do not understand the fluidity of healing for everyone involved. In the western paradigm, our assumptions are based on a separation between "the person who was harmed" and "the person who harmed," or victim and offender, and we do not see relationships at the center of all justice and healing. Although westerners often know it cognitively, it is difficult for people to internalize and live it in a way that healing and justice are interdependent and relational.

The most common forms of indigenous "restorative justice" known to westerners are in the format of peacemaking circles. Examples include circle processes originating from the Tagish and Tlingit peoples of the Yukon territory as popularized in the western context by practitioners like Kay Pranis, Family Group Conferences that originate from the Maori in New Zealand, and circles from the Sioux and Great Plain Indians. Peacemaking is the traditional Navajo way of addressing harm and resolving conflict. As one of the peacemakers, Thomas, explained, "Peacemaking can be problem solving, conflict resolution or dispute resolution; it can be before, during, or after a conflict." Peacemaking is steeped in Navajo thinking. There is a philosophy with strategies and practices that peacemakers learn in order to facilitate these conflicts. These teachings are rooted in the Navajo worldview which is based on their traditions, beliefs, customs, stories, and songs. Peacemaking is happening with referrals from courts, in schools, and for individual family members.

Indigenous communities characterize their own practices in a variety of ways. Peacemaking is not even an agreed upon term. As Judge Perry of the Navajo Nation said, "Peacemaking is not a Navajo word but a word from the Seneca Indians." She said the Navajo word would be the equivalent of "Talking Something Over." Indigenous people have multi-varied, complex and particular circle practices of their own that should not be reduced and simplified as one process. For example, peacemakers in the Navajo Nation do not use a talking piece and neither do the Maori in New Zealand, while the Tagish and Tlingit do. All three are doing a circle process that is specific to their community.

Moving into the future, it is useful for western practitioners to understand that the circle process originating from the Tagish and Tlingit is one form of circle. If westerners use some other form of circle, they are not "doing circle or restorative justice the wrong way." There is a tendency in the western mindset to learn a practice or skill and then assert that it is *the* way or *the* model. This replicates a colonial mindset and erases the many traditions and nuances of different indigenous circle traditions. It fails to see that at the heart of the circle is not the assertion of a model, but a *way of being together* that is non-hierarchical, interdependent, and holistically embedded in a way of life.

Colonization and Cultural Revival

It is impossible to talk about restorative justice in the indigenous context in the Americas without talking about the impact of genocide on the indigenous life-way. In the Navajo Nation listening session, participants spoke deeply about the impact of genocide and colonization on the Navajo people. The Navajo Nation participants agreed that the Fundamental Law of the Diné (Navajo thinking) needs to be infused in every aspect of Navajo life from coloring books to the law school, and that colonization has created major disruption to knowing the Fundamental Law of the Diné. Roger Begay, a peacemaker, said peacemaking is embedded in them from the beginning in the creation stories. Circle and peacemaking are embedded in the Fundamental Law of the Diné.

Gertrude Lee, Chief Prosecutor of the Navajo Nation said, "It seems like peacemaking should come in early, go outside the court and go into schools and be a permanent active program, because there are so many people who don't have this background. Their background is coming from cell phones, TV and music, and they are not learning this; it is not something that grounds them as a person. So just sticking peacemaking in the court system is just a band-aid. We need to get in there ahead of time. Young people are hungry for it."

Melissa Jackson, a Navajo Technical University (NTU) law student expressed her personal experiences. "I don't think that people really look at how much the treaty [of 1868] pulled the rug from under us. We don't even have coloring books that tell us about the Fundamental Law of the Diné. You have to teach us like we are 5 year olds." Melissa went on to share how circle transformed her. "I've been at NTU for three and half years. I was considered the white girl, since I don't speak Navajo. I was a straight-A student. I used to sit in Justice Yazzie's class and he'd draw the circle and I didn't get it. I'd just say 'I didn't get it, I didn't get it.' Then one day I started to understand it. Once I really understood fundamental law, it changed my life forever, and I take it now to my beadwork and to everything I do. The circle saved my life when my sister died; it was the only thing that got me through. I realize that it's not something you just do but it's something that you become inside of yourself, and all your experiences."

Restorative Justice as a Western Paradigm in North America: Social Service, Paradigm Shift, or Social Movement?

Restorative justice, in its western paradigm origins, was primarily conceived of as a *social service*—a legal diversion process aimed at transforming individuals entangled in the criminal justice system, and with the possible by-product of change within families and communities, too. The reasons for this perception of restorative justice as purely a social service are many: the singular focus on improving practice and its application, little theorizing and research undertaken at the time, and its marginal status in the mainstream of the criminal legal system and society at large.

For example, in the early decades, restorative justice meetings between crime offenders and victims were focused on misdemeanant legal offenses and primarily valued as a more effective mechanism to gather restitution than court-ordered fines, as opposed to restorative justice processes being seen as setting a framework for changing social narratives and building stronger communities in order to transform structures. Or, another example would be how in the early decades, restorative justice in schools primarily focused on using a particular practice as one of a number of approaches to choose from in response to student discipline or misconduct issues, as opposed to being seen as a framework for changing whole school systems, policies, pedagogy, and ultimately educational outcomes. There remains a significant number of professionals in the field who would hold to the definition of restorative justice as one more technical skill-set on the menu of multiple social service options and as such *limiting the focus of restorative justice to interpersonal transformation and thereby disregarding its potential for effecting structural change.*

With the publication of *Changing Lenses*,[8] a seminal work on the theory of restorative justice, the idea of a "paradigm shift"[9] was introduced into the field. Zehr and other key leaders in the field began to conceive of restorative justice practice as having the full potential in its theoretical underpinnings, values, principles, and practices to evoke a philosophical transformation of how the criminal justice system responds to harms. However, at this time the concept of a paradigm shift was locked in a modernist worldview that understood change as a linear, mechanical process of developing a logical "blueprint" that methodically detailed the transplanting of an entire system and all its elemental parts by another completely different system and all its elemental parts. This change process was seen as universal, monumental, and cataclysmic for the criminal justice system being discarded.

The consequences of this idea resulted in a deep polarization within the restorative justice field between those who believed that change could only happen from the inside of the system (reformers) and those who believed that change could only happen from outside of the system (revolutionaries). Reformers concentrate their efforts on new legislation that enables restorative justice to be practiced in the criminal legal system more effectively and efficiently, or they may put their energies into changing legal policies and procedures to be more 'restorative' in nature such as programs that tout "restorative prisons" or "restorative courts."

Revolutionaries, on the other hand, focus their efforts on providing complete diversionary or alternative justice processes that are not dependent on the criminal legal system for sustenance. For example, consider urban restorative justice youth projects that refuse to take any referrals or funds from the courts, or the setting up of police-free zones for youth to settle their own conflicts without any interference from state justice authorities. As a result, each of these groups of self-proclaimed restorative justice change-agents have seen the other as "sellouts" (betrayers of the cause), and as a consequence have often refused to work together. In the end, both of these approaches ultimately failed to delink their identities from the criminal legal system as either a complementary or contrasting response to its change as an institution.

In the last decade, another iteration has occurred where upon restorative justice has evolved into a *social movement* in the United States, recognizable by the populist momentum that is giving meaning to it as a frame

8. Zehr, *Changing Lenses.*

9. Kuhn, *Structure of Scientific Revolutions.*

for social change and cohesion. There has been a recent explosion of new research, theory publications, and practice applications coupled with the voices of communities that were previously marginalized which are now entering the conversation with power and clarity. The restorative justice movement embodies a relational justice lifestyle that invites people to live-right, do-right, and make-right through human connection and community for the sake of the "common good." And, the restorative justice movement now reaches far beyond the conventional criminal legal system with new applications being made in all sectors of society, including family, education,[10] community, religion, business, governance, media, and in expressions of arts and culture. *The focus of the restorative justice movement is to hold in tension both interpersonal and institutional change while at the same time moving towards a cultural shift or societal transformation of how justice is understood and practiced for the future.* This vision proffers a form of justice that refuses to be configured around punishment and state-sanctioned violence as a means for social change. Instead, it embraces a future view that requires justice to be socially constructed in relationships defined by accountability, reparations and healing.

Amidst this evolution, a growing set of voices like Dr. Fania Davis[11] and Scharrar and Davis[12] have been evoking restorative justice as having the potential to grow into a *social justice movement*—a transformative force that addresses healing and accountability at personal and structural levels of society, and not only as applied in the present reality of injustices, but also in dealing with the legacies and aftermaths that have transpired as a result of historical harms in the past.[13] The intent is to integrate social justice and anti-oppression values at every level of restorative justice from its values, to theory, practice, and design. It includes a wide range of interventions from factoring in the impact of oppression as a causative factor of interpersonal harm, to truth and reconciliation processes for racial justice at the structural level, to centering indigenous paradigms of peacemaking and community approaches to wrongdoing that precede western conceptions of restorative justice.

In our current reality, restorative justice is being lived as all of the above— a social service, a paradigm shift, a social movement, *and* a social justice movement. Some treat restorative justice as a tool to address

10. Ginwright, *Hope and Healing.*

11. Davis, *Little Book of Race and Restorative Justice.*

12. Davis and Scharrar, "Reimagining and Restoring Justice."

13. Hooker and Potter-Czajkowski, *Transforming Historical Harms*; Hooker, *The Little Book of Transformative Community Conferencing*; and DeWolf and Geddes, *The Little Book of Racial Healing.*

interpersonal harm that is not embedded in a structural and historical analysis of inequity. At the same time, there is a growing momentum to live out restorative justice as a social justice movement.

What Have We Learned from Other Criminal Justice Reform Movements?

Studying restorative justice in light of penal reform movements in United States history can be quite illuminating. Dr. Dana Greene[14] conducted a ground-breaking research study comparing restorative justice with three major reform efforts in the US: the penitentiary, adult rehabilitation, and parole reform movements. What she discovered was startling. Each of these reform impulses when compared with restorative justice, carried a similarity in the sense of urgency, well-articulated vision, populist language, and commonly designed project/program ideas to test their innovations. However, each of these major movements, unlike restorative justice, unwittingly became an extension of the current criminal legal system and its expansion of social control within a decade of their emergence. Why?

According to Greene, there are two distinctions that have kept restorative justice from being totally co-opted by the system. Firstly, restorative justice has brought in the voice of victim-survivor (harmed) communities, whereas the other three movements focused almost exclusively on the crime offender. Secondly, all three of these other movements were translated into broad-based, comprehensive legislation at a national level within a ten-year period of their inception, whereas restorative justice has not been legislated at a national level and therefore it has been able to retain its autonomy and innovative expression albeit on the marginal edge. Thirdly, we would add that another fundamental difference from past reform efforts has been the sustained and deliberate attention to principles and values as opposed to reliance on technical "quick-fix" formulas. In fact, the two points that Greene makes actually flow from this focus on principles and values. In sum, the centrality of the victim-survivor's voice, the lack of uniform national legislation, and the intentionality in maintaining the integrity of ascribed principles and values are three distinctives that have allowed restorative justice to emerge as a social movement as opposed to being incorporated into the dominant criminal legal system. And, as the movement grows it would behoove us to hold onto these distinctive elements.

Not only have these identified "distinctives" kept restorative justice from being co-opted by the criminal legal system, but they have also

14. Greene, "Repeat Performance."

inadvertently allowed restorative justice to exercise its 'bottom-up' approach to justice, to stay in conversation with other social justice movements (e.g. racial, transformative justice), and build relationships and partnerships with indigenous communities that are shaping cultural change and delivering a holistic justice that could be sustained for years to come.

The Structure of This Book

This anthology exposes the reader to a cross-section of the restorative justice movement and the voices it is magnifying at this current moment in time. In many ways, the garnering of different author identities, ideas, writing styles, sectors of work, language, and cultural worldviews, represents the diversity of the movement in all its color, creativity and, at times, chaotic complexity. And, like all social movements, it is bound to morph and change in significant ways in years to come. We liken this collection of writings to a "snapshot" or some sort of temporary container which is holding multiple, yet disparate narratives of the movement in this iteration of its evolution. This anthology is meant to stimulate debate and dialogue, not to bring consensus or agreement on the issues at hand, and it is into this contested space that we invite you as the reader.

Chapters 1–6 integrate topics of movement building, racial justice, and restorative justice in both educational and community settings. **Chapters 7–10** present a series of critical issues such as restorative justice and the natural environment, addressing gun violence, violence reduction in war zones, and meeting the needs of victim-survivors. Each chapter has its own bibliography at the end of that chapter.

The stage is set and the backdrop unfurled with the opening chapter as authors Rose Elizondo and Jovida Ross engage in a powerful and optimistic conversation that frames a hopeful vision of restorative justice as a healing force that transforms individuals and structures alike, and beckons us into the flow of restorative justice as a social movement that imagines a "bigger we"— the space where restorative justice values, principles, and practices nourish the "common good."

Next, in chapter two, Mika Dashman and five other co-authors articulate a clarion charter, calling all white restorative justice practitioners to take seriously the task of dealing with their own white privilege and how they benefit from dominant systems of white supremacy in this nation. The need for white restorative justice practitioners to educate their own communities to embrace racial justice could not be more relevant, and the authors insist that this internal work will bring the critical consciousness necessary to sustain the restorative justice movement into the future.

Looking to the past, Jill Strauss then takes the reader on a journey, outlining how restorative justice gives credence to the processes of collective memorialization, healing, and transforming of historical harms. Using the 'Coming to the Table' (CTTT) movement as a model of engaging racial justice in a restorative manner, Strauss outlines how the ancestors of those who were enslaved and those who enslaved them have come together to face the past, build relationship, collectively heal and take joint action to deal with the persistent legacies and aftermaths of slavery in the United States.

Providing an example of strong practical application, Daniel Rhodes outlines how he utilizes restorative justice frameworks and practices as a liberatory pedagogy for teaching social work students in the Academy. Using the seminal work of Paulo Friere, the author shows how the use of embodied learning results in emancipatory outcomes and is a form of resistance to the traditional "banking system" approach to education where students are seen as empty vessels just waiting to be filled, as opposed to activated agents of change in the world.

In a fast-paced, radical critique of the conventional educational structures as we know them, Jonathan Stith, in chapter five, centers youth organizing and activism as powerful forms of restorative justice practice at a systemic level. Stith challenges us to think "Bigger than a Circle" in our understanding of the socio-political impact of restorative justice and he calls us to enter into a social healing justice where whole educational systems are transformed in legislation, policy, and funding as youth take the lead.

Moving on, Kathy Evans and her co-authors introduce an application of critical race theory in restorative justice education. The authors offer definitions of the concepts of justice and equity as central pillars to the work of restorative justice in school systems. Defying the current and often singular focus on individual student misconduct, the authors instead propose a model of systems analysis that interrogates the structural impediments that keep students from being educated in a holistic manner. The authors provide concrete examples of what a restorative justice educational setting could look like.

Valerie Serrels applies restorative justice thinking and action to our relationship with the natural environment, ecological destruction, and climate change. She works with the term "radical relationalism," and asks us as readers to imagine with her what it would be like to think of the earth and all living plants and creatures as connected and networked. In this way, all living matter could be seen as critical stakeholders in the restorative justice movement. In other words, how could or should we include the natural world as a "victim-survivor" of human harms?

Next, ethan ucker introduces his chapter on gun violence harm reduction by exploring a decolonization strategy for a firearm harm reduction model in the setting of urban Chicago. As a public health issue, harms stemming from gun violence could benefit from community-based services that operate similar to safety-based harm reduction models related to drug use.

Folding in an international application of restorative justice, Mulanda Juma presents a research study on the movement of local peace committees that spread across Burundi. While predominantly using the language of conflict transformation and peacebuilding, Juma makes a case that the establishment and ongoing presence of these peace committees functioned as a restorative justice approach in preventing and intervening in layers of harms experienced by local communities in that post-war context.

Finally, authors Ted Lewis and Mark Umbreit take us back to a central question in restorative justice work: Are we serving the victim-survivors of harm well? This contribution continues the important discussion surrounding the historical and current efforts to ensure that all those harmed by others are being centered in the restorative justice movement. On one hand, institutionalized forms of restorative justice tend to be offender-centric within a framework of case management. On the other hand, recent trends to broaden out victimhood to communities and offending persons may have unintended consequences for some victim-survivors of serious crimes or harms. What needs more consideration is the question of how restorative justice will interface with victim movements and services, be them within the traditional justice system or within realms of restorative work.

We trust you will enjoy this reading journey into the burgeoning restorative justice movement.

Bibliography

Davis, F. *The Little Book of Race and Restorative Justice: Black Lives, Healing, and US Social Transformation.* New York, NY: Skyhorse, 2019.

Davis, F., and J. Scharrar. "Reimagining and Restoring Justice: Toward A Truth and Reconciliation Process to Transform Violence Against African-Americans in the United States." In *Transforming Justice, Lawyers and the Practice of Law*, edited by M. Silver. Durham, NC: Carolina Academic, 2017.

DeWolf, T., and J. Geddes. *The Little Book of Racial Healing: Coming to the Table for Truth-Telling, Liberation, and Transformation.* New York: Skyhorse, 2017.

Ginwright, S. *Hope and Healing in Urban Education—How Urban Activists and Teachers Are Reclaiming Matters of the Heart.* New York: Routledge. 2016.

Greene, D. "Repeat Performance: Is Restorative Justice Another Good Reform Gone Bad?" *Contemporary Justice Review: Issues in Criminal, Social, and Restorative Justice* 16 (2013) 359–90.

Hooker, D. *The Little Book of Transformative Community Conferencing*. New York: Skyhorse, 2016.

Hooker, D., and A. Potter-Czajkowski. *Transforming Historical Harms*. A publication of Coming to the Table (CTTT), in partnership with the Center for Justice & Peacebuilding at Eastern Mennonite University, 2012.

Kahane, A. *Transformative Scenario Planning*. San Francisco: Berrett-Koehler, 2012.

Kuhn, T. *The Structure of Scientific Revolutions*. Chicago: University of Chicago Press, 1962.

Shah, S., S. King, and C. Stauffer. "Restorative Justice Listening Project—Final Report." Zehr Institute for Restorative Justice, a program of the Center for Justice and Peacebuilding at Eastern Mennonite University, Harrisonburg, Virginia, USA, 2017. http://zehr-institute.org/images/Restorative-Justice-Listening-Project-Final-Report.pdf.

Zehr, H. *Changing Lenses: A New Focus for Crime and Justice*. Scottsdale, PA: Herald, 1990.

Prelude

"We're Just Doing Our Jobs"

A Provocation for Restorative Justice Professionals

ETHAN UCKER

We study restorative justice, and demonstrate our mastery of its principles and practices. We receive certificates. We graduate from recently accredited master's degree programs. We attend workshops and summer institutes. Registration fees are steep, but the cost is worth it because the credentials we acquire make us attractive candidates for the jobs we covet.

On email listservs we are excited to announce that our institutions are now hiring. Restorative Justice Community Coordinator; Restorative Practices Coach; Circle Keeper Team Leader; RJ and Community Engagement Specialist; RJ Liaison. Qualified candidates only. Most of the positions we advertise did not exist five years ago.

We are contracted to install peace rooms in public high schools from which Black and Brown students have been getting suspended and arrested. We have a ceremony to cleanse the space. We invite the Junior Reserve Officers' Training Corps instructors who work in the classroom next door and the armed police officers who patrol the school's hallways to smudge sage with us.

The principal calls the students we are working with "the usual suspects" or "the frequent fliers." He prints out charts to show us evidence that their attitudes are improving. He commends us for our work. They are more docile now; they are more compliant. He knows many other principals who are looking for a program like ours; he asks us to consider rolling it out district-wide. "You could really corner the market," he tells us.

The governor sits in a talking circle with young Black men who are incarcerated at a youth prison. He holds an eagle feather in his hand to use as a talking piece, and he tries to pronounce 'Māori.' Journalists take photographs. At a press conference, the governor announces plans to make the state's juvenile justice system more restorative.

A private philanthropic foundation is convinced by our outcomes. The foundation awards us a grant to offer restorative justice-based diversion to 18- to 24- year-olds who are facing nonviolent drug charges. When we tell two 16-year-olds from down the block that they are no longer eligible to participate in our programming, they seem hurt. Hopefully in two years they will be picked up on drug charges and referred to us by the judge so that we can have a relationship with them again. As they leave our office they bump into the new Restorative Justice Supervisor and the new Case Manager and the new Administrative Assistant that we added to our staff with the grant monies.

We get fingerprinted, submit background check forms, take drug tests so that we can work in the jail. We do not have any felonies and we do not use drugs and we have never been incarcerated, and thus we are qualified to work with people who have felonies and who use drugs and who are incarcerated.

At our university research centers, we help non-profit organizations quantify the impact of their restorative justice work. We help them design diagnostic rubrics to track young Black and Brown people's behavior and to measure the ways their behavior changes during a 12-week program cycle. When a young person writes a poem or receives a GED or attends a peace circle or gets arrested or fails a drug test, a staff member from the organization documents it on a form. We feed the information from the forms into a database. The database is swelling. We analyze the data we have collected and publish articles about best practices in restorative justice in peer-reviewed journals. We hope to advance our careers. We eye newly minted tenure-track positions.

We purchase $200 tickets for annual fundraising galas. Executive directors give awards to mayors, state's attorneys, wardens who champion restorative justice. A young Black man is introduced: being part of a restorative justice process helped him turn his life around. He is a success story. He is very articulate. He tells us about growing up poor, without a father, gravitating to the streets, cycling in and out of jail. While he speaks we eat salmon and spaghetti. He shares about a childhood marred by abuse. His pain is made available for our consumption. It is our food, we are slurping it down with the noodles. We clap when the meal is over. We feel satisfied, our stomachs full to bursting. We are contributing to a good cause.

We are experts. We allow ourselves to be called upon for our expertise. We are uniquely qualified to address harm—not just any random person can do what we do. There are a lot of conflicts and harms, and so there is a high demand for our services. We are independent consultants, strategists, entrepreneurs. We form LLCs. We print fliers advertising our upcoming webinars. We facilitate restorative justice trainings at detention centers, police precincts, churches, probation departments, group homes. We submit invoices.

The professional association of which we are members convenes its biennial conference at the downtown Marriott. Attendance has more than doubled from the conference two years ago, and it has swelled nearly fourfold from the conference two years before that. At vendor tables set up in the lobby, we sell our RestorativeChat™ and Safe Space® toolkits. ToolUp before you Circle Up! Buy Restorative Practices Tools Today! The Tibetan Buddhist singing bowls we sell will help you engage clients in restorative activities. We offer our products at a special discount to conference attendees; we will ship them directly to your school or to your program site. Emphasizing that our services are based on Indigenous-inspired principles enhances their marketability and their retail potential. We sell out of our We Will Heal You™© curricula and our restorative justice sweatshirts. Business is booming.

1

Building a Bigger We

A Conversation about Restorative Justice Movement Building

Rose Elizondo and Jovida Ross

What follows is a written conversation between us. The seeds of this conversation were planted on a five-hour drive along Highway 99. We drove from Oakland, California, to a state prison in the Central Valley to participate in a restorative circle. This stretch of highway is California's prison corridor: 15 of the state's 34 prisons stand along this roadway in fields where farm-workers once harvested produce. Seeing busses transporting incarcerated people to these prisons is like witnessing a modern-day "middle passage."[1]

John Steinbeck's novel, *The Grapes of Wrath*, was inspired by what he saw in this valley; the novel explores the injustices of the 1930s to convey deeper lessons. The prisons that now fill this landscape create a new generation of grapes of wrath. The punitive practices of the criminal legal system[2] in the United States harm individuals, families, and communities.[3] The criminalization of poverty and trauma, along with biases in law

1. For an exploration of how mass incarceration mirrors and extends the practice of slavery in the United States, see Alexander, *The New Jim Crow*.

2. We intentionally use the phrase *criminal legal system*, rather than *criminal justice system*, because the current system perpetuates so much injustice. We intend this to refer to all aspects of law enforcement, including policing, prosecution, sentencing, incarceration, and parole.

3. For more on how incarceration is harmful to families and communities, see deVuono-Powell et al., *Who Pays?;* and Wagner et al., *Mass Incarceration*.

enforcement, create a disproportionate impact on communities of color, along with transgender and queer people,[4] making visible the patterns of oppression that our communities face in daily life.

When we are accustomed to the status quo, we often become numb to the injustices that surround us. We might drive down the highway and see the signs for the prisons, but not understand their impact. If we do not recognize the impacts of injustice we can replicate oppression in our own actions. We see this happening within well-intentioned efforts to spread restorative justice practices. The stories and principles we share here are chosen to highlight the strengths of restorative justice values and practices, and to emphasize how incorporating social justice movement-building principles into restorative justice practices could enhance the transformative impact of these efforts.

These insights are drawn from our work. Rose Elizondo is a longtime restorative justice practitioner, with seventeen years of creating and sustaining innovative restorative programs in schools, also co-founding the San Quentin Restorative Justice Interfaith Roundtable,[5] and being an innovator in community work with the North Oakland Restorative Justice Council.[6] Rose is a 2017 Soros Justice Fellow. Jovida Ross has been involved with gender justice movements for more than two decades; since 2012 she has worked with Movement Strategy Center (MSC), where she leads MSC's cross-movement learning and strategy process called the Transitions Initiative.[7]

Social justice movements are collective journeys that take us towards a better world. Building a movement is a process of building a bigger 'We'

4. Transgender and queer people are overrepresented in the prison system and are particularly vulnerable to abuse by police in communities and by law enforcement in custodial settings. See Hunt and Moodie-Mills, "The Unfair Criminalization" and "Standing with LGBT Prisoners."

5. Learn more about San Quentin Restorative Justice Interfaith Roundtable: Haines, "Restorative Justice Program Lets the Healing Begin."

6. Learn more about the North Oakland Restorative Justice Council: Pierce, *What's the Alternative?*

7. Movement Strategy Center (MSC) was started in 2001 to help social justice movements be strategic, collaborative, and sustainable. Since then, the team at MSC has worked with many networks and alliances across different social justice movements. In 2014, MSC launched the Transitions Initiative, a process designed to build multi-systems social change grounded in relationships and personal transformation. The movement building principles shared here come from MSC's work across movements, with gratitude to the people who have led social justice movements and demonstrated these principles in action. Learn more about the work of Movement Strategy Center and access resources to support movement-building on MSC's web site at www.movementstrategy.org.

because shared values and relationships are a key to how movements create change.[8] Intentional reflection on our values and relationships can help us build our movement and create the world we want. Throughout this conversation we offer questions to reflect on restorative justice movement-building practices, to learn through self-awareness, and to strengthen our movement.[9]

Restorative Justice as a Way of Life

Rose: It began with love, it began with loss. The North Oakland Restorative Justice Council (NORJC) started in 2013 through the process of grieving the homicide of a young mother named Donitra Henderson. She was shot near Dover Park in front of her four-year-old son. In shock and grief we gathered family and friends, faith-based leaders, community members, survivors of crime, and people who had spent time in prison for taking a life.

Our collective response was to have a ceremonial tree planting, a potluck lunch, and talking circles. A Baptist minister shared stories about Donitra. A cousin shared how Donitra taught him his ABCs and 123s. African water libations created a sacred space. One by one, we offered shovels full of earth to plant a plum tree near the very place where Donitra's spirit went to a different realm. A spray-painted mural recreated her smiling grin on the redwood fence. In our talking circle, we each voiced what we could do to help bring about change in the community. As we did this, we co-created a circular altar with roses, sunflowers, pinecones, medicinal herbs, candles, and songs, in the tradition of Mexican indigenous people. Through these rituals, we created relationships. The community asked for more gatherings and to learn about restorative justice. Then several of us co-founded the NORJC to explore ways we can use restorative justice to transform harm into healing and put the "neighbor" back in the "hood."

Jovida: What a powerful response to tragedy. It conveys a sense of possibility. What if responses to harm supported healing and learning in everyday life? What if the skills to respond to harm restoratively were widespread?

8. *Transformative movements* recognize that everything gets done through relationships and nothing gets done without them. We are interrelated and interconnected. "A 'bigger we' includes the realization that movements are about people and cultures, our relationships to each other and to the planet," Movement Strategy Center, *The Practices of Transformative Movements.*

9. These reflection questions are based on questions that Movement Strategy Center has developed to support movement-builders, which we have customized in this essay specifically for a restorative justice context.

This possibility also connects with my own exploration, with the community connected with MSC's Transitions Initiative, and with how we can collectively transition from a world of domination and extraction to one of regeneration, resilience, and interdependence.

Rose: Restorative justice can be part of that transition! Envisioning an alternative to retributive or punishing systems that operate in our schools, criminal legal system, and communities is what energizes my community restorative justice work with the NORJC. As my mentor, Fania Davis (cofounder of Restorative Justice for Oakland Youth) states, "We harm people who harm people to show that harming people is wrong. Yet we know that if they are not healed, harmed people go on to harm other people."[10] Fania helped me realize the importance of weaving together personal and interpersonal healing, with advocacy and community healing, while using a cultural framework. We need more than individual healers; we need community and societal healers who empower those most impacted by abusive systems to lead the way toward justice.

Visioning Justice that Heals Harms

Jovida: To lead the way, we need to have a sense of the world we want to create. When I was working with Community United Against Violence (CUAV), I learned that anger and protest can be powerful motivators, but they will not ultimately take us to where we want to go. CUAV was the first organization in the country to focus specifically on violence against and within lesbian, gay, bisexual, and transgender (LGBT) communities, including violence perpetrated by police.[11] When I worked there we celebrated the organization's thirtieth anniversary. Looking back over those thirty years, we noticed how the rates of violence that our communities experienced had not gone down. We realized we had focused so much on stopping what we did not want, that we had not identified what we wanted *instead of* violence. We need to have long-term vision and goals to help us proactively create the world we want.

Rose: My long-term vision is about creating a future inspired by my ancestral traditions. Restorative justice is rooted in the values held within many

10. Learn more about Restorative Justice for Oakland Youth (RJOY) at http://rjoyoakland.org.

11. Learn more about Community United Against Violence (CUAV) at www.cuav.org.

indigenous cultures, including the recognition of our interdependence. To practice restorative justice involves making a fundamental shift in our thinking and actions. In 2010, I had a conversation with Van Jones, co-founder of the Ella Baker Center,[12] where he shared his perspective: "Justice is served when the victim is made whole, the transgressor is redeemed, and harmony is restored to the community." One of the main principles of restorative justice is that everything is interconnected. If we live by this principle, we realize that we each have keys to one another's healing and liberation. Your healing is my healing, and my healing is your healing. By healing myself, I am working on societal healing, and by advocating for policy change to heal social injustices, I heal others and myself. As communities and as a broader movement, restorative justice creates structures, policies, and practices of justice that heal harms and address the needs and obligations arising from those harms.

Jovida: This seems like a true definition of justice. The way our current legal system works does not feel like justice.

Rose: In our current system, when harm happens and the case goes through the legal process, the state takes on the position of the harmed party. This takes away the power of the person who was harmed whose needs are not a primary consideration in the legal proceedings. Instead, the focus is retribution against the person who caused the harm and how they will be punished. A restorative approach looks at how everyone's needs can be met. For example, if there was a robbery, we bring people together, including the person who was robbed, the person who did the robbery, and maybe neighbors who are now afraid because there was a robbery next door. We especially explore the needs of the person who was robbed. It gives them a sense of power. They might think, "I was robbed, yet this process is validating my experience. I can get my questions answered, I can express what I need, and I may be able to get my stolen belongings back."

Jovida: That really resonates with me. As you know, I am a survivor of child sexual abuse. When I first began sharing this as a teen I could tell that if the state got involved, I wouldn't have a say in what happened. Fortunately I had adults in my life who supported me to respond outside the legal system. The approach you described feels so *whole*. It makes me wish that everyone who has ever been hurt could experience that kind of response.

12. Learn more about the Ella Baker Center at http://ellabakercenter.org.

Rose: That might be why restorative justice is expanding quickly in the United States. Returning to wholeness is the goal of peacemaking practices in Native American / Alaskan communities. Many people do not realize how the way we practice restorative justice in the United States draws on ancient and modern peacemaking traditions and practices of many tribes, including the Diné, Lakota, and Tlingit.[13] In non-tribal communities during the 1970s and 1980s, variations of Native peacemaking practices, like circles, were brought into public institutions and called "restorative justice." The cultural context and nuances were lost because western values still prevail in those settings. Now, many schools and school districts are implementing restorative circles and restorative approaches to discipline.[14] In the juvenile system, restorative community conferences offer promising alternatives for addressing wrongdoing and diverting youth away from the criminal legal system while still holding them accountable.[15] In adult criminal cases, restorative justice practices are sometimes used after sentencing. Community restorative justice is also emerging! The North Oakland Restorative Justice Council is blazing a pathway towards community healing after crime or harm occurs. Innovative visions led by those closest to the problems are flipping retributive narratives. The hope is that these varied approaches will grow and provide holistic alternatives to the current punitive system.

Pause for Reflection:

We invite readers to consider how to proactively lead out with their vision for the world. *Imagine a world where responses to harm create healing and restore relationships. What are the qualities of that world? What would family life be like, or schools, or communities, if the skills to respond to harm restoratively were widespread?*

Linking Personal and Political Transformation

Jovida: It is exciting to think about accountability and community-building replacing punishment. Gender justice movements taught me that healing and collective liberation are part of the same process: the personal is political. Successful social justice movements impact all aspects of our lives. They

13. Learn more about indigenous peacemaking practices: Austin, *Navajo Courts*; Yazzie, "Life Comes from It."

14. Frey, "Oakland Ends Suspensions."

15. Learn more about conferencing at Community Works West at http://communityworkswest.org.

shift the way we live, the way we think about ourselves, our socio-political systems and structures, and our culture.[16] It seems like restorative practices hold this possibility. I understand that folks exploring *transformative justice* are considering how healing the impact of violence and trauma is inherently connected with shifting oppressive social conditions.[17] At Movement Strategy Center we are exploring how building social and political power is connected with repairing the harm of trauma; particularly, the impacts of historical traumas such as slavery and genocide.

Rose: Yes, I feel that restorative justice will become a powerful movement when it spreads beyond the court system and schools, into workplaces, neighborhoods and everyday life. Conflict is a natural part of being human. There is an internal shift when we approach conflict in a life-giving way. A question I always ask myself is, "In this moment, am I being a *healer*, or am I being a *jailer* (that is, being punitive)?" We can ask ourselves this simple question whether it is in a personal interaction, with a group, or as a society. We have a choice in every moment. I know the transformative power of this shift because I have experienced it many times. Sometimes, in order to transcend punishment, we need to embrace our own goodness and see goodness reflected in others.

I grew up in South Texas in the 1960s and 70s when the United Farm Workers Movement was very active. Farm workers are paid meager wages and often work in terrible conditions that are essentially economic enslavement. These drastic disparities of power and control, with racialized political power and religion as a tool of oppression, are painful. Historical trauma was repeated over many generations and I carry intergenerational trauma in the very cells of my body from it. To counter this internalized inferiority, the farm worker movement developed a sense of cultural power through a beautiful revitalization of Mexican culture. They also created slogans like "*¡Si Se Puede! Yes We Can!*" to shift from internalized oppression to internalized resilience. This transformation came with an assertion of political power using Gandhian nonviolence.[18] It led to an economic shift as the organizing won new rights.

16. Gratitude to Julie Quiroz and Kristen Zimmerman, who first articulated a version of this thought in *Love with Power.*

17. For more on how transformative justice practitioners connect healing *trauma* and healing *structural oppression*, view webinar with Maccani et al., "Transformative Justice."

18. The leaders of the farm worker movement, including César Chavez, studied the nonviolent approach that Gandhi promoted as well as the way it had been taken up in the U.S. by Dr. Martin Luther King Jr., and intentionally employed nonviolent tactics. See Orosco, *Cesar Chavez.*

During this time, the Chicanxs recognized that, although we were the majority, the white landowners held the political, religious, and economic power. Willie Velazquez had a vision of Latinxs moving from oppression and silence to having a vote, a voice, and actually leading democratic processes.[19] In small towns across South Texas, Chicanxs registered to vote, ran for office, and won![20] My father became a school board member. His best friend became the mayor. They flipped the apartheid-like model of a few people having power over the masses and demonstrated that we had power in numbers and in resilience. The cells in our bodies were collectively saying, "*Si Se Puede.*"

In the community justice work I am doing in North Oakland, we were inspired by these Chicanx political activists. We recently organized to put community members in leadership positions at the police-sponsored Neighborhood Crime Prevention Council (NCPC). In Oakland, the NCPCs have provided a space where residents who already have economic and political power can influence the police, while people of color and the poor are further criminalized. Now, Mustafa Solomon and Max Cadji of the Restorative Justice Council in North Oakland co-chair the NCPC. We changed the name to "Neighborhood Care and Promotion Council." The meetings are about how we can create relationships to know our neighbors, and how we can speak to each other when harm or conflict happens. It is a recent change, so we will see how it plays out.

Pause for Reflection:

We invite readers to reflect on how we can intentionally link personal and political transformation. *As we promote a cultural shift around justice, what political shifts can help us move towards a vision of justice that heals? How can we actively organize for the systemic changes that will help move us towards that vision?*

Restoring a *Just* Balance of Power

Jovida: In both of those powerful stories above, I hear a defining characteristic of *social justice movements*: they are led by the people who directly

19. Willie Velazquez's vision is portrayed in the documentary, *Willie Velasquez: Your Vote is Your Voice*. Directed by Hector Galan.

20. Willie Velazquez's obituary states, "from 1974 when we started to 1987, the number of Hispanic elected officials in the U.S. grew from 1,566 to 3,038, an increase of 82 percent." (Reuters, June 16, 1988).

experience injustice. The people who feel the impact of a systemic social problem have wisdom to offer around what the problem is and what real solutions might be. When we fully claim and act on this wisdom we reclaim our power. Your story of the farm worker movement, Rose, illustrates this so well.

For those of us who may be protected from direct experiences of systemic harm it is important to consider how we can support and celebrate the leadership of those who are directly impacted by that harm. A clear example of this comes from the disability rights movement. In the United States, disability rights advocates popularized the slogan, "*Nothing about us, without us.*"[21] This statement conveys the power to have direct decision-making authority in one's own life, and it affirms the dignity of people living with disabilities. In the process of claiming this power, people with disabilities also developed their leadership, built organizations, and won policy changes that benefit many people.[22] As an able-bodied person, for example, I don't know what it is like to navigate a world that is not designed for access in a wheelchair. I can guess or listen, but I don't have direct experience. If I engage in work promoting accessibility, I would want to take care that my involvement would not take power away from the true leaders of this movement, or else I would be replicating the very social injustices they are working to change.[23] We can support people who are directly impacted by injustice in their leadership, celebrate wins with them, and find joy in experiencing their power. When we accept leadership from people who have lived experience with social injustices we create a more inclusive, just world together.[24]

I think you take this approach already in your work. You talked about your friends and collaborators in North Oakland, like Princess Beverly. Her leadership is a good example.

Rose: Yes, Princess Beverly Williams' story is relevant. She lost her voice when her only son was murdered. She couldn't speak, or work, and

21. Charlton, *Nothing About Us Without Us.*

22. Blackwell, "The Curb Cut Effect."

23. One group leading the way for disability justice is the performance project Sins Invalid. See Lamm, "This is Disability Justice."

24. Involving the human "user" perspective throughout the process of problem-solving is one of the tenets of Human Centered Design (see Thompson, "Why Human Centered Design Matters"). Social justice movements have always taken this approach, and go even further with the idea that those who are directly impacted by an injustice can more effectively *lead the way* towards justice. This is both because lived experience gives insight and wisdom and also because the process of claiming agency and taking leadership towards justice helps restore a more just balance of social power, and in the process addresses some of the root causes of the problems we are seeking to solve.

depression hit her hard. Her son, Lorenzo Ward, was murdered just blocks from the home where she grew up in North Oakland. She was devastated. The NORJC reached out to her, as a survivor of this violent crime, to ask what her needs were. She said, "It's been 18 months, and I never really had a memorial service." So we threw a memorial block party in honor of her son. Of course we had a circle so that Princess Beverly and others could share stories. Malachi Scott and I introduced the basics of restorative justice and together we planted a fig tree to counter her and the neighbors' memories of violence.

At first, Princess Beverly did not understand restorative justice. She was resistant and expressed anger that her son was gone. Because of her honesty, we started a healing circle for people who have survived homicide. I invited Princess Beverly to co-facilitate. We named the group *Healing our Hearts: You Are Not Alone*, in reference to the Michael Jackson song.[25] We used the circle process to listen to each other and we worked on healing through talking circles, cultural traditions, song, and rituals. We also have celebrations so that we do not just focus on the hard experiences. The circle includes people who have lost a family member to long-term incarceration, too. Whether our loved ones have been killed or incarcerated, we have all been impacted by homicide and share experiences of grief and loss. We also host dinners that bring together our group with people who were formerly incarcerated for homicide so that they can hear the truth of each other's experiences.

We met in Dover Park for our circle. Before the circle, there was an opportunity to work in the Phat Beets community garden and harvest vegetables.[26] One day, the godmother of the young man who killed Lorenzo was in the park. Princess Beverly spoke with her, and his godmother explained how the shooter's mother died when he was very young. She talked about the life of neglect and poverty he had lived through, which led him into gang life. In this conversation the phrase "*Black Lives Matter*" took on new meaning for Princess Beverly. Her son's life mattered, and the young man who shot him needed to matter to someone, too. Princess Beverly shared that compassion filled her heart when she heard his story. Now restorative justice made sense. She was being called to live it, to heal, and to even offer healing.

Princess Beverly was frustrated when her son's case was going through court. The court did not keep her updated about the dates and times of the

25. "You Are Not Alone," by Michael Jackson, from the album *HIStory: Past, Present and Future, Book I*, released August 15, 1995.

26. Learn more about Phat Beets food justice programs at www.phatbeetsproduce.org.

trial, and she had to miss work to attend the emotionally painful proceedings. To demonstrate our support, the members of the NORJC showed up at the courtroom in purple t-shirts with photos of Lorenzo printed on them. She wrote a powerful victim impact statement to be read in court, honoring Lorenzo, which included principles of restorative justice as well as values from the Movement for Black Lives.[27] In the statement she spoke to the young man who killed her son and said, "The bullet that took Lorenzo's life will always connect our two families. I can't forgive you now. You really hurt me, and you hurt our community. From my learning about the restorative side of justice, and from my spiritual beliefs, I know forgiveness is needed. I just don't know how to do that yet. I'm getting support to help me in the healing process, and I want you to have a healing journey, too."

In April, Princess Beverly stepped into a new role as an advocate for systems change. She went to the state capitol in Sacramento for the Survivors Speak Conference.[28] She spoke about how the legal system failed her and how the adversarial court process kept her distant by telling her not to talk about the crime. Claiming her leadership in this way brought her a new sense of meaning; she was now giving back, regaining her voice and the power she lost when her son died.

Jovida: This is a beautiful story of someone who has been directly impacted by injustice who ends up leading both at the community level as a co-facilitator and at the systemic level as an advocate. Systems change is most powerful when the people who are negatively impacted by a system have a leadership role in reshaping it. There is a huge potential for people who have been impacted by the legal system to change the nature of that system entirely, which is what Legal Services for Prisoners with Children,[29] the Ella Baker Center, and others, are organizing to do.

27. For information on specific values from the Movement for Black Lives, see the *Black Lives Matter* guiding principles available at http://blacklivesmatter.com and the *Movement for Black Lives* policy platform posted at https://policy.m4bl.org.

28. *Survivors Speak* is produced by Californians for Safety and Justice. The annual conference is held during National Crime Victim's Rights Week, connecting survivors of crime, honor loved ones, and advocate for smart justice policies. Learn more at www.safeandjust.org.

29. Learn about Legal Services for Prisoners with Children at www.prisonerswithchildren.org.

Pause for Reflection:

We invite readers to consider how we can restore a just balance of power. *How can restorative justice practitioners prioritize, support, and genuinely celebrate* leadership *from those most impacted by both structural and personal violence and harm, in a way that restores and heals everyone involved? Since people of color, trans, and queer people are actively targeted for punishment by the criminal legal system, how could we better support their leadership in this work, including our financial practices?*

Grounding Our Work in People, Community, and History

Rose: Princess Beverly is an inspiring leader. She, Aunti Frances, and Malachi Scott lead our community actions. After violence occurs in the neighborhood, we have peace and justice walks to acknowledge the violence and reclaim space for community. On these walks Princess Beverly is often on the bullhorn, leading chants like, "*Ain't no power like the power of the people, 'cause the power of the people don't stop. Say What?*" We draw on chants that are relevant to the people in the neighborhood, like chants from the Black Power movement, since the Black Panthers started in North Oakland.[30]

Jovida: That story illustrates another characteristic of social justice movements, which is that they are about people and relationships, grounded in community and history. When a movement helps us feel deeply connected to each other, and to a sense of existing within the arc of history, we gain a sense of our collective power. A recent example of this is the Water Protectors at Standing Rock. Their sense of community, culture, and history informed both their assertion of sovereignty and the way they established the camp as sacred ceremony space.[31] When you draw on the history of the people in North Oakland, you are also applying this movement-building principle.

Rose: We value our history, elders, and ancestral traditions. In North Oakland, we are fortunate to be the home to many elders from the Black Panther movement. In our community trainings we say at least fifty percent of regular circles should be about relationship building. We enjoy "cooking circles" where we cook to create community and to serve ancestral food to neighbors at block parties. Cooking together is an opportunity to create a

30. Kreitner, "October 15, 1966: The Black Panther Party Is Founded."

31. Learn more about the Standing Rock Water Protectors' choice to practice ceremony, Judith LeBlanc in the recording of the *Love in a Time of Violence* video conference, December 21, 2016. https://www.youtube.com/watch?v=QnsztyZpOOE.

space for casual but intentional cross-generational learning, which builds relationships based on mutuality and reciprocity.

In August of 2015, we had a gumbo fest and block party to remember the anniversary of the murder of Lorenzo Ward, Princess Beverly's son. Several of us from NORJC met in the kitchen of Causa Justa::Just Cause, a grassroots power base-building organization.[32] Making gumbo is a metaphor for mixing things up. We had some master gumbo makers and elders from the neighborhood, like Aunti Frances, Mr. G, and Miss Gerthina. Aunti Frances was part of the Black Panthers' program that provided healthy breakfasts each morning for school kids.[33] As we cooked, the young people connected with history through cutting the okra and vegetables while children ran around, laughing. About midway through, Mr. G. asked us to circle up. Miss Gerthina sprinkled the sacred herbs of gumbo filé on the stew while she called in the ancestors and prayed for the departed Lorenzo and for his mother, Princess Beverly. These rituals create relationships and connect us on many levels.

The next day at the block party, the youth from Urban Peace Movement,[34] a youth-organizing group, paid exquisite attention as Princess Beverly shared the story of losing her son to gun violence. They used Playback Theatre from Theatre of the Oppressed[35] to practice the Zulu acknowledgement, *sawubona*, "*We see you*."[36] It was a deep conversation. In return, Princess Beverly sang a Gospel song and invited us to join in with her.

Pause for Reflection:

We invite readers to consider: *Who are the people and what are the community histories that a restorative justice movement is (or should be) most accountable to? How can we prioritize and take guidance and leadership from those relationships?*

In addition, because there is much to learn from cultures that have been practicing restorative responses to harm for thousands of years — including many Native American tribes, and cultures all over the world who have developed and kept these practices alive — we invite this reflection:

32. Learn more about Causa Justa::Just Cause at https://cjjc.org.

33. Learn more about the Black Panther Party's free breakfast program in Robertson, "The Black Panther Party."

34. Learn more about Urban Peace Movement at www.urbanpeacemovement.org.

35. Boal, *Theatre of the Oppressed*.

36. Bishop, *Sawubona*.

How can we honor cultural traditions that are not our own, in a respectful way, that does not appropriate or commodify them?

Cultivating a Movement Ecosystem

Jovida: This kind of collaboration is a beautiful expression of community resilience. At Movement Strategy Center (MSC), we think about social justice movements as ecosystems. Biologists describe an ecosystem as a system of living organisms in an area that function together as a unit.[37] Like ecosystems, movements involve a diverse community of people, organizations, networks, and alliances interacting within a specific context (which might be a place, or a particular concern, like workers' rights). Healthy ecosystems are interdependent and resilient, and have a diverse web of relationships. The same could be said of movements. When the NORJC collaborates with Phat Beets, Causa Justa::Just Cause, and Urban Peace Movement, each organization is playing a dynamic role in cultivating community resilience and supporting community members to experience the power they hold.

Rose: Right! Plus it is fun, and collaborating clarifies our unique contributions. Another example is the way that NORJC partners with Phat Beets in their kitchen incubator program. In this collaboration, we focus on restorative economics through jobs for women and girls who have experienced violence. We follow the Homeboy Industries model, "Nothing stops a bullet like a job."[38] The way to create a safe community is not through police and prisons: it is through creating local, meaningful economies, and healthy relationships. Restorative economics is about collectively building community-based economies to meet the needs of people who have been most harmed by the capitalism of mass incarceration. It is also about survivors of crime getting their economic needs met. It allows us to provide for our families, and ourselves, in a dignified way. Collaboration helps us to do this well; having diverse perspectives sparks a variety of creative ideas we might not come up with on our own. We also appreciate that the Akonadi Foundation follows an ecosystem grantmaking approach; we all get funding from Akonadi and it helps with these collaborations.[39]

37. Learn about Ecosystem definition from Biology Online at www.biology-online.org/dictionary/Ecosystem.

38. Learn about Homeboy Industries' model from Campbell, "Nothing Stops a Bullet Like a Job."

39. For more on the Akonadi approach, see *Ecosystem Grantmaking: A Systemic Approach to Supporting Movement Building* at http://www.akonadi.org.

Pause for Reflection:

We invite readers to consider if restorative justice is part of a larger social justice movement. *What are the interconnected relationships contributing towards a hopeful future that restorative justice is a part of? Who are the diverse partners we can join with to build that future?*

Building a Bigger We

Jovida: When you cultivate this kind of vibrant movement ecosystem, you are *Building a Bigger We*. Movements are powerful because they can solve problems bigger than one person or organization can address alone. Movements connect a wide range of people who have different experiences, perspectives, and contributions to work towards a common vision or values. This can also mean that we work with people whom we may not fully understand or agree with completely, but with whom we share common purpose.

One of my favorite examples of *Building a Bigger We* is the Strong Families Initiative. It started when Forward Together convened a network of reproductive justice organizations.[40] The group realized that the policies they all opposed reflected an outdated idea of family. The people in the network all felt deeply committed to their families which did not reflect the fantasy of a mom at home and a dad at work. They launched the Strong Families Initiative as "a home for the 4 out of 5 people living in the US who do not live behind the picket fence."[41] Strong Families Initiative connects diverse organizations to collaborate towards a vision that every family has the rights, recognition, and resources it needs to thrive. The network includes efforts focused on racial justice, youth, immigration, LGBT communities, criminal justice reform, and economic justice.

Rose: That makes me think about an experience I had with the San Quentin Restorative Justice Interfaith Roundtable a few years ago. San Quentin, which is a men's prison, is one of the nine California prisons that has been designated to incarcerate transgender people. As the Roundtable grew to 200, more and more transgender women joined. We began to see some "othering" rather than "belonging" within the circles. Inclusivity is one of our values, so we held a daylong symposium on violence against

40. Learn more about Forward Together at http://forwardtogether.org.

41. Learn more about Strong Families Movement at http://strongfamiliesmovement.org/what-we-do.

transgender people. We had two guest speakers who identified as transgender share stories with the group.

Tanesh Nutall was one of our guest speakers. She told us stories about a lifetime of hatred and violence she experienced as a transgender person. The stigma caused her to use drugs and alcohol to numb the pain. She told us, "If you don't agree with another person's beliefs, learn to love them anyway. If you spend time with individuals you may not like, your thoughts will change. You will come to see the person's spirit."[42] Through sharing our personal stories and listening to others with open hearts, we are learning a new way of relating in community. As a group we embraced our varying levels of discomfort. We began to see each other's humanity. I saw people who held closed views about transgender people open up after hearing Tanesh's story. Sitting in weekly restorative circles with diverse people calls us to move beyond biased belief systems. We are consciously choosing and working together to *build a bigger We.*

Pause for Reflection:

We invite readers to consider: *How can we grow a bigger We that can create the world we envision? Would it change* what *we focus on or* how *we go about our work?*

Living in the Future We Want

Jovida: Wow. Because of the work I used to do with Community United Against Violence, I have heard horror stories of the incredible violence transgender women face in men's prisons. I am so glad to hear a story of healing! It is a great example of another strength restorative practices can offer movement-builders: we have to be willing to *walk our talk.* As Brazilian educator and activist Paulo Freire liked to say, "We make the road by walking."[43] When we live our values and consciously cultivate these qualities through regular practice, we generate and experience the world we want. I see this happening within restorative processes, and I'm curious how much you think it is happening outside the formal boundaries of these processes?

Rose: I can give an example of that happening organically. We didn't start out with a diverse group of 200 incarcerated people attending the San

42. Tanesh Nutall spoke to the San Quentin Interfaith Restorative Justice Roundtable on Nov. 21, 2015.

43. Horton, *We Make the Road by Walking,* 1990.

Quentin RJ Interfaith Roundtable each week. In 2005, it started with a handful of incarcerated people who initiated a study group to learn about restorative justice. We had a regular group of thirty or so for around four years. One day we were doing an exercise about our shared values, and one of the men brought up how we needed to embody restorative justice values and principles in our everyday life. We discussed violent reactions if someone hurts us or cuts in front of us in the chow line, even in our thoughts, and how this doesn't build up a restorative way of life. We also explored how we could live as though we are all connected. The indigenous belief that violence happens when we forget we are all connected informs the practice of restorative justice.

Exploring how to live out our values caused a profound shift, and the group really started growing. One man suggested that we reach out to incarcerated people who were different than us and invite them to join the Roundtable. We invited men from ethnic groups that were not already participating, including Polynesians and Filipinos. We made the space welcoming for younger inmates who often do not go to programming. We didn't want to tokenize them, so we also included them in the leadership. There was already an informal restorative justice group for Spanish speakers, and we formalized one with intention. In a few months we doubled in size to seventy-five regulars. As we started addressing intersectional topics like race and restorative justice, or sex trafficking and restorative justice, our group grew to 200. By asking ourselves how we could go deeper, we decided as a group to embody the values we longed for. We used self-reflection, paying attention and observing our actions in order to learn about ourselves. We also decided that through a contemplative practice, we could create space for this learning and transformation. It was hard work to shift our attitudes and actions, but in small, doable steps, we started becoming the change we want to see in the world.

Pause for Reflection: We invite readers to reflect on what we could *do* differently (or how we could *be* different) to grow a movement that reflects our vision. *What are the values that are central to our work, and how could we better practice those values in our everyday interactions? What ways of* being *do we need to embody to create meaningful change that is aligned with our vision?*

Conclusion

Traveling through the prison corridor in California's Central Valley invites reflection on *The Grapes of Wrath*. The novel expresses the pain of many types of injustice, and a yearning to trample out our society's vintage of wrath and punishment.[44] In the book, the main character, Tom, starts out on the road after leaving prison. By the end, he comes to a new understanding: "A fella ain't got a soul of his own, but only a piece of a big one."[45] Through Steinbeck's storytelling, readers get lessons of a bigger We. It is a book of liberation.

We feel this humble chapter is a cry for justice, and it offers a vision, too. We anticipate it will spur conversations. Perhaps this essay will spark openings for people who have lived experiences of systemic and structural harms to lead out, with vision and purpose, and to collaboratively create the world we want. We truly desire that people impacted by injustice can be supported as leaders of restorative justice organizations and of this movement. Embodying the connections between personal transformation and political transformation means that we practice restorative justice as a way of life, knowing that we are connected to everyone and everything. We invite you on this journey. By incorporating movement-building principles into restorative practices, we can "make the road by walking." Together our ecosystem of actions will honor our past as we create the future and build the bigger We.

Bibliography

Alexander, Michelle. *The New Jim Crow: Mass Incarceration in the Age of Colorblindness*. New York: New Press, 2010.

Austin, Raymond D. *Navajo Courts and Navajo Common Law: A Tradition of Tribal Self-Governance*. Minneapolis: University of Minnesota Press, 2009.

Bishop, Orland. *Sawubona*. Online video posted by Global Oneness Project (Feb 8, 2007). https://www.youtube.com/watch?v=2IjUkVZRPK8.

Blackwell, Angela Glover. "The Curb Cut Effect." *Stanford Social Innovation Review* (Winter 2017). https://ssir.org/articles/entry/the_curb_cut_effect.

Boal, Augusto. *Theatre of the Oppressed*. New York: Theatre Communications Group, 1985.

44. The title *The Grapes of Wrath* refers to lyrics from the *Battle Hymn of the Republic*, by Julia Ward Howe. "Mine eyes have seen the glory of the coming of the Lord / He is *trampling out the vintage where the grapes of wrath are stored* / He hath loosed the fateful lightning of His terrible swift sword / His truth is marching on (emphasis added).

45. Steinbeck, *Grapes of Wrath*, 292.

Campbell, Duncan. "Nothing stops a bullet like a job." *The Guardian USA edition* (Nov. 23, 1999). https://www.theguardian.com/world/1999/nov/24/usgunviolence.usa.

Charlton, James I. *Nothing about Us without Us*. Berkeley: University of California Press, 1998.

deVuono-Powell, Saneta, Chris Schweidler, Alicia Walters, and Azadeh Zohrabi. *Who Pays? The True Cost of Incarceration on Families*. Oakland: Ella Baker Center, Forward Together, Research Action Design, 2015. http://whopaysreport.org.

Frey, Susan. "Oakland ends suspensions for willful defiance, funds restorative justice." *EdSource* (May 14, 2015). https://edsource.org/2015/oakland-ends-suspensions-for-willful-defiance-funds-restorative-justice/79731.

Galan, Hector, dir. Documentary film: *Willie Velasquez: Your Vote Is Your Voice*. Latino Public Broadcasting, 2016.

Haines, Juan. "Restorative Justice Program Lets the Healing Begin." San Quentin News (Dec. 10, 2010). http://sanquentinnews.com/restorative-justice-program-lets-the-healing-begin.

Horton, Myles with Paulo Freire, *We Make the Road by Walking: Conversations on Education and Social Change*. Philadelphia: Temple University Press, 1990.

Hunt, Jerome, and Aisha C Moodie-Mills. "Standing with LGBT Prisoners: An Advocate's Guide to Ending Abuse and Combating Imprisonment." National Center for Transgender Equality, 2015. http://www.transequality.org/issues/resources/standing-lgbt-prisoners-advocate-s-guide-ending-abuse-and-combating-imprisonment.

Hunt, Jerome and Moodie-Mills, Aisha C. "The Unfair Criminalization of Gay and Transgender Youth." American Progress (2017). https://www.americanprogress.org/issues/lgbt/reports/2012/06/29/11730/the-unfair-criminalization-of-gay-and-transgender-youth.

Kreitner, Richard. "October 15, 1966: The Black Panther Party Is Founded." *The Nation* (October 2015). https://www.thenation.com/article/october-15-1966-the-black-panther-party-is-founded.

Lamm, Nomy. "This Is Disability Justice." *The Body Is not an Apology* (September 2015). https://thebodyisnotanapology.com/magazine/this-is-disability-justice.

Maccani, R. J., Nathaniel Shara, and Ejeris Dixon. "Transformative Justice." Zehr Institute webinar (Feb. 15, 2017). http://zehr-institute.org/webinar/transformative-justice.

Movement Strategy Center. *The Practices of Transformative Movements* (2016). movementstrategy.org/b/wp-content/uploads/2016/07/MSCPractices_of_Transformative_Movements-WEB.pdf.

Orosco, José-Antonio. *Cesar Chavez and the Common Sense of Nonviolence*. Albuquerque: University of New Mexico Press, 2008.

Pierce, Molly. "What's the Alternative? Restorative Justice Group Discusses Getting Youth out of the Courts." Oakland North (Nov. 19, 2014). http://oaklandnorth.net/2014/11/19/whats-the-alternative-restorative-justice-group-discusses-getting-youth-out-of-the-courts.

Quiroz, Julie, and Kristen Zimmerman. *Love with Power: Practicing Transformation for Social Justice*. Movement Strategy Center (May 2016). http://movementstrategy.org/b/wp-content/uploads/2016/07/MSC-Love_With_Power.pdf.

Robertson, Darryl. "The Black Panther Party and the Free Breakfast for Children Program." *The African American Intellectual History Society* (Feb. 26, 2016). http://www.aaihs.org/the-black-panther-party.

Thompson, Dave. "Why Human Centered Design Matters." *Wired* (December 2013). https://www.wired.com/insights/2013/12/human-centered-design-matters.

Wagner, Peter, and Sakala, Leah. *Mass Incarceration: The Whole Pie.* A Prison Policy Initiative briefing, 2016. https://www.prisonpolicy.org.

Yazzie, Robert. "Life Comes from It: Navajo Justice." *The Ecology of Justice.* Context Institute, 1994.

2

Bringing a Racial Justice Consciousness to the Restorative Justice Movement

A Call to White Practitioners

Mika Dashman, Katherine Culberg, David Dean, Anna Lemler, Mikhail Lyubansky, and Julie Shackford-Bradley

We are a multi-generational, geographically dispersed group of white-identified individuals in the restorative justice movement. We have all been involved in racial justice activism and have participated in various anti-racist white affinity groups. We acknowledge the long history of organizing against racism by people of color broadly and especially by practitioners of color within the restorative justice movement who have been calling for a more explicit focus on the dynamics of race, power and privilege within restorative justice. Our intention is to add our voices to a conversation already in progress because we believe that our silence perpetuates further harm. We come to this conversation with humility and the recognition that we have more questions than answers. We are speaking from our perspective as white-identified people, specifically to and with other white people. We believe that white people have a role to play in the struggle for racial justice, that it starts within ourselves, and that it must continue within the all-white and predominantly white spaces to which we have access. We hope to do this work in the spirit of Stokley Carmichael's 1969 *Black Power* speech, in which he asks, "Can white people move inside their own community and start tearing down racism where in fact it does exist?"

Mika Dashman, the Founding Director of *Restorative Justice Initiative*, a New York City-based advocacy and organizing project, brought this group together. In 2015, she began developing an anti-racist circle model for white people called, "Racism Stops with Me." She presented this model at two national restorative justice conferences, including the Restorative Justice in Motion Conference at Eastern Mennonite University in July 2016 where she collaborated with Anna Lemler and Mikhail Lyubansky. When Mika learned about the "Transforming Whiteness for Racial Justice: A Restorative Approach" workshop that Kat Culberg, David Dean, and Julie Shackford-Bradley offer in the San Francisco Bay Area, she invited them to contribute to this article. In the Spring of 2017 the six of us engaged in fascinating and at times emotional discussions about the role of white people in the restorative justice movement in general and especially in the context of racial justice work. In this article we attempt to capture the most essential aspects of those discussions.

Originally, we considered writing a conventional "academic" piece, but in an effort to honor restorative principles and practices, we decided to hold a virtual circle process in which we agreed on several guiding questions and then took turns responding to each of them, one at a time. In this way, we hoped that we would not only build meaning collaboratively but that we would do so in a way that our different perspectives and voices would be distinguishable to those reading.

In addition, we recognize that academia has itself been shaped by the culture of white supremacy. By writing this *in circle*, we hope to counter the disproportionate value that the academy places on fact-based, rational, and emotionless analysis. Our goal was to speak from the heart as well as the intellect, to share our personal experiences as well as our knowledge, and to demonstrate vulnerability as well as aspiration. Our responses have been edited for brevity, and some of us chose to "pass" when we had nothing more to add to what had already been said.

Question 1: How can white practitioners who engage in anti-racism work contribute to the restorative justice movement?

Mikhail: I think racial justice activists and scholars can contribute by pushing the restorative justice movement to acknowledge the presence and impact of racism and structures that support racism, as well as by insisting that the restorative justice movement attends to power and oppression more broadly. One of my great worries about the future of the restorative justice movement in the United States is that its leaders and practitioners will not attend to these dynamics and, therefore, unintentionally support and/or replicate existing structures that maintain racism and other forms of oppression. As just one example, I worry that well-intentioned gatekeepers will create easier access to restorative practices for some (racialized) groups of individuals than others in a way that is not explicitly racial but will unintentionally wind up being more punitive for some and more restorative for others, based on race.

Mika: I think racial justice and anti-racism work is essential within the restorative justice movement for the reasons Mikhail mentioned, but also because there is a lot of visible white leadership/authorship in this community, and it is important that we are willing to be self-reflective about why this is and what needs to happen to be more welcoming and to create space and opportunities for people of color to be more visible and empowered. And when racism surfaces in restorative justice spaces—and it often does—I think it is important for white practitioners to be prepared to acknowledge it without being defensive, and to make amends. But we need to be able to see it. So there is some "consciousness-raising" work that we need to do among ourselves. This responsibility often falls to people of color in mixed groups, but it shouldn't. I think we have a moral obligation to do this work as restorative justice practitioners.

Restorative justice is based on indigenous practice and philosophy. Anytime we as white practitioners fail to acknowledge the roots of this knowledge, we are engaging in cultural appropriation and in so doing, replicating the same power dynamics and oppression that has shaped the criminal justice system and the broader society. We can and must go into this work with deep humility and respect for the lived-experience of people targeted by racism. We must assume that as white people reared in a white supremacist culture, we don't even know what we don't know. But ending racism is integral to reclaiming our full humanity and being in good relationship with all people, including those who look most like us.

The last point I want to make is about the institutions or systems in which restorative justice is being implemented most commonly, namely schools and the criminal justice system. These systems are major perpetrators of state violence against people of color. We have to acknowledge that and make sure that we are holding space in our circles, conferences, and victim offender mediations not just for a conversation about interpersonal harm but also about systemic/structural harm.

Julie: I have always known the "RJ movement" to be aimed at racial justice outcomes. This may be because I was introduced to it here in the Bay Area, where from the start the goals were to interrupt the school-to-prison pipeline and reduce "disproportionate minority contact" in juvenile and adult criminal justice systems. And that is due to the amazing work of mainly women of color as well as some dedicated white folks who formed a taskforce and were able to shape the future of restorative justice in this area according to their strong vision. But as Mika notes, the systems themselves are extremely problematic to work in (schools, criminal justice, probation for juveniles), and so it is very hard to maintain integrity while doing the work. But I also see that practitioners are working toward a kind of systemic change at the incremental level, day by day, teacher by teacher, kid by kid, and I think that work should be celebrated even as we acknowledge the immense challenges of major systemic change. A lot of people have high expectations that restorative justice will bring that systemic change and when they do not see it right away, they question restorative justice, but it may be that their expectations are too great.

I also see more clearly how white people, including myself, who are facilitating and engaging in restorative justice processes, are not having the necessary and important discussions about race, about inequities, power imbalances and different communication styles, or what it is like to be the one person of color in a circle. Speaking for myself, I could be better about acknowledging those dynamics in ways that don't cause further harm, and that is a process of learning and practicing. I can develop and deepen relationships with other folks of all backgrounds across the campus where I work to show that my goals are aligned with theirs. What I can't do is undo my whiteness or privilege, and so these are the realities that I am challenged by everyday as a white person in the field.

Anna: I agree with Mikhail and Mika's assessments of current racial dynamics institutionally in the restorative justice field (even the concept of it being a 'field' is problematic), and want to highlight that even the most well-intentioned, liberal white practitioners can be doing harm in the name of restorative justice.

This is where the conversation about Transformative Justice feels very important to me. I think we want to believe that inherently the restorative justice process is restorative, but for me, it can't be restorative without it being transformative. While I have much to learn, my understanding is that transformative means that we are including a systemic oppression analysis to our work *all the time*. So, for example, I met a young person a couple months ago in juvenile detention who was being punished for breaking in and stealing a laptop. He seemed to be genuinely lost in life, but we (the system/adults) seemed more concerned about the computer and its owner rather than how adults and society have failed this young person time and time again! No one really focused on the fact that his mom was deported two months prior, or that he had to watch his younger siblings all the time, or that he has now missed so much school that he is literally ashamed and scared to go back. Has any adult ever apologized to this young man for all of that? Have we ever discussed the racist policies that don't allow his mom to live here or his family to get the money they deserve, or for him to be seen as a "bright, driven, future-filled" child? Transformative justice, in my mind, asks us to imagine what it would look like if we held those policy-makers accountable.

The problem is that *we are not taught about systemic oppression, and here specifically about racism, in our restorative justice trainings.* Already white people are intentionally not taught about racism (because why would 'we' want to dismantle something that provides so much benefit to us?), thus making race and racism taboo and uncomfortable to talk about. This means that people are being trained in restorative justice, and are missing this critical lens to their work, and thus perpetuating/recreating the exact systems we claim to want to dismantle.

Kat: I am on a mission to *get comfortable with being uncomfortable* around this conversation . . . to not run from it. Yesterday I spent eight hours giving a "Transforming Whiteness" workshop with a restorative justice approach with Julie and David. The attendees were all white-identified. I'm pretty uncomfortable with our designation of this workshop being "for white people" and yet intuitively, and from experience in multiracial circles talking about race, I know that this space is essential. White people, I have noticed, show up differently in spaces with people of color. It doesn't feel like genuine authenticity, vulnerability, and honesty really happens, because many of us are too invested in defending, denying, intellectualizing, overcompensating or holding on to power and control. I myself had been "running from my own whiteness" for too long, which prevented me from showing up authentically until very recently.

The circle was draining. I left the training to meet up with a friend who is an African American Elder in the Oakland community. He asked me why I seemed so tired. I told him that I had been doing "white work in racial justice/restorative justice with an all-white group all day." "Damn," he said. "I'm sorry for you Kat; I wouldn't want that job. But that's YOUR job, baby, and YOU all need to do it." That's my job, not his. Examining honestly and deeply how we are complicit, consciously or unconsciously, in perpetuating personal, structural, and institutional racism in ALL spaces—including restorative justice spaces—is our job. In fact, I believe restorative justice spaces are particularly at risk of inadvertently perpetuating systemic oppression because we are so well *intended*, indeed, we are "restorative."

Last week I was in the maximum security unit at a juvenile hall doing restorative justice work (chew on that oxymoron). About ten young people, all African American, all going on to hard time, were responding to a question around institutional/structural racism and violence. I was feeling great about the circle. The guys were going deep. I had named my white privilege, and internalized racial superiority as well as how white supremacy continues to benefit me, as I always do, and how my two white sons had done some of the same behaviors as many youth in juvenile hall but were treated differently by society, and on and on. (Note how this framing is all about ME and my whiteness.) At one point the vibe shifted and one of the young men put down the talking piece and said, "None of this matters, Kat. We already know all this." And they do. Most of these young men have a better "critical analysis" of the problems we are talking about than many academics since it comes from a LIVED experience within the school-to-prison pipeline.

Another young man asked for the talking piece. "How does what we know or what we talk about in the circle make a difference to us out there? Nothing changes. We're still going back to the same streets and we are still ending up back here." This scenario highlights two issues. The "white savior," that is, I myself, a white woman who has something *for* you (note the internalized racial superiority), and secondly, the risk of overlooking the fact that the wisdom lies in those communities most impacted by the problem and not within me. Additional harm will be done if we do not pay close attention to how we show up with or without being conscious of these tendencies and norms.

David: If white restorative justice practitioners engage with these topics, we can far more effectively reach our goal of creating opportunities for healing and repair on individual, interpersonal, and structural levels. Personally, I have found I cannot truly embody the philosophy of restorative justice in my own life as a white person without facing the massive historical conflict that I exist in. These days I am learning more all the time about my ancestors' part in horrific racial violence. My ancestors and I have run from the memory of this violence. We have segregated ourselves from it. We have split our consciences, fought these memories through historical revision, fled from them through historical erasure, and frozen in the face of their enduring effects. Coming To The Table (CTTT), an organization that brings together descendants of slave-holders and the enslaved to participate in a process of dialogue and reconciliation, has demonstrated that making restorative justice deeply race-conscious is not only healing for people of color but also the only way that we, as white people, can regain our wholeness. But CTTT does not stop there. Their final step is collective action to create cultural and institutional change in the broader society.

In a similar way, white people in restorative justice need to adopt a racial justice lens not only to create repair on personal and community levels, but also to have the analysis necessary to successfully address structural harm in our world. The actions of the Trump administration made it clear how white supremacy has continually been used, since its inception centuries ago, as a divide-and-conquer tool to advance extreme, unregulated capitalism. By leading white Americans to see black and brown folks as the cause of our problems, it crushes the potential for powerful multiracial coalitions for justice and makes people of all colors more vulnerable to corporate, economic, and environmental exploitation. The enduring strength of white supremacy has left this exploitation largely unchecked, and over time it has produced mass inequality, pollution, and climate change that could ultimately devour everyone. Racism is therefore not a social problem that operates in isolation of others. Rather, it is one of the greatest barriers our country faces in building a better society for all.

The restorative justice movement could take on a large-scale process of group education and processing in racial affinity contexts followed by relationship building and healing across this line of difference in order to revive shattered multiracial coalitions and prepare people to take action for racial justice and freedom from all forms of oppression. Even in settings where restorative justice is not traditionally done in connection to organizing, I believe that we must strive to connect the "repair agreements" that come out of our circles to social action.

Question 2: Why is there a need for all-white, anti-racist, restorative dialogue and healing spaces?

Mika: I feel very fortunate to have done and continue to be doing anti-oppression organizing and healing work in a multiracial community where an emphasis is placed on building honest, authentic, and caring relationships across identities while working toward collective liberation. Within the organization where I have done much of my anti-racist organizing and healing work, there has been an understanding from the beginning that there is value in doing healing work within affinity groups with shared identity and experience.

I grew up in a time, a family, and a culture where I was taught definitively that racism and "racists" are bad. Largely because of my fear of being blamed and humiliated, stemming from my lived experience, I am very careful not to "be racist" in mixed spaces (although I am certain I still am at times). So what is the impact of that? I am sure people of color pick up on my unease, my fear, my caution, and my reticence. How can we build trust and respect across differences when we are not showing up fully? Where are the spaces where we have permission to share our confusion, our fear, and our anxiety around race, however that manifests for us? We should never assume or expect that people of color will reassure us or even hold space for us. But if we are ever going to become more comfortable naming and calling out racism and listening to other people's experiences of racism without denial, defensiveness, or silencing, we need to process our own heartbreak, confusion, and pain stemming from growing up in white families where we were conditioned to participate in this deeply inhuman system.

Anna: I wholeheartedly believe we need caucus/affinity/identity-groups and group education. I also think it is important that no space should ever deny people of color; if a person of color wanted to come to a space aimed at educating white folks, they should, obviously, be allowed and welcomed! Being part of accountable spaces like this have fundamentally transformed every part of my life. Through this work I have begun to identify and understand how pervasive racism is in every aspect of my life and to change my behavior to the best of my ability.

Kat: I believe that by sitting in affinity spaces built on the principles of restorative justice, we can remove an obstacle that is stopping white people in their tracks in racial justice and healing work. We have to first learn to say the *unsayable* ("I did this racist thing; I had this racist thought") and then learn to sit through that crippling discomfort without running from it. For many of us, we don't even have that awareness yet, since we are so deeply entrenched in implicit bias and internalized racial superiority. We do this in white spaces first so that we can get experience, skill, and resilience in saying the *unsayable*, hearing the *unhearable*, to show up with truth and authenticity in mixed-race spaces to do "the work."

Julie: I am thinking about a training I have coming up which will be a mixed space. In the past, we asked the questions: When was the first time you learned about race? When was the first time you learned about gender, or class, and then ask people to tell stories to each other in concentric circles, and thereafter share out to the whole group. In the past some of the people of color shared very traumatic experiences of learning about race through acts of racism aimed at them or their parents or grandparents. Some of the white participants, including myself, talked about when our parents or grandparents were the ones engaging in those horrendous acts of racism toward someone else. Still other participants would bypass race and talk instead about other kinds of harm they experienced based on gender identity or class status. The effect was very asymmetrical. One group is clearly the one that has been harmed while the other group has caused harm, but yet we had not prepared ourselves or the group for a harm circle.

When we lead these discussions, we often have not prepared ourselves for how people will feel pulled and divided, at a loss for words, unheard or misunderstood, growing further apart, rather than closer through the circle process. These kinds of experiences have made me think that a good first step in these multiracial or interracial dialogues involves inviting people to recognize our different experiences of race in our lives and histories in *separate spaces* first, and to begin thinking about what is needed to make cross-racial interactions more humanizing, more about listening and understanding, and more about connecting in ways to develop shared visions for going forward.

David: I think there is a body of healing work that we as white people need to do ourselves—work that is needed for us to embody something different than whiteness, an identity we have been given. Though the idea of white superiority was not a conscious belief I ever had and one directly countered by the words of family, friends, and teachers, I have realized that my sense of self was, in a sense, shaped by it. The messages I received throughout my life and the images I saw everywhere glorified people who looked like me and normalized my people's dominance. My identity became partially dependent on these things. When they were challenged by voices expressing the truth of racism in our society, I experienced a form of existential crisis. As I began to accept this truth, I dealt with this crisis by deeming conservative, southern, or older white folks as the "bad ones." While some cling to a denial of racism, I clung to the myth that I was "the good white person," an exception from the rest. But underneath I still felt rootless and afraid.

When our internalized racial superiority is named and the sanitized history of white American patriotism is discredited, what can we hold on to? How do we make meaning out of our lives? This process of identity development and renewal is one that I think is uniquely ours to do. If we don't, I believe we will hold onto the harmful, false, and fractured ways of understanding ourselves as white people that are currently on the menu.

We must find different soil to root ourselves in. This could mean connecting to the lineage of white anti-racist organizing over time—or what Anne Braden called, "The Other America." I think it also means reconnecting to the indigenous heritages that created meaning for us prior to their loss, prior to our displacement from our ancestral homelands, prior to becoming "white," and prior to our journey forward as foot soldiers of empire. It is important to also understand the specific ways that this transition happened for our particular ancestors. Classist depictions of European history lead us to forget that the vast majority of them lived in communities that opposed an oppressive empire and sought to maintain alternative, more just and sustainable ways of life. All of this is why Jeff Duncan-Andrade, a past professor of mine who teaches at San Francisco State University, has said that "white folks need them some ethnic studies for real!"

Mikhail: When I was first introduced to the concept of white privilege in the 1990s (at the now embarrassing late age of 20-something), I immediately formed two beliefs: 1) the concept had undeniable truth and potential benefit, and 2) it did not apply to me. As an immigrant who struggled socially to fit in throughout his childhood and whose entire friendship network consisted of non-whites until high-school, it was hard to locate myself in whiteness, particularly as part of a privileged class, which, as far as I could tell, wanted nothing to do with me, except maybe as a convenient teasing target. White privilege didn't apply to me, I thought, and I resented anyone's suggestion that it might. These days, I see it a bit differently. Although I did not realize it back then, it is very likely that my whiteness predisposed teachers to believe I was smart, gave me the benefit of the doubt when I got into trouble in school and on the streets, and kept storekeepers and other community adults from making assumptions about my intentions.

The honest conversations about privilege that allowed me to shift my perspective have always been uncomfortable, but I think they are even harder to have in today's political climate than they used to be. Whether it is due to the growing visibility of Black Lives Matter or the relatively new narrative of "white fragility," I seem to hear a lot more white people these days talking about "lack of safety" in reference to interacting with people of color, not only in the context of so-called "anti-racism" and "diversity" work but sometimes in terms of being afraid to disagree or express an opinion, or even just experiencing emotional fatigue at the prospect of yet another conversation about diversity. While a white-only space would not eliminate such fatigue, it could be a place where it could be brought up and discussed, not as a way to justify taking a break or not engaging in the work for other reasons, but as the *appropriate* place to name and receive empathy for the struggle and create strategies for self-care that allow us to keep doing the work that needs doing. Similarly, such spaces could also allow would-be white allies to share and examine their own racist ideas and actions, not to celebrate or even accept such ideas but to make visible what is typically too shameful to bring up, especially in multiracial spaces. White-designated spaces certainly need to have accountability structures (which I know is our next question), but if they allow white people to work through their racism and privilege away from people of color, I believe they can create more safety, not just for white people but for everyone designated or perceived as non-white.

Question 3: What does it look like for restorative justice practitioners gathering in all-white spaces to be accountable to our colleagues of color?

Anna: Internalized Racial Superiority (IRS) is a term I have learned from The People's Institute of Survival and Beyond. Despite being raised in very liberal and diverse community and educational settings, before attending the Undoing Racism training with them I never considered, how have *I* internalized oppression? How does it impact *my* behavior?

The first step in undoing our internalized racism is being able to recognize it. Some manifestations of IRS are: taking up space (verbally, physically, or emotionally), valuing intellect over emotion (and thus suppressing emotions), focusing on individualism, avoiding conflict, prioritizing intentions over impact, perfectionism, defensiveness, either/or thinking, objectivity, assuming a right to comfort, and power hoarding. IRS shows up in all of us (white folks) in some way or another. And it is so internalized in us that if (*when*) we are not taught about it, we are likely recreating racially oppressive dynamics. This question for me is two-fold: (1) what infrastructure can we as a white group put in place to challenge racism, and (2) how can I as the circle keeper hold this space in an "accountable" way?

Some ideas for accountable infrastructure include: at every gathering, ask for (additional) funds to donate to a local organizing group led by people of color as a form of reparations; explicitly name ways we have been racist or how IRS has manifested in us to the group; at the beginning of every gathering, acknowledge the indigenous people whose land you occupy and the history of slavery in that region; set up a culture where both challenging each other and anti-oppression education *will* happen and is encouraged.

The aim of these groups must be to do work on ourselves *in order to* dismantle white supremacy in *all* spaces that we occupy. And we must acknowledge that learning does not stop there. We must educate ourselves for the rest of our lives by listening, listening, and listening some more. I think it is important that groups have action (but of a certain informed type), like, "talk with three of your white friends about racism this week, keep a daily journal identifying your IRS, and read more literature by authors of color than white authors.

The answers to the second part of the question are less clear to me because I think it depends on your relationship with people of color, where you are regionally, and how much work you have done on yourself.

Julie: The Transforming Whiteness workshop is aimed at helping people, including myself, to be accountable for the racism that we ourselves are feeling or enacting. So, after establishing a really safe space, where it is clear that there will be no judging, shaming, and blaming, and where people can be vulnerable and can open up, we ask people to talk about negative assumptions they have made on the basis of race, and to think collectively about the broader question of where those assumptions come from. That is how I see the circle process, as starting with a discussion of our personal experiences and then building on those to develop solidarity and collective action.

In the workshop, we also ask people to talk about another level of individual accountability, namely by talking about the ways in which our family histories intersect with national histories and current structures of racial harm. In the circle space, we work to surface stories and histories with the belief that this is the *first step* in a series of actions that will unfold in the future where we then come together to collectively address those historical harms. The first step in all of this, though, is to create that container where people can open up to different layers of accountability and to acknowledge the kinds of violence and harm that have been enacted throughout history and that we continue to inflict every day in our personal interactions.

Where I get concerned about accountability is when an individual white person, say, is asked to "be accountable" for this sweeping history and all of the political and economic dynamics past and present, or even to "be accountable" for all the ways in which they have experienced privilege in their lives. In my view, this creates an impossible situation where the person expected to "be accountable" experiences a sense of being overwhelmed, of existential panic, or perhaps a sense that "this is not who I am; I am a good person," while the person demanding accountability will also be disappointed or even harmed by the encounter because they may face defensiveness, minimization of their harms, or an array of other responses. I don't think that this antagonistic approach will bring about the kinds of transformation we are all seeking. There has to be a better way, and I think we are trying to figure it out collectively by trying out different strategies and tactics in different kinds of gatherings. We start with questions such as, How do we create spaces where people are moved out of their comfort zone but not placed in the panic zone? How can accountability be discussed collectively in ways that lead to an outcome that moves us forward? How do we agree to start from where we are now to move forward, acknowledging the inequities and the asymmetries and the crimes of the past, but not letting those be a barrier for thinking about moving forward?

Kat: A mentor and a dear friend—a black woman with whom I do restorative justice work—said to me the other day, "Internalized white superiority to white folks is like water to fish. It's all you all know. It's as normal to you as water is to fish; you're swimming in it . . . You can't even see all the ways internalized white superiority plays out in your thoughts and behaviors because you were born in that water." She didn't say this in a way that was shaming. She said it simply as a truth. The sky didn't fall and the ground didn't give way underneath me. It resonated so completely.

I believe that unless we can see this water we are swimming in, we, as white people, will not know how to get out of and take those actionable steps of accountability towards truth, reconciliation and racial healing. And I believe that this understanding and insight will come more effectively and meaningfully with restorative justice principles and practices than it can in a punitive environment.

Some Recommendations for White Practitioners

In closing, we offer some practical recommendations—micro and macro—for white restorative justice practitioners to ensure that we are centering racial justice in our work.

The first way is to **create and maintain a community value** that restorative justice practitioners (and scholars) should be actively engaged in doing their own work around understanding intersectional systems of oppression and racial bias. This is essential because without a certain level of competence in these areas, restorative justice has the potential to cause substantial harm by reinforcing rather than challenging racial hierarchies and inequities. While it is tempting to conclude that this would be best done by including these topics (e.g., privilege, bias, oppression) in restorative justice trainings, there is a risk that restorative justice trainers are not necessarily sufficiently experienced and versed in this realm, especially in the United States, where the restorative justice movement has so far largely eschewed any kind of licensure and credentialing. This leads to the question of how restorative justice can support inclusion and access over professionalism, while still promoting certain competencies throughout restorative justice that are aimed at reducing harm and meeting the needs of all who participate.

The second way is to **create restorative spaces** in which those who see themselves as white can critically examine whiteness and unlearn racism. Although such spaces exist outside the restorative justice movement, for a variety of different reasons, these non-restorative spaces are too unfamiliar, too threatening, and too vulnerable for many white people to be able to engage. In these spaces, the analyses, the discourses and the language of today's anti-racism movement can be addressed and embraced in ways that emphasize "head and heart" approaches and personal accountability. As we discovered through the process of writing this article, restorative spaces are conducive to unpacking terms like "privilege," "white supremacy," "white fragility," "accountability," "cultural appropriation," as such terms have been developed and applied through anti-racism discourse and through our own personal responses to them. Strategies such as "shaming and blaming" can also be discussed and debated in terms of their effectiveness in different contexts. Through these conversations, the analyses that these terms, concepts and strategies bring can be fully engaged and interpolated in ways that reduce the likelihood of negative reactions, such as defensiveness and denial, which obstruct true growth and transformation.

The third way is by committing to **work through our own racial conflicts**, both interpersonally and organizationally. Social justice organizations (like other organizations) are often distracted or untracked by internal conflict because the work they are doing is often stressful and, for many, is tied up into their sense of self. Though the long-term goals are often shared, there may be passionate disagreement about strategies, as well as anger and hurt feelings about how power and privilege are expressed within the organization. We have seen this happen first-hand in different social justice organizations and we continue to mourn the harm that was never repaired. Restorative practices can support those doing anti-racism work in working through these kinds of interpersonal and organizational conflicts and repairing the harm and misunderstandings that are inevitable when human beings work closely together.

The final way restorative justice can center anti-racism work is to **prioritize institutional diversity and address racial disproportionality**. Research data show that interacting with people who are racially different is more strongly associated with cognitive growth than either coursework or workshops.[1] Moreover, Pettigrew and Tropp found that reducing anxiety and increasing empathy toward outgroup people were both more effective in reducing prejudice than increasing knowledge about the outgroup.[2] Both of these findings point toward the need for racial diversity in both the restorative movement and in the many contexts in which restorative justice

1. Bowman, "College Diversity Experiences and Cognitive Development."
2. Pettigrew and Tropp "Does Intergroup Contact Reduce Prejudice?"

systems are being developed. It is important that those who are in leadership positions in restorative justice make it a priority to recruit and support (financially and otherwise) people from all backgrounds. It is imperative that people in the restorative justice movement track and address racial disproportionality both within our own restorative organizations and (again) in the different contexts in which we do our work. Thus, for example, those working in the school systems must not only focus on reducing suspensions and other forms of punitive discipline, but also invite people from the groups most targeted to learn about and engage in restorative processes in ways that are beneficial for their communities.

As restorative justice practitioners, we cannot effectively facilitate the healing of harm if we do not understand one of the greatest sources of harm in our society, white supremacy. We must also recognize and address the psychosomatic effect that white supremacy has had on us as white people. As human beings we are hardwired for connection. Our role as the dominant group in this violent system has created a painful and traumatic violation of our humanity that is passed from one generation to another. It is precisely because 'hurt people hurt people' that white restorative justice practitioners must engage in ongoing learning, healing and accountability practices around race, power and privilege. As Fania Davis of Restorative Justice for Oakland Youth has written, "To move toward a reconciled America, we have to do the work ourselves. Reconciliation is an ongoing and collective process. We must roll up our sleeves and do the messy, challenging, but hopeful work of creating transformed relationships and structures leading us into new futures."[3] We hope that this article will serve as an invitation to our fellow white practitioners to do exactly that: "our work."

Bibliography

Bowman, N. A. "College Diversity Experiences and Cognitive Development: A Meta-Analysis." *Review of Educational Research* 80 (2010) 4–33.

Davis, Fania. "The US Needs a Truth and Reconciliation Process on Violence against African Americans." *YES Magazine*, December 4, 2014. https://truthout.org/articles/the-us-needs-a-truth-and-reconciliation-process-on-violence-against-african-americans/

Pettigrew, T. F., and L. R. Tropp."Does Intergroup Contact Reduce Prejudice? Recent Meta-Analytic Findings." In *Reducing Prejudice and Discrimination: The Claremont Symposium on Applied Social Psychology*, edited by Stuart Oskamp, 93–114. Mahwah, NJ: Erlbaum, 2000.

3. Davis, "The US Needs a Truth and Reconciliation Process."

3

Shared Legacies

Narratives of Race and Reconciliation by Descendants of Enslavers and the Enslaved

Jill Strauss

Introduction[1]

In August 2017, the white supremacist, nationalist, self-proclaimed "Alt Right" travelled from all over the United States to a rally at the University of Virginia in Charlottesville. They marched with their faces uncovered, and while carrying burning torches, swastikas, Confederate flags, and weapons, Klansman clashed with anti-racist counter-demonstrators; many people were injured and one person died. During their demonstration, Neo-Nazis chanted anti-gay slurs, "Black lives do not matter," and Jews will not replace them. This was an extreme but by no means isolated incident.

Atlantic Monthly writer Ta-Nehisi Coates has called for a national "collective introspection" in his seminal article "The Case for Reparations."[2] Many of us would like to have this difficult conversation because we recognize the connections between slavery in the past and racism in the present, but we feel we need guidance to initiate and facilitate the discussion. Others of us have been taught in school and through the media to think and experience our lives as disconnected events rather than understanding them as

1. Support for this chapter was provided by a PSC-CUNY Award, jointly funded by The Professional Staff Congress and The City University of New York.

2. Coates, "The Case for Reparations."

interrelated in terms of "causality, significance, and consequence."[3] Therefore, it can be difficult to engage people on issues that happened historically because they believe these issues have nothing to do with contemporary social issues or the future. In fact, the past and how we remember the past in the present has everything to do with what is to come. Likewise, some do not believe that we, in the present, should be held accountable for what our ancestors did, or they think that discussing a family's connections to slavery would be somehow disloyal. Moreover, acknowledging slavery at a national level brings into question the very creeds of the nation and, by extension, our cultural identity. This is why many of us would prefer to avoid the difficult conversations required of reckoning with the past despite the reality that we cannot have reconciliation[4] and real justice without truth-telling and accountability. As historian James Livingston notes in his article on universities with historic connections to slavery, "it's only when we acknowledge that we ourselves are the barbarians that we can stop running from the past and start learning from it."[5]

Coming To The Table (CTTT) is one organization that seeks to find "meaning and healing in the process of creating justice and promoting accountability"[6] by remembering the past in the present for healing, acknowledgment, and action (repair) at local and national levels. This chapter describes how CTTT applies the principles and values of restorative practices for "repairing the harm as much as possible, both concretely and symbolically"[7] for a sustainable transformation to a more fair and equitable society. Coming To The Table is unique in its understanding of trauma and healing and how this understanding can break the cycles of violence. CTTT is based in the Center for Justice and Peacebuilding (CJP) at Eastern Mennonite University. CJP started out as the Conflict Transformation Program, created by scholar practitioner John Paul Lederach in the 1990s. Although the name has been changed, the effort for the transformation of conflict as well as the deeper, more contested, historical issues, is fundamental to restorative justice theory and practice. Restorative justice is focused on repairing harm by creating the conditions to express human needs, develop relationships,

3. Wagner-Pacifici, *What Is an Event?*

4. The term 'reconciliation' implies that there was some kind of relationship in the past, and in the context of righting historical wrongs, how can there be reconciliation between people in the present who have never met? However, I agree with Weyeneth that the interdependent, complicated relationships between masters and their slaves shaped each other and our nation up to the present day

5. Livingston, "Don't Repress the Past."

6. Umbreit et al., "Restorative Justice in the Twenty-First Century."

7. Zehr, *Little Book of Restorative Justice.*

enable accountability, and foster growth. This theory and practice inform CTTT and its mission and vision by furthering the restorative justice field to include efforts at historical dialogue for reconciliation, societal transformation, and the generative possibilities of taking action.

What Is Coming to the Table?

Founded in 2006 by descendants of slaveholders and enslaved people, and with the continued guidance and support of the Center for Justice and Peacebuilding, Coming To The Table envisions the United States as "a just and truthful society that acknowledges and seeks to heal from the racial wounds of the past—from slavery and the many forms of racism it spawned."[8] Examining our history of settler colonialism and slavery through a restorative lens allows for a framing of "collective introspection"[9] to uncover and reflect upon the complex and painful truths of a racial past in order to determine what is possible in the present to address and repair the wrongdoing, and thereby shape a new legacy.

The framework for Coming To The Table is founded on four interrelated areas of practice:

1. **Facing History**—researching, acknowledging, and sharing personal, family, and community histories of race with openness and honesty;
2. **Making Connections**—connecting to others within and across racial lines in order to develop and deepen relationships;
3. **Healing Wounds**—exploring how we can heal together through dialogue, reunion, ritual, ceremony, the arts, apology, and other methods;
4. **Taking Action**—actively seeking to heal the wounds of racial inequality and injustice and to support racial reconciliation between individuals, within families, and in communities.[10]

These four areas were developed out of racial justice theory and practice through a restorative justice lens combined with the methodology of Strategies for Trauma Awareness and Resilience (STAR), another CJP initiative.[11] STAR was designed to develop awareness of the impacts of trauma, interrupt cycles of violence, and increase resilience at all levels of society. Created to

8. CCCT website at http://comingtothetable.org/about-us/vision-mission-values/

9. Coates, "The Case for Reparations."

10. Learn more about CTTT at http://comingtothetable.org/about-us/coming-table-approach/.

11. Yoder, "Desire to Address, Heal, Traumatic Legacy."

address the trauma of the events of September 11, 2001, STAR "equip[s] community leaders to understand the dynamics of trauma and healing, and their linkage to issues of conflict, justice and peace."[12] To engage in the difficult conversations of slavery and racism, CTTT uses the peacemaking circle process[13] to face history, make connections, heal wounds, and take action.

The circle process is an indigenous model integrated with contemporary practices of consensus-building, dialogue, and conflict transformation. The talking piece (any item that has special meaning to the facilitator and/or the group) and the circle format both serve to equalize power relationships, allowing everyone to be heard through storytelling. The one who holds the talking piece has their turn to speak while others listen and support the speaker.[14] "How we are treated, how we participate, who is involved, how we are heard: these factors give us a sense of whether or not we have experienced justice."[15] CTTT was founded on the belief that all voices matter. When we feel respected and heard, we tend to be more open to hearing other viewpoints and considering the larger picture. Furthermore, what begins in dialogue has the potential to move to collective action for positive social change.

I first learned about Coming To The Table while attending trainings at the Center for Justice and Peacebuilding (CJP) at Eastern Mennonite University (EMU). I participated in my first STAR training in 2004 which happened to coincide with meetings between the descendants of Sally Hemmings and Thomas Jefferson. These historic events did not go unnoticed at CJP, given its vision and mission, not to mention its location in Virginia, also the home of Jefferson's Monticello where many of those meetings initially took place. When I returned to EMU two years later to take a course at the Summer Peacebuilding Institute, I learned of the founding of Coming To The Table. CTTT was to be based there since it was started by EMU's grounds-supervisor, Will Harrison, whose ancestors were slaveholders, along with Susan Hutchison who is a Jefferson descendant. Coming To The Table is the first national organization bringing together descendants with a shared history and heritage of slavery and racism to *engage with the past in the present for a different future.*

12. Learn more at STAR at http://www.emu.edu/cjp/star/training/

13. Learn more about circles at Living Justice Press website, http://www.livingjusticepress.org/index.asp?Type=B_BASIC&SEC=%7B51F9C610-C097-445A-8C60-05E8B4599FE7%7D.

14. Learn more about circle processes at http://www.tolerance.org/blog/talking-circles-restorative-justice-and-beyond.

15. Pranis et al., *Peacemaking Circles.*

I had followed Coming To The Table from its inception but only joined in 2014 when an open invitation was made to all who recognize the injustice of slavery and racism in the past and present, and who want to work for racial healing and social change. Being part of CTTT has inspired me to do genealogical research into my own conflicted German Jewish history and heritage. In fact, there is considerable evidence and literature comparing, contrasting, and linking the black and Jewish ethnic and social experience, so this journey I am undertaking is not unprecedented. For example, slave spirituals, "expressed a yearning for a better life [and] claimed identification with the children of Israel."[16] Likewise, depending on when and where Jews have lived in the United States, they have been assigned to the white race and at other times an "off-white race," which shares the "experience of marginality" with blacks and other minority power groups.[17]

I do not think it is useful to compare trauma. However, efforts by second- and third-generation Germans who have worked to acknowledge and make amends for an inherited legacy of wrongdoing are models worth looking at as we in the United States find our ways to address the legacies of slavery and racism in the present. I am a woman, Jewish, and white. As a Jewish woman, I have experienced sexism and anti-Semitism along with the privilege that comes from being European American in the United States. These are complex, interconnected issues requiring both an internal journey about my personal heritage and an external journey regarding the heritage of my country. What can I learn from my German peers to make amends for my white privilege that often goes unacknowledged and from which I frequently benefit? What can we, as a nation, learn from third-generation Germans who offer us fifty years of "collective introspection,"[18] repair, and action?

Writing Projects at Coming To The Table

A "collective introspection" can take any number of forms. Coming To The Table has working groups focused on reparations, trips to sites significant to slavery and the civil rights movement, a writer's group, monthly dialogues, meditation, inspiring the next generation of activists, and a group for linked descendants (African Americans and European Americans with shared

16. Learn more about spirituals at http://www.umc.org/resources/part-of-history-african-american-spirituals-still-heal.

17. Brodkin, *How Jews Became White Folks*.

18. See Bar-On, *Legacy of Silence*; Bar-On and Kassem, "Storytelling"; Bar-Siman-Tov, *From Conflict Resolution*; Krondorfer, *Remembrance*; Ohsako, "German Pupils".

ancestry). In addition, CTTT members are prolific authors and poets, documentary filmmakers, artists, presenters, and activist public historians, offering genealogy research support, and advocating for the recovery of slave cemeteries. When there are few or no traces left, these creative projects take on the added challenge and responsibility of "historical representation."[19] At the same time, preservation and documentation can be healing and empowering when histories that have been all but lost or forgotten are recovered through (re)constructed and memorialized word, image, and ritual.

For instance, the Linked Descendants working group maintains the Bittersweet: Linked Through Slavery blog.[20] As CTTT member Felicia Furman notes, the organization "places a high value on these links because personal connections can create a compelling and intense desire for healing and reconciliation."[21] Members and others are invited to share their stories of doing genealogical research, approaching linked relatives, and having the opportunity to respond to the posts of others who generate important online dialogues about racism and justice. These 500-to-1000-word pieces describe the power of genealogy, blood, place, and story[22] as well as the frustrations of trying to find documentation. Thus they piece together a narrative based on educated assumptions about the personalities and behaviors of ancestors, along with the rationalization of slavery–what Grant Hayter-Menzies describes in *End of the List* as "a combination of imagination and logic suggests a scenario."[23]

As challenging as it can be for descendants of enslavers to find information about their ancestors, it can be that much harder or nearly impossible for descendants of enslaved people. To aid her healing process, Sharon Morgan developed a database called Our Black Ancestry to help African Americans find their history in honor of her ancestors–enslaved, enslavers, and lynching victims.[24] Morgan's database has a special section for descendants of enslavers where they can contribute information about the people their family enslaved, people who are often discovered in family papers such as deeds and wills. Morgan also co-authored Repairing the Breach of Slavery with Prinny Anderson[25] for the Bittersweet blog, which

19. Hartman, "The Time of Slavery."

20. Learn more about Bittersweet: Linked Through Slavery at https://linkedthroughslavery.com/our-stories/.

21. Source: https://linkedthroughslavery.com/2015/06/28/just-like-family/.

22. https://linkedthroughslavery.com/2015/12/01/linked-through-stories-and-history/.

23. https://linkedthroughslavery.com/2015/09/09/end-of-the-list/.

24. Sharon Morgan. Our Black Ancestry. https://ourblackancestry.com/about.php.

25. https://linkedthroughslavery.com/2016/02/10/repairing-the-breach-of-slavery/.

describes the CTTT monthly conference call as a venue for "what linked descendants say about making connections across the divide." The blog post describes participant satisfactions as well as their frustrations with trying to contact and create relationships with their linked family members. Then, the blog post reader is asked, "What would YOU like to say to or ask of people with whom you are linked by slavery?"

This invitation to the reader to add their story to the blog is also an invitation to those who have not yet begun their own family history (re) search to take on the task to further repair the divisions and estrangements that are also an inheritance of settler colonialism and slavery.

The monthly conference call is another example of how Coming To The Table works to maintain connections between biannual conferences. One conference call in September 2014 was focused on developing a Coming to the Table writers' group. Several on the call voiced a similar need to write their stories in community because they were new to the writing process. Others felt prepared to take on the challenge but expressed a concern that they did not think they had enough in their respective story for a whole book or did not have the time for such an endeavor. This conversation sparked the idea of a collection of non-fiction essays by descendants of enslavers and the enslaved to be published in one volume. There are many commendable books on slavery in the United States,[26] but none of these texts takes a multiple-perspective approach. This opportunity is something that Coming To The Table members could do and should do in keeping with the organization's efforts to challenge and transform the legacy of slavery and racism.

Most Coming To The Table efforts are co-led by an African American and a European American, so I partnered with journalist Dionne Ford, a descendant of both enslavers and enslaved to co-edit the anthology. Dionne is also researching and writing her own memoir called *Finding Josephine* that is about Dionne's journey to discover and recover her biracial heritage.[27] As co-editors, we created the title, *Slavery's Descendants: Shared Legacies of Race and Reconciliation*.[28] While Dionne and I had thought about the positive contribution the anthology will have for those who read the book, as it turns out, writing the respective narratives has had a cathartic effect for several contributors. Literature, be it prose, poetry, fiction, or nonfiction, has a powerful role to play in the reconciliation process for authors as well as readers. Narratives can be transformative for authors when we are able

26. See Ball, *Slaves in the Family*; Branan, *The Family Tree*; DeWolf, *Inheriting the Trade*; Gordon-Reed, *Thomas Jefferson*; Hartman, *Lose Your Mother*; Horton, *Slavery*; Wiencek, *The Hairstons*.

27. Ford. *Finding Josephine*.

28. Ford and Strauss, *Slavery's Descendants*.

to make meaning of our experiences and find shared meaning with others. Making connections based on communal experiences can be particularly healing for groups such as African Americans who "have experienced political repression, historic violence, or marginalization, [whose] voices and experiences have usually been excluded from mainstream understanding of that particular period of history."[29] Coming To The Table members, however, are not only crossing racial divides. Many are also seeking out ways to find the humanity in their own ancestors. For some of the European Americans, this is a particularly challenging part of their journey. Whereas descendants of enslavers often feel guilt, African Americans may feel shame and even a kind of inherited trauma termed "Post Traumatic Slave Syndrome"[30] as a consequence of being descended from enslaved people.[31] CTTT members are not just attempting to walk in another's shoes; we are attempting "to walk back in someone's footsteps,"[32] and this requires empathy and imagination as well as a sense of obligation for what happened in the past.

The telling observation that she was "walking back in someone's footsteps" was made by Crystal Rosson, a participant in one of CTTT's Slave Dwelling Project overnight events led by CTTT member Joe McGill.[33] This event was held at Thomas Jefferson's Poplar Forest plantation. McGill has arranged Slave Dwelling Project overnights across the country to raise awareness and discussion, as well as encourage protection of extant slave dwellings. Empathy and understanding are created through first-hand experiences of sleeping in the same spaces and in the same ways as the enslaved did, namely on the floor. "It's being a part of and going through the same thing that they went through and feeling what they felt, and through that, understanding just a glimpse into that world."[34] Hamber maintains that genuine healing is communicated through the context and process, and also through the relationships engendered around the rituals and actions of righting the wrongs of the past and the present.[35] However, as discussed at the beginning of this chapter, there are many reasons for an unwillingness or inability to engage in these processes. Cohen points out that while there can be a "mismatch between people's need to tell their stories and express their suffering, and

29. Hooker and Czajkowski, *Transforming Historical Harms.*

30. Leary, *Post Traumatic Slave Syndrome.*

31. Carten, "How the Legacy of Slavery."

32. Schkloven, "Visitors Spend."

33. Learn more about the Slave Dwelling Project at http://slavedwellingproject.org/

34. Schkloven, "Visitors Spend."

35. Hamber, "Public Memorials."

'the other's capacity to listen.'"[36] Reading someone else's experience can seem less threatening, leaving the reader more open to taking in the narrative even when it is counter to their understanding of the world or identity. This initial willingness to accept the experience of the other as valid is a first step toward reconciliation and even forgiveness.

What forgiveness and literary activity share, then, is an act of submission and active risk-taking in so far as one person opens up to the possibilities brought into existence through contact with another person. For just as in writing, where the author must relinquish the desire to predetermine the reader's comprehension in any definitive way, so also in giving and offering forgiveness, participants must make themselves vulnerable to the interpreting activity of the other.[37]

As it turns out, I went through this interpreting activity myself as co-editor of *Slavery's Descendants*. I am writing a chapter titled, "What a Legacy of Slavery and Racism has to do with Me," which explores our present-day dilemma and debate on the purposes and consequences of revisiting the past through the lens of my own story. Like all the contributing authors, I am doing genealogical research and collecting information from relatives. In addition, writing this chapter coincides with an opportunity to do onsite research in Michelfeld, Germany, the hometown of my grandfather and my ancestors going back to at least the 1700s. My guides are the townspeople who are researching and memorializing my great-grandparents who were the last Jews in the village and the last to leave in 1937 or 1938. I also plan to go to the surviving home of my great-grandparents which my father remembers visiting as a young child. I will write about the experience of having pieces of my lost ancestry returned to me by those who descend from the ones that tried to take it away. In the process, I will create my own narrative of a past of forced displacement and migration that in turn creates a sense of place and a new belonging for me. Hopefully I will also build new relationships with those who are doing the hard work of researching and documenting our shared past.

Coming To The Table members are enthusiastic about the idea of an anthology. From the original thirty proposals we now have a collection of more than two dozen essays that collectively give a more nuanced perspective on our national inheritance of slavery and racism. *Slavery's Descendants* includes essays by contributors like Sarah Kohrs who writes about restoring a cemetery in her community where many enslaved were buried. Karen Branan and Stephanie Harp reconstruct their families' participation

36. Cohen, "Engaging with the Arts."

37. McGonegal, *Imagining Justice*.

in separate lynchings, and recount their work to memorialize the victims. Phoebe and Betty Kilby tour the country, discussing their families' connection through slavery.[38]

The narratives included in *Slavery's Descendants* expand the time frame associated with our country's history of slavery. The wide range starts with Grant Hayter Menzies' narrative which connects his family's roots to the first 1555 slave route from Africa to England which thereafter became an established practice carried over to the 'new world.' At the other end of the time continuum is Elisa Pearmain's narrative that probes the accepted relationships established by the institution of slavery which remained in her family in the body of a cook all the way through the 1960's and the Apollo Mission to the moon. The essays return to the Americas with Fabrice Guerrier who emigrated to the United States from Haiti as a teenager when he "first discovered that he was black [sic]." To comprehend what it means to be a Black man in the United States, Fabrice looked to W.E.B. Dubois, and then found healing at the Center for Justice and Peacebuilding through Coming To The Table activities. These essays also enlarge our understanding of where slavery existed, which includes Rhode Island (DeWolf) and Oregon (Noakes). Some of the narratives reframe who we assume to have been touched by slavery. For example, Rodney Williams recounts unearthing that his ancestor was the son of a slave and a Quaker, a religious group thought of as pacifist and egalitarian. These and the rest of the essays by descendants of enslavers and the enslaved are uncomfortable and sometimes harrowing, filled with recurring themes of displacement (literally and figuratively), identity, trauma, shame and guilt, memory and silences across generations, along with generosity, gratitude, and love. Throughout the book, the various contributions challenge readers' understanding of history while uncovering personal and collective truths.

Conclusion

In his January 2017 Farewell Address, President Barak Obama said, "Race remains a potent and often divisive force in our society."[39] Coming To The Table, with its mission and vision, is expanding the restorative justice field by including efforts of historical dialogue for expression of harms, both past and present, and to determine obligations for inherited and present-day wrongs. Moving beyond guilt, shame, and blame, and on to imagining

38. Ford and Strauss, *Slavery's Descendants*.

39. https://www.nytimes.com/2017/01/10/us/politics/obama-farewell-address-speech.html.

possibilities can have the added benefit of giving citizens an opportunity to not only break open the many facets of our national story, but also to determine together what Bell calls a "collective meaning" of our shared history and legacy. In the absence of a national truth-telling process, CTTT is taking the first steps by adapting restorative justice models at the grassroots, offering examples for how we can use restorative practices in more situations and contexts in society.

Coming to the Table also emphasizes the creative, generative possibilities of taking action for societal transformation. For there to be true, national self-examination or "collective introspection" (if such a thing were possible), we will need organizations like CTTT that are creating the conditions for accountability and for what author Jill Scott calls "poetic forgiveness" that "arises as the product of human creative communication . . . this forgiveness constructs us. It speaks to us as we speak in creative ways."[40] At CTTT, we believe that by learning our history, we can forge a new sense of identity and use that knowledge to educate others and create solidarity.

Bibliography

Ball, Edward. *Slaves in the Family.* New York: Farrar, Straus & Giroux, 1998.

Bar-On, Dan. *Legacy of Silence: Encounters with Children of the Third Reich.* Cambridge: Harvard University Press, 1989.

Bar-On, Dan, and Fatma Kassem. "Storytelling as a Way to Work through Intractable Conflicts: The German–Jewish Experience and Its Relevance to the Palestinian–Israeli Context." *Journal of Social Issues* 60 (2004).

Bar-Siman-Tov, Yaacov. *From Conflict Resolution to Reconciliation.* New York: Oxford University Press, 2004.

Bell, Vikki. "Contemporary Art and Transitional Justice in Northern Ireland: The Consolation of Form." *Journal of Visual Culture* 10 (2011) 324–53. http://doi:10.1177/1470412911419760.

Bennett, Milton J. *Basic Concepts of Intercultural Communication: Selected Readings.* Yarmouth: Intercultural Press, 1998.

Berlin, Ira. "Coming to Terms with Slavery in Twenty-First-Century America." In *Slavery and Public History: The Tough Stuff of American Memory*, edited by James Oliver Horton and Lois E. Horton. Chapel Hill: University of North Carolina Press, 2009.

Branan, Karen. *The Family Tree: A Lynching in Georgia, a Legacy of Secrets, and My Search for the Truth.* New York: Atria, 2016.

Brodkin, Karen. *How Jews Became White Folks and What that Says about Race in America.* New Brunswick, NJ: Rutgers University Press, 1998.

Carten, Alma. "How the Legacy of Slavery Affects the Mental Health of Black Americans Today." 2015. http://theconversation.com/how-the-legacy-of-slavery-affects-the-mental-health-of-black-americans-today-44642.

40. Scott, *A Poetics of Forgiveness.*

Coates, Ta-Nehisi. "The Case for Reparations." *The Atlantic* 313/5 (2014) 54.
Cohen, Cynthia. "Engaging with the Arts to Promote Coexistence." In *Imagine Coexistence: Restoring Humanity after Violent Ethnic Conflict*, edited by Antonia Chayes and Martha Minow, 267–79. San Francisco: Jossey-Bass, 2003.
DeWolf, Thomas Norman. *Inheriting the Trade: A Northern Family Confronts Its Legacy as the Largest Slave-Trading Dynasty in U. S. History.* Boston: Beacon, 2008.
Ford, Dionne, and Jill Strauss, eds. *Slavery's Descendants: Shared Legacies of Race and Reconciliation.* New Brunswick, NJ: Rutgers University Press, 2019.
Ford, Dionne. *Finding Josephine.* New York: Putnam, 2020.
Gopnik, Adam. "The Spanish Inquisition Revisited." *New Yorker* (Jan. 16, 2012).
Gordon-Reed, Annette. *Thomas Jefferson and Sally Hemings: An American Controversy.* Charlottesville: University of Virginia Press, 1997.
Gutman, Yifat, Adam D. Brown, and Amy Sodaro, eds. *Memory and the Future: Transnational Politics, Ethics and Society.* Palgrave Macmillan Memory Studies. Hampshire: Palgrave Macmillan, 2010.
Hamber, Brandon. "Public Memorials and Reconciliation Processes in Northern Ireland." Paper delivered at Trauma and Transitional Justice in Divided Societies Conference, Warrington, Virginia. 2004.
Hartman, Saidiya. "The Time of Slavery." *South Atlantic Quarterly* 101 (2002) 757–77.
Hartman, Saidiya. *Lose Your Mother: A Journey along the Atlantic Slave Route.* New York: Farrar, Straus & Giroux, 2007.
Hooker, David Anderson, and Amy Potter Czajkowski. "Transforming Historical Harms." Harrisonburg, VA: Eastern Mennonite University, 2012.
Horton, James Oliver, and Lois E. Horton. *Slavery and the Making of America.* Oxford: Oxford University Press, 2006.
Krondorfer, Björn. *Remembrance and Reconciliation: Encounters between Young Jews and Germans.* New Haven: Yale University Press, 1995.
Leary, Joy DeGruy. *Post Traumatic Slave Syndrome : America's Legacy of Enduring Injury and Healing.* Portland, OR: Uptone, 2005.
Lewis, Ted, and Mark Umbreit. "A Humanistic Approach to Mediation and Dialogue: An Evolving Transformative Practice." *Conflict Resolution Quarterly* 33 (2015) 3–17. doi: 10.1002/crq.21130.
Livingston, James. "Don't Repress the Past." *The Chronicle of Higher Education*, Nov. 20, 2015.
Martin, Michael T., and Marilyn Yaquinto, eds. *Redress for Historical Injustices in the United States: On Reparations for Slavery, Jim Crow, and Their Legacies.* Durham: Duke University Press, 2007.
McGonegal, Julie. *Imagining Justice: The Politics of Postcolonial Forgiveness and Reconciliation.* Montreal: McGill-Queen's University Press, 2008.
Ohsako, Toshio. "German Pupils and Jewish Seniors: Intergenerational Dialogue as a Framework for Healing History." In *Linking Lifetimes: A Global View of Intergenerational Exchange*, edited by Matthew S. Kaplan, Nancy Z. Henkin, and Atsuko T. Kusano, 209–19. Lanham, MD: University Press of America, 2002.
Parry, Marc. "Stained by Slavery." *Chronicle of Higher Education* 63 (Mar. 2, 2017): B6-B9. 2017.
Pranis, Kay. *The Little Book of Circle Processes: A New/Old Approach to Peacemaking.* Intercourse, PA: Good Books, 2005.

Pranis, Kay, Barry Stuart, and Mark Wedge. *Peacemaking Circles: From Crime to Community*. St. Paul: Living Justice, 2003.

Schkloven, Emma. "Visitors Spend the Night at Poplar Forest as Part of Slave Dwelling Project." *The News & Advance* (2017). http://www.newsadvance.com/lifestyles/visitors-spend-the-night-at-poplar-forest-as-part-of/article_4a33dd19-09cd-5b10-8fa8-6560fdd1090b.html.

Scott, Jill. *A Poetics of Forgiveness: Cultural Responses to Loss and Wrongdoing*. New York: Palgrave Macmillan, 2010.

Strauss, Jill. "The Art of Acknowledgement: Re-imagining Relationships in Northern Ireland." In *Reparation for Victims of Crimes Against Humanity: The Healing Role of Reparation*, edited by Jo-Anne M. Wemmers, 169–82. London: Routledge, 2014.

Umbreit, Mark S., Betty Vos, Robert B. Coates, Elizabeth Lightfoot. "Restorative Justice in The Twenty-first Century: A Social Movement Full of Opportunities and Pitfalls." *Marquette Law Review* 89 (2005) 251–304.

Wagner-Pacifici, Robin Erica. *What Is an Event?* Chicago: University of Chicago Press, 2017.

Wiencek, Henry. *The Hairstons: An American Family in Black and White*. New York: St. Martin's, 1999.

Weyeneth, Robert R. "The Power of Apology and the Process of Historical Reconciliation." *The Public Historian* 23/3 (2001) 9–38. doi: 10.1525/tph.2001.23.3.9.

Yoder, David. "Desire to Address, Heal, Traumatic Legacy of U.S. Slavery Sparks Growth in Coming to the Table Group." Eastern Mennonite University (2014). https://emu.edu/now/news/2014/06/desire-to-address-heal-traumatic-legacy-of-u-s-slavery-sparks-growth-in-coming-to-the-table-group/.

Zehr, Howard. *Changing Lenses: A New Focus for Crime and Justice*. Edited by Inc NetLibrary. Scottdale, PA: Herald, 1990.

———. *The Little Book of Restorative Justice*. Revised and updated ed. The Little Books of Justice and Peacebuilding. New York: Good Books, 2015.

Zierler, Wendy. "My Holocaust Is not Your Holocaust: 'Facing' Black and Jewish Experience in *The Pawnbroker*, *Higher Ground*, and *The Nature of Blood*." *Holocaust and Genocide Studies* 18 (2004) 46-67. doi: 10.1093/hgs/dch039.

4

Pedagogy of Circles

Teaching Restorative Justice to Social Work Students

Daniel Rhodes

After my meditation beads return to me, I sit holding them silently for a few minutes to let the shared stories sink in for everyone. I then request that the students prepare for the closing ceremony—our moment of mindfulness—inviting the mindfulness bell as we sit silently. These are senior social work students in the final year of their studies. Being at a public, mid-sized Southern university, these students are steeped in what Freire calls the "banking" model of education.[1] The first day of class is to be detailed and ordered: here is the syllabus . . . these are the readings . . . these are the assignments . . . this is the grading scale . . . this is the rubric upon which you will be evaluated . . . this is the attendance policy . . . etc. Anything else creates an ambiguity that makes students uncomfortable. Education is "suffering from narration sickness."[2] For students, "the teacher talks about reality as if it were motionless, static, compartmentalized, and predictable. Or else he expounds on a topic completely alien to the existential experience of the students."[3] As I ring the mindfulness bell for the closing ceremony, the sound resonating and fading, I reflect on the Peace Circle and the student's reactions.

1. Freire, *Pedagogy of the Oppressed*, 72.
2. Freire, *Pedagogy of the Oppressed*, 71.
3. Freire, *Pedagogy of the Oppressed*, 71.

Using the Circle process to teach restorative justice helps transform the anti-dialogical narrative that students have been institutionalized in up to this point. The Circle is distinct in asking questions such as:

- How can we move towards healing?
- What can be done to repair the immediate harm and to prevent further harm?
- What wounds and circumstances—past and present—prevent us from having healthy relationships, both with ourselves and with others?
- What steps can we take to understand these wounds and to aid healing?[4]

These are questions that social workers should be addressing in communities. Social work students must have restorative justice concepts integrated into the curriculum from the very beginning, and therefore "it is in the interest of social work to take a leadership position in advancing restorative justice principles and restorative processes."[5] Having social work students engage in a Circle process fuses these ideas together: the dialogical engagement with each other and the community, the integration of the Social Work Code of Ethics, and the working towards healing within communities through restorative justice. As Mark Umbreit and Marilyn Amour best explain it, "Peacemaking circles are based on the process of dialogue, relationship building, and the communication of moral values in order to promote accountability, healing, and compassion through community participation in resolving conflicts."[6]

Radical Acts: Transforming the Classroom

I came to the classroom early that day to prepare for our Circle. This is an arduous process since classrooms are replete with obstacles that discourage educators from engaging in anything except the banking model of education. Official placards are in every classroom with diagrams of how the classrooms are to be arranged in precise detail. Desks are heavy, bulky and cumbersome to move. It takes me twenty minutes before students arrive for moving, placing and stacking desks around the edges of the room, then arranging the chairs in a circle. Meanwhile a sign is posted in my room: "Please do not move desks or furniture."

4. Pranis et al., *Peacemaking* Circles, 11.
5. Beck, *Social Work*, 6.
6. Umbreit and Armour, *Restorative Justice Dialogue*, 86.

Historically, classrooms are arranged in straight rows with chairs facing frontward for specific reasons, so that, "Teachers and students have few opportunities to be in the liberatory classrooms."[7] Classes are designed to maximize space so that students are situated in cramped settings that restrict movement or interaction with each other; they are to remain static and to maintain their attention directly ahead. Students are to be passive recipients, "and since people 'receive' the world as passive entities, education should make them more passive still, and adapt them to the world."[8] Education is to be hegemonic, and thus transforming the physical classroom is itself a radical act.

Students are institutionalized in this form of education early in their lives. Jonathan Kozol discusses this in his work, *The Shame of the Nation*, where schools in the United States have adopted the "Taylorism" model of education.[9] Taylorism is based on the philosophy of Frederick Taylor and his "primitive utilitarianism" which was used to manage factory workers in the early 1900s and thereafter replicated in the classroom.[10] With Taylorism, students are objects to regulate and control, with the structure of the classroom helping to facilitate this management model of education.

By breaking from this tradition of classroom management, I literally transform the classroom, disrupting the rows and columns and creating a circle, thus invoking Baldwin's ideas:

> A circle is not just a meeting with the chairs rearranged. A circle is a way of doing things differently than we have become accustomed to. The circle is a return to our original form of community as well as a leap forward to create a new form of community.[11]

In the middle of the Circle, I position a sacred item, the *Circle of Friends*, which is a small stone statue of human figures holding hands and encircling a lit candle. As Zimmerman and Coyle note, "Lighting a candle in the center before beginning invariable evokes a sense of ceremony, because fire has been the center of tribal and community circles throughout the world since ancient times."[12] Natural light floods the room with blinds open and the fluorescent overhead lights turned off. Students were perplexed when they filter into the

7. Shore and Freire, *Pedagogy for Liberation*, 17.
8. Freire, *Pedagogy of the Oppressed*, 76.
9. Kozol, *Shame of the Nation*, 56.
10. Kozol, *Shame of the Nation*, 68.
11. Baldwin, *Calling the Circle*, 26.
12. Zimmerman and Coyle, *Way of Council*, 15.

first day of the traditional classroom, all designed for the "bureaucratizing of the mind,"[13] only to see the desks stacked up in the corners and the chairs arranged into a circle. They position themselves, reluctant to sit close to me since I am the professor. Late arrivals have no other choice. I am, after all, the authority figure they want to avoid. Students fidget and squirm, unsure about what the next three hours will entail, whispering to each other and looking at their cellphones as I sit quietly and they settle in.

My Approach (Methodology): Engaged Pedagogy

Before I begin this process with students, I am mindful to balance my role as a Circle facilitator and educator. In the classroom, I am an educator and mentor to future social workers, but also an authority figure. I want to educate students in this process and I encourage them to engage in it authentically. This will only work if students feel that this is "less about power-over and more about power-with."[14] This requires preparation on my part; it means "attending to our own personal growth, through self-examination, self-reflection, and inner questioning is essential to Circle work."[15] My role as an educator, a social worker, and a Circle facilitator all come together in my educational philosophy. This is what bell hooks calls "Engaged Pedagogy."[16]

For Hooks, by synthesizing the works of educator Paulo Freire and Vietnamese Buddhist monk Thích Nhất Hạnh, "Engaged Pedagogy" is a learning process that "comes easiest to those of us who teach who also believe that there is an aspect of our vocation that is sacred; who believe that our work is not merely to share information but to share in the intellectual and spiritual growth of our students."[17] It will not do for me to have social work students be passive recipients of information in the classroom, only to expect them to turn around and engage with those in the community in dialogue. Students should understand that "the active nature of students' participation in the learning process must be stressed."[18] I must be vigilant in understanding my position as an authority figure while simultaneously encouraging students to engage in authentic dialogue. "The great potential

13. Freire, *Pedagogy of Freedom*, 102.
14. Pranis et al., *Peacemaking Circles*, 14.
15. Pranis et al., *Peacemaking Circles*, 53.
16. hooks, *Teaching to Transgress*, 13.
17. hooks, *Teaching to Transgress*, 13.
18. Giroux, *Theory and Resistance*, 202.

of council is its power to draw out the wisdom each person brings to the circle—and that, after all, is what education is all about."[19]

History of Council and Peace Circle Structure

With students settled in the classroom, I welcome everyone. Pointing out that the classroom is arranged differently, I inform them that we will be breaking the traditional first day of class where a teacher just disseminates information. Instead, we will be engaging in a Peace Circle. I explain to them the overall physical structure of the Circle. As Pranis notes,

> Participants sit in a circle of chairs with no table. Sometimes objects that have meaning to the group are placed in the center as a focal point to remind participants of shared values and common ground. The physical format of the Circle symbolizes shared leadership, equality, connection, and inclusion. It also promotes focus, accountability, and participation from all.[20]

I request that they put all items and cell phones away; I want everyone to be fully present and mindful for this process. We then go around the Circle with each of us introducing ourselves and saying something unique about who we are. I begin with myself, reflecting on who I am to provide an example for students and to let them know that I am not only facilitating this process, but engaging in it with them. This lets them know that I want it to be authentic. "Authenticity and a focus on *personal revelation* rather than philosophical reflection helps everyone stay attentive and honors the circle further by showing a willingness to take risks."[21] By me disclosing aspects of myself, I am also taking risks and thus requesting students do the same. "How can I motivate students unless they act with me? Inventing a course in-progress with students is both exciting and anxiety-producing."[22]

After introductions, I briefly explain to the students what the Circle process is, reviewing its historical roots in Indigenous or First Nations peoples, as well as religious and secular practices, and that "the Indigenous origins of the Circle process are the source of key teachings that are foundational to the process."[23] I also want students to understand why the classroom has been physically changed. As Baldwin notes,

19. Zimmerman and Coyle, *Way of Council*, 179.
20. Pranis, *Little Book of Circle*, 11.
21. Zimmerman and Coyle, *Way of Council*, 29.
22. Shore and Freire, *Pedagogy for Liberation*, 7.
23. Boyes-Weston and Pranis, *Circle Forward*, 28.

> When we come into a room and rearrange the seating, it causes us to rearrange our expectations also. Creating the space for council in a way indigenous peoples have come together since time immemorial. Moving our bodies from rows to circles, and our self-interests from the center to the edge, enable each of us to reclaim our innate knowledge of circle and carry it forward consciously.[24]

I also discuss the terms used to describe this process, noting that "the term 'sentencing circle' gave way to the more inclusive term of 'peacemaking circle,' reflecting the larger aim to bring peace by building communities."[25] Even though I am calling this a Peace Circle, I am following the Community-Building Circle model that Kay Pranis expands on. "The purpose of a Community-Building Circle is to create bonds and build relationships among a group of people who have a shared interest. Community-Building Circles support effective collective and mutual responsibility."[26] Social work is a community engagement project, yet social work students are not guided on how to engage each other in community; beginning a class with a Community-Building Circle is an essential step towards this engagement. Through the Circle process, I am establishing community building in class, countering the anti-dialogical and hegemonic educational process that has been imposed upon them, and restoring students to their inquisitive educational nature. This process also helps social work students to develop ways to address harms within communities. For this reason, it is important for me to name it a Peace Circle for students.

Restorative Justice

I explain to students that the Circle process is also a way to introduce them to restorative justice, a concept most social work students have never heard of despite the fact that they will be engaging in restorative practices in the community. As social work students, they will be leaving our program to engage communities with disadvantaged populations which have historically been oppressed. Social workers are to adhere to a Code of Ethics from the National Association of Social Workers (NASW) that expects them to engage in the values of human rights and social justice. "As a social reform movement, restorative justice is social justice in action."[27] Students can-

24. Baldwin, *Calling the Circle,* 57.
25. Pranis et al., *Peacemaking Circles,* 21.
26. Pranis, *Little Book of Circle,* 16.
27. Umbreit and Armour, *Restorative Justice Dialogue,* 43.

not ethically impose the very anti-dialogical, hegemonic structure of the classroom onto the community. As Paulo Freire notes,

> Internalizing paternal authority through the rigid relationship structure emphasized by the school, these young people tend when they become professionals (because of the very fear of freedom instilled by these relationships) to repeat the rigid patterns in which they were miseducated. This phenomenon, in addition to their class position, perhaps explains why so many professionals adhere to anti-dialogical action.[28]

This "anti-dialogical action" that social workers engage in with the community reinforces the negative stereotypes of social workers, especially the "disconcerting myth about social work practice is that we are a profession of 'baby snatchers' who take children away from their families."[29] As social workers, we are to be restorative justice practitioners who address issues of harm in the community, not reinforce or impose it.

Peace Circle Guidelines

Guidelines for our Peace Circle are posted and I direct our attention to them, enumerating each one as a way to generate dialogue about what they mean. I adopted the four main guidelines from Zimmerman and Coyle's text, *The Way of Council*: 1) speaking from the heart; 2) listening from the heart; 3) being "lean of expression," and 4) spontaneity.[30] I want my students to contemplate each one of these guidelines before beginning the Circle process. We start with, speaking from the heart and reflect on what this means. In my attempt to generate conversation, most sit silently, feeling unsure how to respond. Some answer sheepishly, concerned that they may get the answer 'wrong' and will be called out because of it. I am encouraging them to engage in dialogue, not just with me but with each other. I want students to be thoughtful in their understanding and responses to these guidelines because, "the correct method lies in dialogue" and not in what student just think I want to hear.[31]

Social work education creates a cognitive dissonance for students. Positioned in a traditional education setting, students are continuously reinforced to be objective. Following the Western scientific model of

28. Freire, *Pedagogy of the Oppressed*, 155.
29. Kropf, "Justice, Restoration," 26.
30. Zimmerman and Coyle, *Way of Council*, 28–34.
31. Freire, *Pedagogy of the Oppressed*, 67.

"technocratic rationality,"[32] education emphasizes a reductionist approach to learning; students are to think in terms of 'third person' and eschew ideas tainted by emotions. In social work, we adhere to an 'objective,' Western model of education, while simultaneously telling students that they must follow a Code of Ethics that highlights empathy as an essential part of social work. One of the main components of the Code of Ethics in social work is "the importance of human relationships."

> Social workers understand that relationships between and among people are an important vehicle for change. Social workers engage people as partners in the helping process. Social workers seek to strengthen relationships among people in a purposeful effort to promote, restore, maintain, and enhance the well-being of individuals, families, social groups, organizations, and communities.[33]

This is exactly Howard Zehr's point when he notes how "Restorative Justice reminds us of the importance of relationships."[34] We are expecting social work students to engage in the activity of strengthening relationships and developing empathy and compassion, while reinforcing in the classroom that they need to be objective yet passive learners. When I review the first guideline of speaking from the heart, I immediately see the cognitive dissonance and their struggle to process this information. Professors do not ask students what it means to *speak from the heart*, not even social work professors.

Acknowledging and validating each response from the students, I press them to reflect deeper. Once students express their ideas on the first guideline, I then share my perspective of what it means, integrating their responses into mine. You can tell through their answers that they are reinforcing their roles as obedient learners, struggling to get the answer 'right'. I want them to understand that speaking from the heart means that their voice matters. As Umbreit and Armour note, "Consequently, all participants, regardless of role or status, age, or experience, are of equal importance, with equal voice."[35] This is where the philosophy of Engaged Pedagogy is important with its emphasis on undoing what traditional education has imposed. It is the restorative nature of Engaged Pedagogy which makes it a restorative practice. With traditional education, speaking from the heart is considered anathema to the process; one is to be objective and

32. Giroux, *Theory and Resistance*, xx.

33. National Association of Social Workers: Code of Ethics.

34. Zehr, *Changing Lenses*, 246.

35. Umbreit and Armour, *Restorative Justice Dialogue*, 179.

unfeeling. In the Circle process, speaking from the heart is essential; "to repress our feelings is to repress ourselves."[36]

We continue with the guidelines. Students slowly begin to open up but are still hesitant to respond freely, afraid of being chastised if they answer incorrectly. Listening from the heart is a vital component of what it is to be a social worker. To listen from the heart is to demonstrate that "social workers respect the inherent dignity and worth of the person."[37] Inability to listen deeply and mindfully means that social workers are inadequate in doing their job effectively and competently, and thereby unable to develop empathy or connect with clients and communities in ways that they should. This is also reflected in the NASW Code of Ethics where "Social workers treat each person in a caring and respectful fashion, mindful of individual differences and cultural and ethnic diversity."[38] Listening from the heart also determines how well the Circle process will go. "The success of council is largely determined by the quality of listening in the circle."[39]

We continue with the third and fourth guidelines, namely being lean of expression and allowing for spontaneity. The students struggle with the tension they are feeling, "but it's a creative tension."[40] Students are having to take a leap of faith with this process, opening themselves up and honoring those around them, which is challenging for them, given their history of education. Ultimately, social work students "must learn to look at the world holistically in order to understand the interconnections of the parts to each other."[41] Altogether, these guidelines help students in their understanding of the impact that harm does to the whole community.

My role as an authority figure is also transforming into a facilitator, and our reflection of these guidelines becomes an Engaged Pedagogy. I invoke Kay Pranis who wrote how "guidelines help participants put their personal values into practice. In this context, guidelines are seen not as rigid rules imposed from without but rooted in each person's own values."[42] These guidelines connect students to their social work values and Code of Ethics, including the principles of "dignity and worth of the person; importance of human relationships; and integrity."[43] Once again, this process

36. Thích Nhất Hạnh, *Awakening of the Heart,* 148.

37. National Association of Social Workers: Code of Ethics.

38. National Association of Social Workers: Code of Ethics.

39. Zimmerman and Coyle, *Way of Council,* 29.

40. Baldwin, *Calling the Circle,* 34.

41. Giroux, *Theory and Resistance,* 202.

42. Pranis, *Little Book of Circle,* 104–5.

43. National Association of Social Workers: Code of Ethics.

must be experiential, not just theoretical. "This is why liberatory learning cannot be standardized. It has to be situated, experimental, creative."[44] These guidelines, culminating in students being spontaneous, defies the traditional educational setting of regulation and order, and allows students to engage in learning actively.

Talking Piece

While discussing all of this with my students, I hold in my hand the talking piece I will use for our Peace Circle: my own meditation beads. These are small bone beads that I have possessed for years which I often use as a talking piece. "If a group is meeting in council for the first time, the leader may want to choose a familiar object as a talking piece."[45] Directing our attention to the talking piece, I explain to students what it is and the purpose is serves. I describe how we will conduct the Circle process, with the talking piece passed around for everyone to use and that participants speaking only when they have this talking piece. I illustrate to students that "the talking piece slows the pace of conversation and encourages thoughtful and reflective interactions among participants."[46]

I want to be clear and guide students through their understanding of the importance of the talking piece since this is new for most of these students. I reinforce for students that, "holding the talking piece silently while making eye contact with everyone in the circle, can be a profound part of the practice."[47] I emphasize for students that holding the talking piece without speaking, or choosing to pass are options. Students have been reinforced in education that they are to only speak when spoken to, and that when singled out they need respond with the 'correct' answer. I want students to know that, "whatever the reason, expressing oneself through silence is always acceptable."[48] As Paulo Freire notes,

> The importance of silence in the context of communication is fundamental. On the one hand, it affords me space while listening to the verbal communication of another person and allows me to enter into the internal rhythm of the speaker's thought and experience that rhythm as language. On the other hand, silence makes it possible for the speaker who is really committed

44. Shore and Freire, *Pedagogy for Liberation*, 26.
45. Zimmerman and Coyle, *Way of Council*, 19.
46. Pranis, *Little Book of Circle*, 35.
47. Zimmerman and Coyle, *Way of Council*, 79.
48. Zimmerman and Coyle, *Way of Council*, 79.

> to the experience of communication rather than to the simple transmission of information to hear the question, the doubt, the creativity of the person who is listening. Without this, communication withers.[49]

In a conventional classroom, a student's understanding of silence only comes from being a passive recipient of information. For the Circle process to work, I need students to know how to actually be silent while still being actively engaged. I do this through teaching them about mindfulness and using a moment of mindfulness as the opening ritual of the Peace Circle for class.

Opening Ceremony: Moment of Mindfulness

Each Circle process begins and ends with a ceremony or ritual. Umbreit and Armour have described how this can work.

> Some type of ceremony is used to open and close the circle. The opening ceremony sets the time and space for the circle apart from the usual hustle and bustle of the day. It establishes the tone for the circle and moves participants themselves and others in different ways. It centers the person psychically and shifts his or her perspective inward from head to heart and from a focus on outer concerns to unseen forces that provide a sense of the universal connectedness of all that is. It fosters a sense of community and connection with others.[50]

My background is in community and clinical social work and I am trained in forms of cognitive-behavioral therapy such as Dialectical Behavioral Therapy (DBT). DBT integrates mindfulness skills in working with people who experience emotional suffering. Mindfulness techniques have been demonstrated to be highly effective in working with a multitude of emotional and mental health issues, as well as pain management and trauma.[51] Not only do social workers need to develop mindfulness skills, so they may be present and in the moment with those with whom they work; they also need to know these techniques so they can pass them on to clients and communities to help address issues of trauma and harm in communities. As Marsha Linehan,

49. Freire, *Pedagogy of Freedom*, 104.
50. Umbreit and Armour, *Restorative Justice Dialogue*, 189.
51. Briere and Scott, *Principles of Trauma Therapy*, 189.

creator of DBT notes, "Mindfulness in its totality has to do with the quality of awareness that a person brings to activities."[52]

Anapanasati, or awareness of breath, is a simple mindfulness technique that helps guide participants towards breath awareness and calming of the mind.[53] Mindfulness is an important part of my teaching strategy and I begin every class period with a moment of mindfulness to help introduce and reinforce these skills to social work students. This is most easily introduced to participants though the counting of their breath. As the Vietnamese Buddhist monk Thích Nhất Hạnh instructs, "Counting is an excellent technique for beginners. Breathing in, count 'one.' Breathing out, count 'two.' Continue up to ten and then start counting over again. If at any time you forget where you are, begin again with 'one'.[54]

For me, having our opening ceremony be a moment of mindfulness is a way to encompass aspects of the Circle process for students. The 'moment of mindfulness' is a ritual that can "create atmospheres in which other spiritual components can be actualized."[55]Mindfulness moments also serve as "inclusive, nondenominational, nonthreatening rituals to help move people into the Circle space and then out of it again. Ceremonies promote a sense of community—of pulling together around shared visions, aim, and endeavors—within the Circle."[56] These are ideas I must balance when working with students from different ethnicities, backgrounds, spiritual beliefs and ideas. "The language used to describe council and introduce themes should be as secular as possible."[57] In other words, I want to create an atmosphere that "combines this ancient tradition with contemporary concepts of democracy and inclusivity in a complex, multicultural society."[58]

Mindfulness also reinforces the importance of listening from the heart. I explain to students that listening from the heart means to listen mindfully and respectfully. "Respectful interaction refers both to respect for the participants and respect for the process. In their preparatory meeting and in the dialogue session, facilitators remind participants to be respectful listeners."[59] Listening mindfully cannot be an abstract concept for social work students; it must be a tangible and lived experience. The process

52. Linehan, *Cognitive Behavioral Treatment,* 146.
53. Thích Nhất Hạnh, *Awakening of the Heart.* 15.
54. Thích Nhất Hạnh, *Awakening of the Heart,* 81.
55. Umbreit and Armour, *Restorative Justice Dialogue,* 77.
56. Pranis et al., *Peacemaking Circles,* 82.
57. Zimmerman and Coyle, *Way of Council,* 163.
58. Pranis et al., *Peacemaking Circles,* 3.
59. Umbreit and Armour, *Restorative Justice Dialogue,* 103.

of learning and integrating the guidelines, along with participating and engaging in the Circle process, helps to reinforce mindfulness and listening from the heart. Paulo Freire does well to connect the ideas of speaking from the heart and listening from the heart.

> The person who knows how to listen demonstrates this, in obvious fashion, by being able to control the urge to speak (which is right), as well as his or her personal preference (something worthy of respect). Whoever has something worth saying has also the right and the duty to say it. Conversely, it is also obvious that those who have something to say should know that they are not the only ones with ideas and opinions that need to be expressed.[60]

Mindfulness is also where I do more than just teach. I demonstrate my commitment to this process and reinforce the work I have done to prepare myself for this kind of activity. Engaged Pedagogy cannot be a theory that I expound on; it too must be my lived experience. I cannot just tell students how to be mindful listeners or how to listen from the heart; I must respect the process itself and model mindfulness to them. The banking model of education is useless in this endeavor. If I do not do this work myself and believe it in myself, then I am of no use to the students who are learning this.

The Circle Process and Reflections

After reviewing the Circle process and instructing students on the technique of mindfulness, I request that students prepare themselves for our opening ritual. As Baldwin notes, "Opening a circle with ritual is essential to help people drop their expectations that the circle is just another name for a committee meeting, a task force, or a project team"[61] or in this case, just a class. Ringing the mindfulness bell, we settle in, directing our awareness towards our breath and centering ourselves, becoming present and being in the moment. After a few minutes, I ring the mindfulness bell again, indicating the ending of the opening ritual and the beginning of the Circle process.

Sitting silently for a few moments, holding the talking piece, I reflect on how I want students to authentically engage. I really want students to engage in the process and reinforce the importance of speaking and listening from the heart. I also do not want to dictate their responses or have them just

60. Freire, *Pedagogy of Freedom*, 105.

61. Baldwin, *Calling the Circle*, 31.

answer questions they think I want to hear. This process must be open and I should be mindful of my role in not influencing student responses.

> The role of the facilitator as nondirective and nonjudgmental during the dialogue meeting is a measure of the respect accorded the parties and the fact that the dialogue and its outcome belong to them. The facilitator's nondirectiveness also empowers the participants to engage with each other.[62]

Our social work students are often asked, "Why do you want to be a social worker?" We even have them write an essay prompted from this question in our introductory course. Even though this is a valid question, it does not solicit deep reflection and a student's standard response when asked in class is often, "To help people." I am trying to build community in this class and introduce complex ideas of restorative justice. I want students to really process and reflect. I shift this standard question they are often asked to one that requires a more complex and thoughtful response. I pose the question, "What brought you to social work?" I then place the talking piece in the middle of the Circle for a time of silence. As simple as this may seem to restructure the question, it places students in a position to be more contemplative.

After a few moments, a student approaches the center and picks up the talking piece. The changing of that question changes the dynamics of student answers and places them in a position to think about the personal aspects of their lives that brought them to their current point. As the talking piece passes around, students begin to open up and disclose their personal connections to social work. For some, this becomes cathartic. Many reflect on their first experience with a social worker, or some event in their lives where someone helped them. Some begin to connect ideas of human rights and social justice to their responses. The talking piece gets to me and I disclose my own personal background, history and the events in my life that brought me to social work. I cannot have students open themselves up without me doing the same. This is what Engaged Pedagogy is really about.

After questioning students on what brought them to social work, I then have students do an exercise where they write down two values on a piece of paper that they feel are important to them. We send the talking piece around and students reflect on what two values they chose and why they are important to them. It is through this process that I am working with students to understand their own values in relation to social work values, especially the values of "social justice, the dignity and worth of the person, the importance

62. Umbreit and Armour, *Restorative Justice Dialogue*, 82.

of human relationships, integrity, competence, (and) human rights."[63] Once they share their values and the importance of them, they place the sheet in the middle of the Circle. By the time the talking piece circles around, everyone's values are in the middle, symbolically becoming the "shared" values that we will have in class as we move forward. We will continue to process this values exercise throughout the semester.

We engage in this Circle process for around an hour and a half, and then we prepare for our closing ceremony. We end with another moment of mindfulness in the closing ceremony, and as the sound of the mindfulness bell fades, I find that I am not very mindful as my own thoughts wander to the way the students participated. Once the bell stops, I sit quietly for a few moments and then tell the students that we will take a short break, and thereafter reconvene to reflect on the Circle process.

Students return from the break and settle in and we begin to process our experience with the Circle. Interestingly, some students reflect on the discomfort they felt because of the ambiguity of the environment. Students reinforced their preconceived expectations of the first day of class, and how just entering into the traditional classroom, transformed into a Circle, was anxiety provoking. This makes me think of educator Ira Shore's response to the resistance he received from students when he transformed the classroom. "Still others were actively hostile, challenging me in ways to stop the critical thrust of the class. They were committed to tradition and saw the class as a threat to their established values."[64] Transforming the class on the first day of the semester and having students engage in an experiential process such as the Peace Circle generated anxiety and some resistance, and as Baldwin notes, "experience is not always a comfortable teacher."[65] Most students, however, are able to reflect on how powerful the overall experience was, noting that they learned aspects of themselves and their classmates that they had never known before.

When I am introducing ideas of community building and restorative justice to students, I have to break from the traditional educational setting and have students engage in a process that is authentic, experiential and liberatory. Teaching restorative justice cannot happen in the standard classroom where I am the authority figure expounding on theories that are alien to student's lived experiences; we have to engage in this process together. For students steeped in the banking model of education, becoming active

63. Learn more about the Council on Social Work Education (CSWE) Values and Ethics at https://www.cswe.org/Events-Meetings/2019-APM/Proposals/2019-APM-Tracks/Values-and-Ethics.

64. Shore and Freire, *Pedagogy for Liberation*, 25.

65. Baldwin, *Calling the Circle*, 150.

participants as opposed to passive recipients can be unsettling, but once engaged it can be very liberating. "Liberatory education is fundamentally a situation where the teacher and the students *both* have to be learners, *both* have to be cognitive subjects, in spite of being different."[66]

I am asking students to liberate themselves from the confines of traditional education and engage in a process that defuses the hierarchal, power dynamic in the class, and "instead of granting power to a leader, the circle requires that participants trust the process and not force its direction or its outcome."[67] Drawing again from the philosophy of Engaged Pedagogy, Paulo Freire feels that education has to be liberatory as opposed to oppressive. Utilizing Engaged Pedagogy as a teaching philosophy in restorative justice and beginning a semester-long social work class with a Peace Circle, "students—no longer docile listeners—are now critical co-investigators in dialogue with the teacher."[68]

Conclusion

Restorative justice is not a concept that can be taught using the banking model of education; it is something that must be experienced and must be experiential. Mark Umbreit writes that "Restorative justice is more of a process than a product."[69] That is why engaging social work students in a restorative justice process is essential in dismantling the banking and anti-dialogical nature of education, and thus changing student interactions with communities. "The context for transformation is not only the classroom but extends outside of it. The students and teachers will be undertaking a transformation that includes a context outside the classroom, if the process is a liberating one."[70] Having social workers engage in restorative justice with communities also changes the dynamics of how social workers are often perceived. "Circles also break down barriers between professionals and the community, allowing the community to see the professional as more than 'just a badge.' Professionals reintegrate with their communities beyond their roles."[71]

Utilizing my philosophy of Engaged Pedagogy in conjunction with using a Peace Circle to start a class becomes a restorative process for students.

66. Shore and Freire, *Pedagogy for Liberation*, 33.

67. Umbreit and Armour, *Restorative Justice Dialogue*, 180.

68. Freire, *Pedagogy of the Oppressed*, 81.

69. Umbreit and Armour, *Restorative Justice Dialogue*, 22.

70. Shore and Freire, *Pedagogy for Liberation*, 33.

71. Pranis et al., *Peacemaking Circles*, 27.

> It is fundamental for us to know that without certain qualities or virtues, such as a generous loving heart, respect for others, tolerance, humility, a joyful disposition, love of life, openness to what is new, a disposition to welcome change, perseverance in the struggle, a refusal of determinism, a spirit of hope, and openness to justice, progressive pedagogical practice is not possible.[72]

Restorative justice and the Circle process are alien to students who have been indoctrinated in a paternalistic, hierarchical and anti-dialogical method of education. This traditional form of education directly opposes the values, ethics, human rights and social justice components of social work. Engaging in a Circle process with social work students counters this and demonstrates to students that, "Restorative justice encounters (between people) create empathy and mutual understanding."[73]

Bibliography

Baldwin, Christina. *Calling the Circle: The First and Future Culture*. New York: Bantam, 1994.

Beck, Elizabeth. "Introduction." In *Social Work and Restorative Justice*, edited by Elizabeth Beck et al., 3–14. New York: Oxford University Press, 2011.

Boyes-Weston, Carolyn F., and Kay Pranis. *Circle Forward: Building a Restorative School Community*. St. Paul: Living Justice, 2015.

Briere, John, and Catherine Scott. *Principles of Trauma Therapy: A Guide to Symptoms, Evaluation, and Treatment*. Thousand Oaks, CA: Sage, 2013.

Freire, Paulo. *Pedagogy of Freedom: Ethics, Democracy, and Civic Courage*. Translated by Patrick Clarke. Critical Perspectives Series. Lanham, MD: Rowman & Littlefield, 1998.

———. *Pedagogy of the Oppressed*. Translated by Myra Bergman Ramos. New York: Bloomsbury, 1970.

Giroux, Henry A. *Theory and Resistance in Education: Towards a Pedagogy for the Opposition*. Critical Perspectives in Social Theory. Westport, CT: Bergin & Garvey, 2001.

hooks, bell. *Teaching to Transgress: Education as the Practice of Freedom*. New York: Routledge, 1994.

Kozol, J. *The Shame of the Nation: The Restoration of Apartheid Schooling in America*. New York: Three Rivers, 2005.

Kropf, Nancy P. "Justice, Restoration, and Social Work." In *Social Work and Restorative Justice*, edited by Elizabeth Beck et al., 15–30 New York: Oxford University Press, 2011.

Linehan, M. *Cognitive Behavioral Treatment of Borderline Personality Disorder*. Diagnosis and Treatment of Mental Disorders. New York: Guilford, 1993.

72. Freire, *Pedagogy of Freedom*, 108.
73. Umbreit and Armour, *Restorative Justice Dialogue*, 72.

National Association of Social Workers: Code of Ethics. https://www.socialworkers.org/pubs/code/default.asp

Nhất Hạnh, Thích. *Awakening of the Heart: Essential Buddhist Sutras and Commentaries*. Berkeley, CA: Parallax, 2012.

Pranis, Kay. *The Little Book of Circle Process*. Intercourse, PA: Good Books, 2005.

Pranis, Kay et al. *Peacemaking Circles: From Crime to Community*. St. Paul: Living Justice, 2003.

Shore, Ira, and Paulo Freire, *A Pedagogy for Liberation: Dialogues on Transforming Education*. Critical Studies in Education Series. Westport, CT: Bergin & Garvey, 1987.

Umbreit, Mark, and Marilyn Peterson Armour. *Restorative Justice Dialogue: An Essential Guide for Research and Practice*. New York: Springer, 2011.

Zehr, Howard. *Changing Lenses: Restorative Justice for Our Times*. Harrisonburg, VA: Herald, 1990.

Zimmerman, Jack M., with Virginia Coyle. *The Way of Council*. 2nd ed. Las Vegas: Bramble, 2009.

5

Bigger Than an RJ Circle

Youth Organizing for Restorative Justice in Education

JONATHAN STITH

Prelude

THIS ESSAY WAS INSPIRED from a speech named "Bigger Than A Hamburger," which was delivered by Black Freedom Movement and Civil Rights Organizer Ella Baker after she organized a student leadership conference to bring together Black youth who had initiated sit-ins across the south in April 1960.[1] *The conference led to the creation of the Student Nonviolent Coordinating Committee (SNCC) and the resurgence of the Civil Rights movement. In her speech, Ella Baker challenges the audience of well-meaning adults to see the political significance of the young people sitting in at lunch counters as more than them trying to meet the physical need of hunger.*

Rooted in the legacy of Ella Baker and the lineage of youth organizing she birthed, I now seek to affirm the political significance of the youth organizing efforts of Black and Brown high school students in the expansion of restorative justice in education. The essay poses youth of color as both radically imaginative political actors and expert restorative justice practitioners who have blended the restorative justice principles of justice and equity with youth organizing to create a transformative insurgency and a democratic movement for education justice. At the close of her speech, Ella Baker offers an invitation for youth and adults to work together to provide genuine leadership based on

1. Baker, "Bigger Than a Hamburger," 1960.

principles of cooperation and trust to build an intergenerational movement capable of realizing freedom. And as Ella Baker did then, this essay is an invitation for restorative justice practitioners in education to reimagine themselves and radicalize their practice as part of this insurgency with *young people of color as a powerful and transformative intergenerational movement to disrupt and dismantle the school-to-prison pipeline.*

RiiiinnnnGGGGG!! It is the final bell of the day, signaling the end of another school day. As Black and Brown high school students spill out of the building swiftly, about a dozen students form a circle with one young person in the middle. She yells "Mic Check!!!" The circle responds back "Mic Check!!!" Then she smiles and spirals to see everyone in the circle. Other youth, reminded, quickly fall in and the circle naturally expands to include them. Curious youth and adults stand a few paces away, indirectly observing the circle. She begins again this time with all bravado that embodies Black Girl magicness. "Miiiiiicccccc Chhhhhhheeeeccckkkk!" All parts of the circle enliven with laughter and meet her energy. "MIIIIIICCCC CCHHHEEECCCKKK!!!"

"Why are we out?" The facilitator pauses and pivots. One student blurts out, "Because we are not criminals. We want to go to college." She affirms his answer. "Let's start on the left." As the next student begins answering, she joins the circle standing next to another classmate. One by one, they go around the circle answering the question. Some say they are there because a friend brought them or they got offered extra credit by a teacher. Others mention the buzzwords: school-to-prison pipeline, restorative justice, and mass incarceration. A few share stories of being unfairly suspended or witnessing an injustice in the classroom that went unaddressed. Instead of a traditional rally, where a few charismatic leaders get to speak and all others listen, youth organizers have blended the restorative justice practice of circles into their organizing praxis to acknowledge the inherent leadership of all and to build collective leadership of the group.

The youth organizers are preparing for a "Walk-In," a direct action to demand their school principal to adopt and implement restorative justice. They have four demands. They want the principal to agree to a moratorium on suspensions for willful defiance, start a restorative justice program with part of the school's budget, approve youth-led professional development for teachers, and allow youth involvement on the school's safety committee. They have chosen to do their walk-in afterschool, starting in the courtyard as an act of defiance. The students are occupying space where they are normally rushed about and pushed out of every day by the school's security into the waiting stare and snare of the local police department.

In 2016, similar walk-ins also happened in New York, Los Angeles and Chicago. In New York, Black and Brown students walked into the office of the school resource officer and demanded that the security staff attend a mandatory professional development training on restorative justice. In Los Angeles, students walked into the office of their School Board representative, demanding that the representative sign on to a letter calling for the LAUSD school police to return the military-grade weapons they received from the Federal 1033 Program. In Chicago, students walked into an office to affirm their human right to an education against state budget cuts, stating that they are "more than a number on a spreadsheet." These stories are snapshots from a youth-led movement to dismantle the school-to-prison pipeline and advance education equity, a movement fueled by the power of youth organizing.

Youth Organizing and Restorative Justice

Youth organizing is a youth development and social justice strategy that involves young people in community organizing and advocacy to alter power relations that lead to meaningful institutional change in their communities.[2] It is the dynamic praxis of youth-led activities like research, policy creation, leadership development, political analysis, and direct action that brings young people together in defining issues for themselves, constructing youth-driven membership organizations that take collective action, and working together long-term to bring about strategic, sustainable and systemic change. By centering the power and leadership of youth acting on issues impacting them and their communities, young people transform the way they view themselves and the way adults view young people.[3]

The Alliance for Educational Justice (AEJ) is a national network of 30 youth and intergenerational groups organizing to shift local, state and federal policy away from punitive discipline and towards restorative justice in order to dismantle the school-to-prison pipeline. The Alliance congealed in 2008 around the political moment of the new Obama administration and the pending reauthorization of No Child Left Behind. The original 19 organizations first formed the Alliance after arriving at a shared analysis through their local organizing campaigns that No Child Left Behind was being used as a shield to defend discriminatory school discipline and mask other education inequities by local decision-makers and school leaders.

2. Funders Collaborative on Youth Organizing (FCYO) Occasional Paper #1.
3. Funders Collaborative on Youth Organizing (FCYO) Taj James paper.

By 2008, the national youth-led movement against the school-to-prison pipeline grew to be so powerful that the concerns of youth organizers and their allies was a top priority of the Federal Department of Education. Under the Obama administration, the Department of Education spent eight years disavowing Zero Tolerance as federal education policy, requiring and reporting discipline data from schools along the intersections of race, gender and ability. The Department targeted egregious districts and used legal strategies like consent degrees to encourage cities and states to take responsibility and make right by those directly impacted by the school-to-prison pipeline while shifting federal resources and policies towards restorative justice. In 2011, the Supportive School Discipline Initiative was launched, an interagency collaboration between the Department of Education and the Department of Justice, created to "address the school-to-prison pipeline and the disciplinary policies and practices that can push students out of school and into the justice system."[4] A year later, youth organizers would win the first ever Senate hearing on the school-to-prison pipeline.[5] Two years later, the Supportive School Discipline Initiative announced a series of federal guidelines aimed to help school districts and stakeholders to remedy racial discrimination in school discipline at Frederick Douglass High School in Baltimore, MD. During his speech, Secretary of Education Arne Duncan affirmed the youth organizers who present and their insurgency, and stated how "the school-to-prison pipeline must be challenged every day" and identifying that "it is adult behavior that needs to change."[6] The work of youth organizers was a critical catalyst to this moment which established a powerful platform for ongoing organizing at the local level.

Young people in AEJ-member organizations (Alliance for Educational Justice) are responsible for the presence of restorative justice within dozens of schools and school districts across the United States by winning radical changes in school discipline policy and practice, pushing systems to invest more in education than incarceration. In New York City, youth organizers in the Urban Youth Collaborative won the elimination of suspensions for defying authority. In addition, they won $2.4 million from the New York City Council for investment in a citywide Restorative Justice Initiative.[7] After more than eight years of struggle in Miami, the youth of Power U Center

4. See https://www.ed.gov/news/press-releases/us-departments-education-and-justice-release-school-discipline-guidance-package-

5. Press Release, "Durbin Holds Hearing on Ending the School-to-Prison Pipeline." U.S. Senate. https://www.durbin.senate.gov/newsroom/press-releases/durbin-holds-hearing-on-ending-the-school-to-prison-pipeline.

6. See https://www.ed.gov/news/speeches/rethinking-school-discipline.

7. See http://www.urbanyouthcollaborative.org/ending-school-to-prison-pipeline/.

for Social Change won district-wide implementation of restorative justice in Miami-Dade County Public Schools, the third largest school system in the country.[8] Padres y Jovenes Unidos, an intergenerational organizing group, won the creation of the Denver School-Based Restorative Practices Partnership, a three school restorative justice project that serves as a local and national teaching and learning site.[9] In Los Angeles, a collaborative of youth organizing groups including the Youth Justice Coalition, Labor Community Strategy Center, Inner City Struggle, and Community Coalition-South LA, waged effective campaigns to end police citations for minor student offenses like tardiness. They also moved the Los Angeles Unified School District to adopt the School Climate Bill of Rights in May 2013 and to commit to implementing restorative justice practices in all schools by 2020.[10]

These and other campaigns happening in cities across the United States constitute a movement for restorative justice in schools and communities that is primarily led by young people of color. However, these efforts are not entirely new. The Alliance for Educational Justice is the flower of a nearly 20-year struggle led by youth of color to end the school-to-prison pipeline. Moreover, this youth-led movement for education justice is part of an even longer tradition of young people of color organizing for civil rights, freedom, democracy and dignity within and outside of educational institutions. In words remixed from civil rights leader Ella Baker, the grandmother of youth organizing, the goals of these struggles are even bigger than winning alternative school discipline policies or bringing Peacemaking Circles to classrooms.

Race, Violence, and the Pipeline

If the premise is true that education is the civil rights issue of our time, then for nearly two decades, Black and Brown youth have waged an intergenerational insurgency in education in the United States to challenge and defeat racist school discipline policies that have developed in reaction to the promise of Brown vs. Board of Education and codified in the Gun Free Zone Act of 1994 that made Zero Tolerance federal posture and policy, and laid the foundation of the school-to-prison pipeline.[11] In this light, the school-to-prison pipeline

8. See http://poweru.org/our-schools/.

9. See http://localprogress.org/wp-content/uploads/2016/01/Restorative-Practices-Insights-From-3-Denver-Schools.pdf.

10. See https://achieve.lausd.net/cms/lib08/CA01000043/Centricity/Domain/293/Restorative%20Justice%20Statement.pdf.

11. https://en.wikipedia.org/wiki/Zero_tolerance_(schools).

is the modern machination of Jim Crow education that racializes educational policies, inequitable funding and teaching practices to deny youth of color their dignity and their human right to an education. It is state violence and the first form of violence that many youth of color face. It is government power that harms, government power that hurts. Schools are agencies of state violence which promote the violent indoctrination that in America, for Black and Brown children, learning means learning to stay in your place. The same lesson the Little Rock Nine learned when trying to integrate Central High School almost over half century ago is the same one youth learn today. The national guard of yesterday has been replaced with school police armed with military grade weapons provided by the Federal 1033 Program. The #AssaultAtSpringValley is a grabbing example of the pedagogy of immediate annihilation or compulsory assimilation used to teach Black and Brown youth their place. At its depth is the genocidal impulse first found in the history that held enslaved Africans under the penalty of death for learning to read, and the forced assimilation of Native Indian children into schools that sought to "Kill the Indian in him, and save the man." In its modernity, the school-to-prison pipeline has widened to extend well beyond the boundaries of race to push Black girls, LGBQT, immigrant, disabled and poor youth out of school and towards mass incarceration. The school-to-prison pipeline is a continued commitment of America's education system to mentacide, namely the deliberate and systematic destruction of an oppressed people's capacity for cognitive agency and collective action.

Led by Black and Brown students, LGBQT, Disabled and Immigrant youth have fashioned an uprising through youth organizing and intergenerational alliances to massively interrupt the functioning of the country's education system, and thereby force a rearrangement of roles, authority and power.[12] In cities like New York, Miami, Philadelphia, Denver, Chicago, New Orleans, Boston and Oakland, Baltimore, Los Angeles, and Detroit, youth organizing groups have interrupted the school-to-prison pipeline. Every victory against the school-to-prison pipeline created more space for restorative justice in our schools. These high school activists and movement builders are crystal clear that their national movement, comprised of local and state-wide campaigns and federal action, are concerned with something much bigger than a restorative justice circle. Like the Student NonViolent Student Coordinating Committee youth who fueled the sit-in movement, the youth of our day are seeking to rid education of the scourges of racial injustice, not only in the classroom, but in the world.

12. Gillen, *Educating for Insurgency*, 16.

When you listen deeply to the call for restorative justice by today's youth, you will hear how they want the world to know that they no longer accept the position of being second-class students. What we see time and time again is how Black and Brown youth understand that school and society are in a mutually influential relationship. Society shapes schools and school shapes society. The schools they attend are reflections of the oppressive society that created them. Is it not then the student's job, as it is the citizens in the world, to make schools a better place? They have been courageously willing to challenge racist, punitive and criminalizing education policy, face ridicule by peers, be looked down upon by teachers, and even suffer physical violence at the hands of school police to demand a first-class education. And some have died . . .

In Remembrance of the Radical Imagination of George Carter III

George Carter III was an AEJ youth leader from Rethink-NOLA. He was loved and renowned for his imagination and tender toughness. He was the embodiment of big things coming in little packages. His life and his death is a constant reminder of what is at stake and what will be lost if we do not make restorative justice a political, social and cultural imperative in education. The not-guilty verdict in the murder of Trayvon Martin was dropped in the news during the last night of the Alliance's annual conference. Shocked, scared and saddened, AEJ youth leaders stuffed the living room area of my hotel room. Each young person shared a story or sentiment on the impact of the murder of Trayvon Martin. Many of them expressed fear of the George Zimmermans of their communities. When it came time for him to share, George Carter III talked of another fear. He spoke of the fear he felt living in his New Orleans neighborhood since the time of recovery after Hurricane Katrina. He was not afraid of any George Zimmermans. Rather, he was afraid of being shot by a police officer or another desperate youth trying to survive a post-apocalyptic New Orleans. His neighborhood had been transformed into a confluence of state and intercommunal violence since people returned after Katrina. "And they haven't even opened our school back," he lamented. A few months later George was murdered on his way to catch his 7:00 AM school bus by another youth in an act of intercommunal violence. The circumstance of his murder and his postmortem criminalization is one of the inspirations of our national movement to end state violence in education.[13] George and other AEJ youth leaders imagined schools

13. "Anti-blackness is the paradigm that will not only kill a black person, but

where restorative justice is all about preparing them to govern themselves and society by learning to build and keep peace or to make things right after harm has happened. "Can you imagine a school with mood detectors, instead of metal detectors?" he asked. George Carter III dared to transform where others only seek reform. He re-imagined schools where instead of being suspended or arrested, you got sent to pick strawberries in the school's garden. Young people are winning more than a restorative justice circle. With radical imagination, they are daring to dream out loud, waging love to build a transformative insurgency to liberate education.

An Invitation to Restorative Insurgency

Restorative Justice Education (RJE) practitioners have a critical and important role in this insurgency to dismantle the school-to-prison pipeline and build a better world. As young people and their organizing asserts, it is bigger than an RJ circle. To align this restorative insurgency, RJE practitioners must orient themselves to be prefigurative and transformative in their praxis as, according to Vincent Harding, "practitioners in an education system that does not exist yet."

Restorative Justice in Education (RJE) must adopt anti-racism as a core competency in the profession and practicum to address the historic and current anti-blackness in America and its schools. Most of the schools that RJE will be entering are not just and equitable learning environments for Black and Brown students where their respect and dignity ought to be nurtured. White supremacy is deeply ingrained in America, in education, and even in the field of restorative justice. In spite of successes in policy that decreased the number of suspensions of Black and Brown youth, the racial disparity has remained the same. Moreover, since the 2016 elections, there has been an upsurge in racialized bullying in schools of Black and Brown students by White students and teachers. Without anti-racism as a competency, RJE practitioners will pat themselves on the back for getting a Black student to apologize to a White student in a circle for fighting after being called the N-word repeatedly. Believing they have restored justice, they have only reinforced White supremacy. The RJE field must challenge its own inherent anti-blackness and not only acknowledge the indigenous roots of restorative justice in the Americas but also its African roots as a transplanted practice carried by Black people into the Western Hemisphere.

---

will then use their image and even their death as a hollow symbol to represent everything they stood against" (Nicholas Brady). https://progressivepupil.wordpress.com/2014/02/27/right-to-death-defining-anti-blackness/.

Contemporary Black restorative justice practitioners should be accorded the same dignity and right to self-determination over what is restorative and what justice looks like within their communities.

RJE practitioners must see themselves as politicized healers,[14] view restorative justice in education as the antithesis to the school-to-prison pipeline, and understand restorative justice as a prefigurative practice place of the society we seek to transform. Every one of the 145 documented #Assault[15] incidents since and including the #AssaultAtSpringValley could have been prevented if the school had a culture of restorative justice or a restorative justice program. In its politicization, Restorative Justice in Education must also break the criminalizing binary 'offender-victim' framework that continues to characterize restorative justice practice within the criminal legal system and beyond. In education, the leading cause of school suspensions is not intercommunal crime or violence between students or by a student toward a teacher, but "willful defiance." The tolerant acceptance of racially-biased student discipline codes and culture can lead to reinforcing power and structural inequalities, which determine who gets to define what is right (and even what is making things right) in a way that only mirrors the world as it is and not as it should be. In doing so, we miss the transformative impact of restorative justice on school culture and society.

The Restorative Justice in Education field and practitioners must actively support young people's contributions to restorative justice not only as activists, advocates and policymakers, but also as theoreticians, practitioners and experts of their own experience. Both practitioners and organizations that gain from the expansion of restorative justice in education have an obligation to give back with their time, tithe and talent to further this youth movement. RJE practitioners and organizations can aid youth organizing campaigns to win restorative justice by publicly endorsing, financially supporting and joining them in advocacy activities such as testifying at hearings, writing op-eds and sign-on letters. RJE organizations should insist that school systems which are implementing restorative justice need to collect rigorous data and stories that it are publicly reported. Also, those working with schools districts must support the right and responsibility of students of color and their parents to participate in the shaping and implementation of any and all restorative justice programs in their schools. *Nothing about youth without youth* should be the mandate and the praxis of every restorative justice practitioner and organization working within a school system,

14. I heard this term from Mama Lisa (Mawulisa Thomas-Adeyemo) in a BOLD training.

15. An AssaultAt is when a school police officer (SRO) harms or hurts a student for any reason.

if the true goal for restorative justice is to root itself and transform education. This requires that young people should have access to meaningful opportunities to learn and develop their proficiency and mastery in restorative justice both in and out of school.

Young people, specifically Black and Brown youth organizers, have been on the frontlines, winning campaigns to implement restorative justice in schools. They understand the political significance of restorative justice as a social change strategy to transform schools and reshape society. For them, it is *bigger than a circle*. Like their SNCC forerunners during the Civil Rights movement, they are attempting to fulfill their generation's destiny to build a new world through organizing, starting in their schools with restorative justice. Their invitation to reimagine education and change the world with restorative justice comes with this final radical request. "If you have come here to restore us, you are wasting your time. But if you have come because your restoration is bound up with ours, then let us circle together."

Bibliography

Advancement Project and Alliance for Educational Justice. "We Came To Learn: A Call for Police Free Schools." Report. 2017. https://wecametolearn.com/.

Baker, Ella. "Bigger Than a Hamburger." *Southern Patriot* 18 (June 1960). http://www.historyisaweapon.com/defcon1/bakerbigger.html.

Funders Collaborative on Youth Organizing (FCYO). Occasional Paper #1: "An Emerging Model for Working with Youth: Community Organizing + Youth Development = Youth Organizing." 2003. https://fcyo.org/. See also, https://www.racialequitytools.org/resourcefiles/YouthOrganizingPipeline.pdf.

Gillen, Jay. *Educating for Insurgency: The Roles of Young People in Schools of Poverty.* Edinburgh: AK Press, 2014.

Grant, Joanne. *Ella Baker: Freedom Bound*. New York: Wiley, 1998.

Payne, Charles M. *Teach Freedom Education for Liberation in the African-American Tradition*. Teaching for Social Justice Series. New York: Teachers College Press. 2008.

Ransby, Barber. *Ella Baker and the Black Freedom Movement A Radical Democratic Vision*. Durham: University of North Carolina Press. 2003.

Stith, Jonathan."#EndWarOnYouth: Building a Youth Movement for Black Lives and Education." 82–91. From *"Lift Us Up, Don't Push Us Out!" Voices From the Frontlines of the Educational Justice Movement"* by Mark R. Warren with David Goodman. Boston: Beacon. 2018.

6

Critical Race Theory and Restorative Justice in Education

KATHY EVANS, BRENDA MORRISON, AND DOROTHY VAANDERING

A study about white privilege and restorative justice which examines how critical theory can challenge implicit bias in restorative justice processes in school settings.

Introduction

THERE IS NOTHING EASY or magical about implementing restorative justice in society today. The issues we face are complex, historic, and ever evolving. Many of us find ourselves orienting toward restorative justice as a way to forge a path forward and fix the ills of our societies. While restorative justice promises to provide processes for resolving conflict and moving toward healing, there are risks to our work. Many of us who work in restorative justice belong to a dominant sector of society where we can safely shift our thoughts away from ongoing discrimination and prejudice and lean into the privilege of living in relative comfort, free from fear.[1]

As restorative justice continues to gain momentum in educational settings, it is important that the movement not be compromised by restorative practices that fail to promote justice and equity. It is also important that we, as restorative justice practitioners committed to the

1. Sensoy and DiAngelo, *Is Everyone Really Equal?*

transformation of society, continue to challenge ourselves and our work in ways that promote equity and justice.

As authors of this chapter, we acknowledge that we belong to this dominant, privileged sector that knows *about* racial disparity, but hasn't a clue as to what it feels like. As white, educated women residing in Canada and the United States, we realize we are privileged and that we uncomfortably venture into this space of exploring the power dynamics implicit in restorative justice. We do so in an attempt to hold a mirror to ourselves and others with whom we share privilege, considering how we might actually be using restorative justice to perpetuate harm, and thus we challenge ourselves to reflect critically on how we practice restorative justice.

Critical race theory guides us. In particular, we continually examine our own actions and thoughts by asking, *Who is benefiting? Who is bearing the burden?*[2] When applied to race and power, critical race theory deepens our questioning.[3] This theoretical framework, when combined with the essence of restorative justice,[4] provides opportunity to bridge divides that often seem insurmountable. Our primary responsibility as privileged researchers and educators is to observe, listen, and critically examine our own perspectives and experiences and those we witness. This chapter describes some of our learning. It is only a beginning.

To date, our separate journeys as educators have led us to a common understanding that restorative justice in education (RJE) is not merely a set of practices, but rather a philosophical stance, a theoretical framework through which educators view their classroom, their students, and their whole lives.[5] Within this perspective, education is viewed as a relational framework where nurturing and maintaining healthy relationships, establishing just and equitable school/classroom environments, and addressing harm and transforming conflict are three crucial components for establishing an effective learning community where disparities for vulnerable populations are eradicated.[6] This view of RJE sees student behavior ecologically as a reflection of many variables, including but not limited to the climate of the learning environment. Thus, student behavior does not occur in a vacuum, but often reflects unmet needs, unresolved conflict,

2. Kincheloe and McLaren, *Rethinking Critical Theory*, 303–42.

3. Bell, *Faces at the Bottom of the Well;* Ladson-Billings and Tate, *Toward a Critical Race Theory of Education*, 47–68.

4. Wadhwa, *There Has Never Been a Glory Day in Education for Non-Whites.*

5. Boyes-Watson, *Peacemaking Circles and Urban Youth*; Morrison, *From Social Control to Social Engagement*; Rosenfeld, Quinet, and Garcia, *Contemporary Issues in Criminology Theory and Research.*

6. Evans and Vaandering, *Little Book of Restorative Justice Education.*

trauma, inappropriate instruction, and inequitable learning environments, among other things.[7] Restorative justice in education focuses on addressing the unmet needs of students, as well as those of educators, and creates spaces for solving problems *with* students and other stakeholders, rather than *for* or *against* them.[8]

In this, restorative justice in education moves away from a sole emphasis on addressing issues of school discipline, to creating learning environments that are healthy and safe for all students, including those who are often marginalized based on race, ethnicity, language, ability, sexual orientation, or gender. While research has demonstrated the effectiveness of restorative justice at reducing suspensions and expulsions, our experiences and research serve to uncover the reality that without a comprehensive understanding of 'justice,' restorative justice cannot address issues of power and inequity that often create toxic learning conditions for vulnerable populations.

Defining Justice

To date, restorative justice has been implemented in educational settings across the globe; in many places, people have been reticent to use the language of restorative justice and instead named their work as restorative practices, restorative approaches, or restorative discipline. For some, the language of *restorative justice* is reserved for responsive approaches to harm while *restorative practices* are seen as the everyday preventative interventions. For others, the use of *restorative practices* reflects an unwillingness to use the language of justice, viewing *justice* as too tied up with the language of the justice system, or too complicated by the baggage associated with the term *social justice*, which could alienate a broad swath of stakeholders who might have otherwise bought into an alternative to punitive discipline.

Acknowledging the reality that implicit and explicit bias is rampant in our school systems, our search for understanding has led us to reclaim the term *justice* in *restorative justice* as having two branches, primary justice and secondary justice. Primary justice is present in social relationships when no one is wronged and the worth of the other is placed in the forefront of our attention in respectful ways; secondary justice addresses situations where

7. Morrison, *From Social Control to Social Engagement*; Rosenfeld, Quinet, and Garcia, *Contemporary Issues in Criminology Theory and Research*.

8. Morrison, *Restoring Safe School Communities*; Larson, Sawin, and Zehr, *Handbook of Restorative Justice*, 41–58; Evans & Vaandering, *Little Book of Restorative Justice Education*.

wrong or harm has occurred such that the worth of the other is diminished.[9] By including and emphasizing primary justice in restorative justice, the context required for healthy relational communities is recognized as necessary for secondary justice to be effective. Primary justice is significant as it highlights the reciprocal pursuit of what everyone needs for their individual and collective well-being. It addresses hierarchical relationships, makes explicit areas of privilege and power, and seeks to balance and share power. Primary justice considers what people need in order to thrive. Primary justice works to interrupt injustices wherever they show up. And they show up in lots of places and in lots of ways: interpersonal, intrapersonal, community, structural, and systematic. Lederach's framework in *The Little Book of Conflict Transformation* is helpful here as a framework that acknowledges all the levels that need to be attended to from intrapersonal to systemic.[10]

Further, Social Identity Theory (SIT) and Self-Categorization Theory (SCT) have been influential in the study of psychological links between individuals and the social groups to which we belong.[11] Our social identities are the psychological link between who we are as individuals and who we are as members of social groups, namely gender, social roles, occupation, and race. In the post-Holocaust era, many social psychologists were interested in understanding the psychology of intergroup relations, particularly the negative effects of intergroup processes. Many theorists understood these processes to be irrational, intrapsychic or interpersonal; SIT and SCT challenged these individualistic ideas of human nature.

The foundational work of Tajfel and Wilkes (1963) argued that the mere use of salient 'us and them' distinctions changes the way people perceive each other, enhancing similarities within the group (e.g. Caucasian) and differences between the groups (e.g. Caucasian and African American).[12] Categorization, in terms of group membership, changes the way people see themselves and others through activating a different level of one's self-concept. Social identities derive from social categories to which individuals belong, defining an individual's emotional and evaluative consequences of group membership. Social identities are sensitive to social context, perceiver readiness, and power relations.[13]

9. Wolterstorff, *Teaching Justly for Justice*, 23–37.

10. Lederach, *The Little Book of Conflict Transformation*.

11. Sindic and Condor, *Social Identity Theory and Self Categorization Theory*, 39–54. Richeson and Sommers, *Toward a Social Psychology of Race and Race Relations*, 439–63.

12. Tajfel *and* Wilkes, *Classification and Quantitative Judgment*, 101–14.

13. Hornsey, *Social Identify Theory and Self-Categorization Theory*, 204–22; Morrison, *From Social Control to Social Engagement*; Rosenfeld, Quinet, and Garcia,

Social Identity Theory was the "first social psychological theory to acknowledge that groups occupy different levels of a hierarchy of status and power, and that intergroup behavior is driven by people's ability to be critical of, and to see alternatives to, the status quo." For Tajfel, social identity theory was at its heart a theory of social change. In contrast to theories that are "increasingly 'micro' in their scope, the social identity approach is a rare beast, a meta-theory that is ambitious in scope but ultimately rests on simple, elegant, testable, and usable principles."

Social Identity Theory has been applied to educational contexts to frame issues from bullying to school climate. Schools are both intra- and inter-group systems. We must be critically reflective of, and engage with, these systems at all levels—intrapersonal, intragroup, intergroup and structural. Each level offers distinct opportunities to understand and respond to equity differences in power and status, from knowledge mobilization to behavior. Racial identities are not merely reflections of societal relations within educational contexts, benignly formed within them; rather, racial identities are actively constructed within educational settings. Educational institutions implicitly and explicitly give power and status to some social groups, while denying others. In other words, educational institutions can be agents of assimilation or diversification.

The practice of restorative justice must attend to this agency within schools. Circles, for example, are active and fluid structures of belonging within schools. At the most basic level, they create a normative field of belonging. They have the power to hold the space between us. Without an understanding of power and the way power shows up in educational spaces, Circle processes have the potential to inadvertently perpetuate injustices and maintain hierarchical disparities.

Restorative justice has been sensitive to power imbalances at an interpersonal level, in the context of interpersonal harms such as bullying, domestic violence, and sexual assault. We need to be equally sensitive to power imbalances at the intergroup level. Social Identity Theory helps us to frame and understand these processes at an intergroup level. In other words, we need to be critically mindful about assumptions of whose identities, cultures, values, and knowledge are superior. We also need to be mindful of the superordinate context in which those power relations are being played out; i.e., who is 'fitting in with' or 'catching up' with whom?

It is not unusual for educators to push back against this perspective, suggesting that in order to maintain authority in the school or classroom, there has to be a hierarchy. We too have had to examine this way of understanding

---

Contemporary Issues in Criminology Theory and Research.

power and authority that is embedded in our teacher education degrees and experiences. In challenging ourselves to reconsider these structures, we recognize that restorative justice paradigms make clear a distinction between *authoritativeness*, which is necessary to create a respectful space where participants are reminded by the facilitator/teacher to adhere to the Circle guidelines established together, and *authoritarianism*, seen as power for power's sake. This is evident in the many Indigenous communities from which the field of restorative justice has received much of its foundation, where space created in talking Circles as guided by elders, for example, honors every voice. In sum, justice is not a zero-sum game, nor is power. If I give you some of my power, I do not suddenly have less. Conversely, I might actually have less power when I try to hold on to it with a tight fist.

Defining Equity

Likewise, we define equity as fairness or impartiality, not necessarily in how people are treated but rather in the potential for fair and impartial outcomes.[14] Many of the zero tolerance policies that emerged in the 1990s were grounded on the notion that everyone should receive the same treatment for the same offenses. This focus in schools on equality as everyone being treated alike, would be fine if we all started at the same place. We do not, however, and when we seek to treat everyone the same, we overlook the uniqueness of each student, we gloss over their struggles, we force everyone into a standardized box, and, as we saw with zero tolerance policies, it does not work. According to Sullivan and Tifft, "We develop our potentialities as human beings and enhance our collective well-being when our needs are respected, expressed, listened to, defined with care, and ultimately met."[15] Thus, within a restorative justice process addressing harm, we start with questions about who has experienced harm, what *needs* emerged because of that harm, and who is obligated to meet those needs.

For us, the language of equity is crucial in educational settings. We believe that much of what has been framed as misbehavior, and often labeled with vague and imprecise language such as "noncompliance," "insubordination," or "oppositional defiance," might actually reflect students' resistance to what they perceive to be unjust and inequitable treatment in schools.[16] Because of the way these vague and imprecise disciplinary codes have resulted in disproportionate rates of suspensions and expulsions, some school

14. Evans and Vaandering, *Little Book of Restorative Justice Education.*

15. Sullivan and Tifft, *Restorative Justice.*

16. Fine, *Framing Dropouts.*

districts, and the entire state of California, have worked to remove these categories from school disciplinary procedures. Rather than suspending students who exhibit challenging behaviors, restorative justice has been implemented. However, in many situations, while overall rates of suspensions and expulsions have been reduced, the rates of disproportionality have remained the same. In other words, schools that have implemented restorative justice practices may see a reduction in exclusionary discipline yet continue to see students of color suspended and expelled at rates significantly above those of white students.[17] This observation should then drive us to examine what we mean by the effectiveness of restorative justice and to reflect critically on how it might be possible that students of color are being suspended for resisting what they perceive to be unjust and inequitable school practices even in a school committed to RJE.

The following examples make the need for critical theory and critical race theory explicit. Several years ago, I (Kathy) received a phone call from a disability rights attorney who was working in a large city that had an active restorative justice program in their school district. He had been approached by the parent of a child with autism. The child had hit another student and while the school offered restorative justice informed victim-offender mediation, administrators in the district had disqualified this student from participating because the child used a facilitated communication device and the restorative justice coordinators were uncomfortable facilitating a circle process with a student who didn't speak. The attorney was looking for restorative justice facilitators who might be comfortable incorporating facilitated communication.

The student with autism who was not invited to the circle experienced harm—at the hands of the restorative justice program. The very exclusion purported to be prevented by restorative justice was in fact reinforced by the circle. This was not an anomaly; in a recent study, Kincaid and Sullivan (2019) claimed that despite varying understandings of disability, youth with identified disabilities are and have been consistently overrepresented in school discipline and in the juvenile justice system. Further, official data on special education needs and suspensions collected in Ontario for ten years indicate that during the 2014–15 school year, 46.5% of suspended students had identified learning needs.[18]

As we engage in restorative justice in school settings, what if *we* are the offender, the one who excludes or the one who perpetuates injustice?

17. Gregory et al., *An Examination of Restorative Interventions and Racial Equity*, 167–82; Yusem, *Implementing Whole District and Whole School Restorative Justice*; Winn, M. *Justice on Both Sides*.

18. Kincaid and Sullivan, *Double Jeopardy?*, 1–18.

And even when we are not directly culpable, what are we doing to address systemic discrimination such as ableism in our schools and classrooms? Adapting our practices to meet the needs of students, and adults, who have varying cognitive, communicative, and social-emotional strengths and weaknesses is an issue of justice and equity, and the field of restorative justice needs to do this better.[19]

As a second example, there has been a strong focus, extensive research, and a great deal of discussion about racial disproportionality in school discipline and the ways in which zero tolerance policies have perpetuated the school-to-prison pipeline. For example, in Chicago, black students make up 45% of the student enrollment but account for 78% of school suspensions. Similar statistics show up in most of our larger cities in North America: Charlotte, NC, Prince George's County, MD, and Philadelphia, PA, all report that 70% or more of their suspensions are African-American and Latino students. In Canada, as of 2012, most schools did not compile disciplinary statistics by race or ethnicity.[20] However, Ontario, which has agreed to begin collecting data on race and suspension rates, reports that in Toronto, 48% of suspended students identify as black, and only 10% identify as white.[21] In neither country do we know how significantly Aboriginal students are impacted. By way of extrapolation, when black and brown students are being suspended at rates two and three times higher than those of white students, and most suspended students have special needs, one could speculate that systemic racialized injustice is at core of the issues to be unpacked and addressed.

Anne Gregory's research on restorative justice, as a process to dismantle the school-to-prison pipeline, has been instrumental in making the case for replacing zero tolerance policies with restorative justice practices.[22] This is good work and we need to continue to see restorative justice as a way to tackle racial disproportionality in school discipline. But we need to do so in ways that align with our commitment to justice and equity. Several months ago, I (Kathy) received a call from a school district inquiring about implementing restorative justice because they were in trouble with the Office of Civil Rights (OCR) for having suspension rates that were too high and that disproportionately impacted students of color. We had a long conversation about justice and equity.

19. Burnett, Thorsborne, *Restorative Practice and Special Needs.*
20. Teklu, *Canada's Forgotten Children.*
21. James and Turner, *Towards Race Equity in Education.*
22. Gregory et al., *The Promise of Restorative Practices,* 1–29.

If our primary motivation for implementing restorative justice is as a way to comply with the Office for Civil Rights, or with the Human Rights Commission in Canada, it is doubtful that we will be effective. We might see a reduction in suspension rates, but we will still likely maintain racial disproportionality, because we have not addressed the underlying issues. Anne Gregory's research supports this. According to her findings, when restorative justice was implemented with fidelity (i.e., a focus on building effective relationships and promoting engaged learning opportunities), it reduced the rate of disproportionality in school discipline. When it was implemented just as another tool, without considering the larger structural issues of racial equity, restorative justice practices were not effective, as measured by the persistence of disproportionality even while the rate of suspensions decreased.[23] Simply addressing suspension rates is insufficient if we are going to effectively support just and equitable learning environments in schools.

As a third example, consider issues of representation in education. Research suggests that elementary students do better on standardized tests when they have a teacher who is of the same racial identity. And yet, only seven percent of public school teachers in the United States are black and only 24 percent of black teachers are male.[24] In March of 2017, researchers from three universities published findings from a study suggesting that having one black teacher in grades 3–5 increased the graduation rate of black students by 29% and by 39% for black male students from economically disadvantaged communities.[25] Representation matters. It is not everything, but if we are serious about building more just and equitable environments, it is something we need to pay attention to as restorative justice practitioners.

We are not suggesting that white teachers cannot be effective with children of color. We are suggesting that those of us with privilege due to our skin color need to become more critically conscious. We have to identify our own racialized identity and pay attention to the ways in which implicit bias (and sometimes not so implicit bias) impact our ability to connect with students of different races and ethnicities. We are also suggesting that we need to advocate for hiring educators that represent the student/family demographic. Further, as noted above, white leaders of restorative justice initiatives also must not only consider our implicit bias, but also consider issues of representation in our organizations and schools.

23. Gregory et al., *The Promise of Restorative Practices*, 1–29.

24. Taie and Goldring, *Characteristics of Public Elementary and Secondary School Teachers in the United States.*

25. Gershenson et al., *The Long-Run Impacts of Same-Race Teachers.*

What is our responsibility to students who feel those inequities and respond with anger and frustration or who shut down, drop out, or push back? Who is responsible for this type of harm? What needs are represented here and who is obligated to advocate for more just and equitable learning environments?

Getting Concrete

We asked restorative justice facilitators who work in educational contexts to comment on what schools might look like that had worked to establish just and equitable learning environments. What follows below are some concrete ideas that were suggested. We offer them here as a sample of practical ways to consider justice and equity in schools seeking to implement restorative justice practices. We suggest that these practices truly impact the overall climate of a school, decisions about curriculum and instruction, safety and school discipline, issues of representation, and the support offered to faculty and students.

Overall School Climate:

- There are spaces within the school where conversations about equity, justice, and social issues are taking place among teachers, among students, and between teachers and students.
- Adults in the school consistently ask what they can do to make the school environment more just and equitable for all students.
- Healthy relationships among adults at the school are modeled, their conflicts are handled using restorative practices, and they build community using restorative practices such as circles among themselves.
- Students' differences are not simply tolerated, but rather embraced and celebrated—more than just for one month of the year.

Respect for Diversity:

- Students and school personnel, as well as policies and procedures, demonstrate respect and dignity for all members of the learning community, regardless of race, ethnicity, language, sexual orientation, gender, economic status, or any other area of diversity.

- There are a variety of student-led clubs that support students' social engagement and promote all students' sense of belonging (i.e. gay-straight alliances, Muslim Student Association, etc.).
- If the religious holidays and cultural traditions of one group are observed, they are observed for all students.
- Teachers use inclusive language to talk about students' families, including non-gendered language: for example, the grownups you live with, rather than "your parents or "your mom and dad," in that some children may live with grandparents, foster parents, aunts, two dads, etc.
- There is at least one acknowledged gender-neutral restroom in the school where transgender students are not afraid of the repercussions of using the restroom of their choice.
- Education on and modelling of gender appropriate pronouns.
- Teachers push back against gender stereotypes in the professions; for example, talking about women who are scientists and mathematicians.
- Posters in the hallways and classrooms reflect the diversity of the school environment and present that diversity in a positive light.
- Adults in the school have engaged in professional development related to diversity and demonstrate cultural awareness in their teaching, communication, and other interactions with each other and with students.

Curriculum and Instructional Practices:

- The curriculum takes into consideration the human rights of those being studied; for example, the plight of Native Americans is discussed when talking about the Westward Expansion in the United States or the history of slavery is not whitewashed by talking about "forced immigration."
- The curriculum takes into account the cultural backgrounds of the students it serves.
- Children's books include a variety of cultures, ethnic groups, languages, family designs, religions, and races.
- Instruction is presented in ways that meet the needs of all students.
- Students who are English Language Learners know that language supports will be offered in all of their classes, including the opportunity

to receive instruction in their first language and to be assessed in their first language when appropriate.

- Learning materials are offered in a variety of formats to support diverse learners, including hands-on activities, pictures to support language development, audiobooks, etc.
- Students are able to move about in the classroom at a level appropriate for their age.

Safety and School Discipline:

- School "rules" are structured as expectations for building a healthy learning environment; there is not a separate code of conduct that only applies to students, but rather a shared expectation for all members of the learning community; all members of the school community are able to articulate those expectations.
- Student behaviors are seen as communication, and attempts are made to understand that communication through active listening, not simply as inappropriate behaviors.
- There is an absence of metal detectors, security cameras, and personal searches; if the school has school resource officers or other security personnel, they are taught restorative justice practices and participate in the overall restorative climate of the school.
- Students know that if they are experiencing conflict or bullying, someone will be there to support them and to intervene with a restorative justice process that is well-known and practiced regularly.
- Discipline hearings focus on who was harmed and what needs emerged from the harm, rather than what rule was broken and what punishment the offending party deserves; accountability measures are designed to support students' growth relying on increased self-regulation rather than external regulation.

Representation:

- The school is viewed as a learning community that includes caregivers, students, administrators, teachers, and school staff; these members hold different, but equally important roles in the community. Attempts are made to minimize asymmetrical relationships and promote equal respect for all members. Teachers feel respected by administration and by students. Students feel that teachers and administrators like them, respect them, and are interested in them as human beings, not just as students; students are often invited to participate in decision-making; parents and caregivers feel respected and included by school personnel and are invited to be a part of decision-making

- Advanced placement courses are offered and all student groups are equally represented in those courses.
- Adults see youth as "problem-solvers and assets to school communities,"[26] and work to involve students in the decisions of the school and classroom.
- Discipline and academic data suggest that there is proportional representation of all students regardless of race, ethnicity, language, gender, ability, sexual orientation, or economic status.

Student and Faculty Support:

- Students who have experienced trauma are met with educators who understand the role that trauma plays on learning and who attend to social and emotional needs, not just academic ones.
- Students with specific learning needs are integrated in the general education classroom; they are not simply in the room, but actively participating with their peers.
- Support services, such as health, counseling, occupational therapy, physical therapy, speech therapy, social work, and career counseling, are available to all students as needed.
- Translation services are available to support communication between school and home.
- Students who struggle academically have access to support in the way of differentiated learning, tutoring, and remediation.
- There are physical spaces where students and faculty can go and have conversations about issues they face.

26. Knight and Wadhwa, *Expanding Opportunity through Critical Restorative Justice*, 11–33.

- All students and faculty feel safe at school, physically, emotionally, socially, psychologically; when they don't, there is a place to go to find help.
- Practices of self-care are encouraged for restorative justice practitioners, teachers, and students.

Getting concrete about nurturing just and equitable learning environments is complex. The suggestions given above are not the final solution, but only steps towards making changes if we are willing to take each of them as an opportunity for embedding justice and equity into our way of being.

Final Thoughts

In conclusion, we stress that our work as restorative justice educators requires that we continuously participate in our own critical reflection, questioning the ways in which we are potentially perpetuating injustice and inequity. Most starkly this includes questioning, as we asked earlier, if we as restorative justice practitioners, might be the offenders? How can we learn from our harmful actions how to do this work better? As restorative justice educators who are white, educated, and privileged in so many ways, we would suggest that we have a greater responsibility to promote just and equitable spaces where everyone can show up. Conferences, such as the Restorative Justice in Motion conference, are spaces where we can hold each other accountable for promoting justice and equity.

In her article entitled, "Decolonizing Restorative Justice," Denise Breton examines the ways in which restorative justice has been promoted within Indigenous communities and suggests that it is hypocritical and unconvincing for white restorative justice practitioners to hold a Navajo youth accountable for stealing a car when we have stolen his entire country.[27] We would echo that when restorative justice educators fail to take into consideration injustices in schools such as racism, sexism, homophobia, ableism, etc., ignoring students' very real experiences with these forms of oppression, all of our attempts to address these students' behavior will likely be met with contempt, resistance, and skepticism. Moreover, we need to acknowledge that we will be perpetuating the harm that students are already experiencing, exacerbating their pain and, in turn, their behavioral responses to that pain. Then, when agreements are not kept after such a circle for serious harm, as practitioners/facilitators we need to first examine our role rather than the role of the participants involved. The very nature of restorative justice can be challenged and dismissed by educators, students, and caregivers if we use

27. Breton, *Decolonizing Restorative Justice.*

our privilege to manipulate circle planning, facilitation, and outcomes. In so doing, we can inadvertently promote a limited and skewed view of how restorative justice practices can cement relationships, keep people accountable for harm, and create a more just world.

For this reason, we suggest the following principles for this type of critical reflection. First, we make an assumption that in general, we are all doing the best we know and that if we knew better, we would do better. It is our hope that through mutual concern for one another, we might make supporting and holding each other accountable common practice and thereby learn to do better restorative justice work in the world.

Second, we believe that partnership among students, teachers, administrators, and school counselors can inform our work. Most of the above examples come from practicing educators who are working diligently on behalf of justice and equity. We also need to consult with youth who are knowledgeable and committed to justice and equity in school settings.

Third, this cannot be a box we decide to check off and call it good. Our commitment to justice has to be an integral part of our work as restorative justice practitioners. It's not a once and done training, but rather an ongoing move toward more justice and equity, accompanied by lots of honest reflection, humility, and accountability by our colleagues.

Fourth, it is not the job of people of color to teach their own humanity to their white peers. It is not the job of LGBTQ identified folks to advocate for their right to be acknowledged, hired, or provided with equitable opportunities. We have to educate ourselves. Read. We suggest reading educational books by authors who represent marginalized communities. There is wisdom there that those of us from dominant cultures simply do not have. We must include the perspectives of all members of the learning community as we work toward creating more just and equitable learning spaces.

Fifth, we have to start with ourselves. As we do the work of restorative justice, it is important to consider that we have to be restorative with ourselves. We have to do the work of justice starting from the inside before we can work for others. We must attend to the work of justice in our relationship with self, in our relationship with others, in our relationship with place and land. This needs more attention.[28]

As we continue to promote restorative justice in educational settings, and as restorative justice gains traction in schools, it is imperative that we address issues of injustice and inequity in schools. Critical theory, with its insights into power, helps us to move toward more just expressions of education and restorative justice. In their restorative justice work in Boston

28. Evans & Vaandering, *Little Book of Restorative Justice in Education*, 68.

public schools, Knight and Wadhwa noted the importance of "focusing not just on the success of each individual case-by-case basis but on how structures such as institutionalized racism affected [students] as individuals and impacted the community and society writ large. By connecting curriculum to the historical context of economic and racial inequality in this country, students were able to reflect on their own experiences with power structures as they played out through school disciplinary practices."[29]

The concrete examples provided above represent only some of the ways in which we might promote more just and equitable school and classroom environments. We have much work to do.

Acknowledgements

We are grateful for the educators who responded to emails inquiring about concrete expressions of restorative justice that prioritize justice and equity. We are especially grateful to Dr. Anita Wadhwa who read through drafts of this chapter, offering critiques and suggestions along the way, and who is living out so much of what we talk about in this paper in her work in Houston.

Bibliography

Bell, Derrick. *Faces at the Bottom of the Well: The Permanence of Racism*. New York: Basic Books, 1992.

Boyes-Watson, Carolyn. *Peacemaking Circles and Urban Youth: Bringing Justice Home*. St. Paul: Living Justice, 2008.

Breton, Denise. "Decolonizing Restorative Justice." In *Unsettling Ourselves: Reflections and Resources for Deconstructing Colonial Mentality*. Edited by The Unsettling Minnesota Collective, 2009. https://unsettlingminnesota.org

Burnett, N., & Thorsborne, M. *Restorative Practice and Special Needs: A Practical Guide to Working Restoratively with Young People*. Philadelphia: Kingsley, 2015.

Evans, Katherine, and Dorothy Vaandering. *Little Book of Restorative Justice Education: Fostering Responsibility, Healing, and Hope in Schools*. Justice and Peacebuilding. New York: Good Books, 2016.

Fine, Michelle. *Framing Dropouts: Notes on the Politics of an Urban Public High School*. SUNY Series in Teacher Empowerment and School Reform. Albany: State University of New York Press, 1991.

Gershenson, Seth, Cassandra M. D. Hart, Joshua Hyman, Constance Lindsay, and Nicholas W. Papageorge. *The Long-Run Impacts of Same-Race Teachers. IZA Institute of Labor Economics: Discussion Paper Series*, 2017. http://legacy.iza.org/en/webcontent/publications/papers/view Abstract?dp_id=10630.

29. Knight and Wadhwa, *Expanding Opportunity through Critical Restorative Justice*, 27.

Gregory, Anne, Kathleen Clawson, Alycia Davis, and Jennifer Gerewitz. "The Promise of Restorative Practices to Transform Teacher-Student Relationships and Achieve Equity in School Discipline." *Journal of Educational Psychological Consultation*, 26 (2016) 325–53.

Hornsey, M. J. "Social Identify Theory and Self-Categorization Theory: A Historical Review." *Social and Personality Psychology Compass* 2 (2008) 204–22.

James, Carl E., and Tana Turner. *Towards Race Equity in Education: The Schooling of Black Students in the Greater Toronto Area*. Toronto: York University Press, 2017.

Kincaid, Aleksis P., and Amanda L. Sullivan. "Double Jeopardy? Disproportionality in First Juvenile Court Involvement by Disability Status." *Exceptional Children* 85 (2019) 453–75.

Kincheloe, Joe L., and Peter McLaren. "Rethinking Critical Theory and Qualitative Research." In *The Sage Handbook of Qualitative Research*, edited by Norman K. Denzin and Yvonna S. Lincoln, 303–42. 3rd ed. Thousand Oaks, CA: Sage, 2005.

Knight, David, and Anita Wadhwa. "Expanding Opportunity through Critical Restorative Justice: Portraits of Resilience at the Individual and School Level." *Schools: Studies in Education* 11 (2014) 11–33.

Ladson-Billings, Gloria, and William F. Tate. "Toward a Critical Race Theory of Education." *Teachers College Record* 97 (1995) 47–68.

Larson Sawin, Jennifer, and Howard Zehr. "The Ideas of Engagement and Empowerment." In *Handbook of Restorative Justice*, edited by Gerry Johnstone and Daniel W. Van Ness, 41–58. Portland, OR: Willan, 2007.

Lederach, John Paul. *The Little Book of Conflict Transformation*. Intercourse, PA: Good Books, 2003.

Morrison, Brenda. "From Social Control to Social Engagement: Enabling the 'Time and Space' to Talk through Restorative Justice and Responsive Regulation." In *Contemporary Issues in Criminology Theory and Research*, edited by R. Rosenfeld et al. Florence, KY: Wadsworth, 2012.

———. *Restoring Safe School Communities: A Whole School Response to Bullying, Violence and Alienation*. Sydney: Federation, 2006.

Morrison, Brenda, and Dorothy Vaandering. "Restorative Justice: Pedagogy, Praxis, and Discipline." *Journal of School Violence* 11 (2012) 138–55.

Richeson, Jennifer A., and Samuel R. Sommers. "Toward a Social Psychology of Race and Race Relations for the Twenty-First Century." *Annual Review of Psychology* 67 (2016) 439–63.

Sensoy, Özlem, and Robin DiAngelo. *Is Everyone Really Equal? An Introduction to Key Concepts in Social Justice Education*. Multicultural Education Series. New York: Teachers College Press, 2012.

Sindic, Denis, and Susan Condor. "Social Identity Theory and Self-Categorisation Theory." In *The Palgrave Handbook of Global Political Psychology*, edited by C. Kinvall et al., 39–54. Basingstoke, UK: Palgrave Macmillan, 2014.

Sullivan, Dennis, and Larry Tifft. *Restorative Justice: Healing the Foundations of Our Everyday Lives*. Monsey, NY: Willow Tree, 2005.

Taie, Soheyla, and Rebecca Goldring. *Characteristics of Public Elementary and Secondary School Teachers in the United States: Results from the 2015–2016 National Teacher and Principal Survey First Look*. NCES 2017-072. Washington, DC: National Center for Education Statistics, 2017. https://nces.ed.gov/pubs2017/2017072.pdf.

Tajfel, Henri, and H. Wilkes. "Classification and Quantitative Judgment." *British Journal of Psychology* 54 (1963) 101–14.

Teklu, Moya. *Canada's Forgotten Children: Written Submissions to the Committee on the Rights of the Child on the Third and Fourth Reports of Canada.* African Canadian Legal Clinic, 2012.

Wadhwa, Anita K. "There Has never Been a Glory Day in Education for Non-Whites: Critical Race Theory and Discipline Reform in Denver." *International Journal on School Disaffection* (2010) 21–28.

Winn, Maisha T. *Justice on Both Sides: Transforming Education through Restorative Justice.* Race and Education Series. Cambridge: Harvard Education Press, 2018.

Wolterstorff, Nicholas. "Teaching Justly for Justice." *Journal of Education & Christian Belief* 10/2 (2006) 23–37.

Yusem, David. "Implementing Whole District and Whole School Restorative Justice: Pre-Conference Training Session." *Sixth National NACRJ Conference*, June 15, 2017.

7

Radical Relationalism

Restorative Justice with the Earth

Valerie Luna Serrels

"We need acts of restoration, not only for polluted waters and degraded lands, but also for our relationship to the world. We need to restore honor to the way we live."—Robin Wall Kimmerer

Preface

This essay has roots in an indigenous understanding of the world. As a descendant of white European settlers on Native American territory in the 1700's, I approach this with my feet in two worlds—from my own Indigenous earth-honoring Gaelic/Celtic tradition prior to domination by the imperialist church and state power, and as a white person with Christian roots and settler ancestors that make me complicit with that same power, too. I recognize the complexity of my background, connected with the subjugation and genocide of Native Americans, the stealing of land, and the enslavement of African and African-American peoples. I approach this work acknowledging and honoring the great wisdom traditions of the original inhabitants of this land who have kept alive the reality of human interconnection with the rest of creation. The great Oren Lyons, Turtle Clan of the Seneca Nations of the Iroquois Confederacy, canonized this in his address to the United Nations in 1977,

> You call yourself the United Nations. I do not see a delegation for the four footed. I see no seat for the eagles. You call yourself the United Nations and all you've got here are human beings. What about the millions of species on the earth that are nations just as holy? . . . We forget and we consider ourselves superior, but we are after all a mere part of the creation.[1]

These are the bones upon which this essay is built. While radical relationalism might seem 'radical' to us today, it is the normal and natural way of relating to the earth that millennia of Indigenous Peoples have understood. It behooves all of us involved in the restorative justice field, and to anyone invested in planetary wellbeing, to learn from our indigenous sisters and brothers.

❧ ❧ ❧

Environmental crises and conflicts are escalating and could trigger the greatest global security disaster the world has known.[2] The increasing threat to life implores us to ask every institution, system and field to consider what each is called to do to change the course of destruction. The environmental movement has battled for protections and conservation of biosystems, awakening people to our symbiotic connection with the Earth. Still, deaf ears and delusion of corporate elites and government leaders continues to threaten life as we know it. Yet, in the midst of a time of collapse, a new culture is slowly emerging on the edges, shaped not by a vision of industrialization and constant growth, but by co-creating a living society in relationship with the Earth, across perceived boundaries, race, nationality, and species.

This crisis presents an opening in the cultural fabric for change. During prolonged crises, we are asked to look beneath the surface to unveil hidden assumptions and values at the core of the problem. This chapter focuses on how restorative justice is well positioned to address the core problem beneath the environmental crisis, namely the illusion of separation between humankind and nature. As such it will be guided by a valuation framework termed *radical relationalism*.[3] Einstein called the idea of

1. Lyons, Address to the United Nations.

2. The Department of Defense has released reports naming climate change as a serious national security risk, and the World Economic Forum has named the global water crisis as the "biggest threat facing the planet over the next decade." See National Security, "Implications," and Ganter, "Water Crisis."

3. The concept of *radical relationalism* is gleaned from an academic paper by Dr. Barbara Muraca, Oregon State University, who calls for a new environmental axiology framework that she terms *radical relationalism*, to replace the dichotomy of the usual

a separate self an "optical delusion of consciousness,"[4] and Martin Luther King, Jr. noted that we are all connected in an "inescapable network of mutuality."[5] If King were alive today, I imagine he would expand this to include the whole community of the natural world.

This emerging yet ancient framework has affinity with the values of restorative justice, and could "mark an alternative understanding of our relation to 'nature,' and thus a different way of addressing the ecological crisis . . . that would assemble around the idea of cooperation, Gestaltung, interaction, co-creation, transformation, and ultimately inhabitation of a common, shared world."[6] Guided by such a framework, practices and processes could catalyze restoration and justice for all members of society, human and non-human, rooted in a kindred relationship with the Earth. Restorative justice is already oriented toward relationalism, as it addresses harm by valuing all members related to an incident, including the wider community, based on an unstated but apparent lens of interconnectedness. The environmental crisis compels the inclusion of all victims and members of the living world into processes of addressing harm, and to imagine new and expanded processes and roles for environmental conflict prevention.

Underlying Environmental Valuation Frameworks

The industrialization of our planet derives from a particular seed of thought about what we value and why, as do many strategies that seek to protect this worldview, namely that 'nature' is a backdrop for human affairs, useful for our economy, our health, or our enjoyment A society built on the perception of humans as somehow being other than and above nature leads to objectification, with the resulting commodification and colonization of 'resources.' History has witnessed this same objectification of women and black and brown people. A shift from industrial society to living society is not possible from this worldview.

Environmental conflicts, and the enfolding crises, are basically conflicts of value. There are generally two frameworks of value, *instrumental* and *intrinsic*, that guide the global justice movement as well as environmental law and policy. Instrumentalism views nature as 'natural resources,' as a means to an end, which leads to the protection of the land solely for the benefit of human industrial use and profit, and/or human enjoyment Intrinsic frameworks

instrumental and intrinsic valuations.

4. Calaprice, *New Quotable Einstein,* 206.

5. King, "Letter from a Birmingham Jail."

6. Muraca, "Radical Relationalism," 36.

view the protection of water, land, and living beings for their own benefit, by virtue of their inherent worth. While this framework might seem more inclusive, it also positions the rest of the world as separate from humanity, as if human interaction with nature has no value or relevance.

> The language of intrinsic value is not the opposite of instrumental language, but shares a kinship relationship with it. Both are rooted in the concept of a bifurcated nature and the myth of an independent, separate subject, and in the neglect of the fundamental relationality that constitutes it.[7]

In both cases, nature is viewed as "something separated, distinct, and independent from humans."[8] Evidence of how embedded this valuation is in our culture is revealed in our language. No pronouns exist for nature aside from the inanimate 'it' which frames 'natural resources' as objects to be used or protected, monitored or destroyed. "Using 'it' absolves us of moral relational responsibility and opens the door to exploitation."[9] This language, in turn, reveals the faulty underlying axiology, that is, the story of separation between the human and non-human world.

Catholic priest and eco-theologian Thomas Berry wrote of his vision of "The New Story" based on his understanding that the ecological crisis was rooted in examining and changing our underlying worldview.

> In Berry's view, a central cause of the West's ecological hostility was its separation from nature—a separation that was at once spiritual, religious, psychological, emotional, intellectual, and philosophical. The root of the eco-destruction was an anthropocentric Western worldview that saw an existential gulf, a 'radical discontinuity,' between human and the natural worlds.[10]

Radical relationalism flips this 'radical discontinuity,' and offers the foundation for crafting a new story that many in the ecological movement have been envisioning for decades. This new story is needed—*a shift in consciousness shaped by radical relationalism to restore humans to our primary identity as people of the Earth, transformed by and transforming nature in a reciprocal relationship that values the good of all.* There is good synergy between restorative justice and radical relationalism, with similar roots in indigenous worldviews, and by virtue of the relational values descriptive of both. For restorative justice, this story can 1) expand processes of

7. Muraca, "Relational Values," 33.

8. Muraca, "Relational Values," 32.

9. Kimmerer, *Braiding Sweetgrass*, 2.

10. Dellinger, "Change the Worldview," 30–34.

addressing environmental harms and conflicts to restore whole communities, including nature, and 2) shape practices of healing and experiential kindred relationship with the land as conflict prevention.[11]

A Look at the Root Cause of Illusion of Separation

"Our origins are of the earth. And so there is in us a deeply seated response to the natural universe, which is part of our humanity."
—Rachel Carson

Our language and worldview are shaped by our accepted science, religion, socio-economic, political and cultural experiences, including how we understand the human relationship with the earth. For hundreds of thousands of years before industrial civilization, 'science' was simply understanding the technologies of nature, which guided social, economic and religious orientation. Humans lived in rhythm with the natural world, interdependent and connected at the most primal level, shaped on a daily basis by the forces of nature: the call of coyote, the circling of raven, the rains, rivers and rock formations. These experiences "were integral not only to our own survival, but also to the very shaping of our souls. Now, in the shortest wisp of a moment, the perennial conversation has been silenced for the vast majority of us."[12]

Gradually, beginning in the Agricultural Revolution and culminating in the Industrial Revolution, our innate interdependence with the natural world shifted toward people claiming sole subjectivity in the universe, being separate from all other beings. This shift emerged as populations grew and tribes became empires, which required economic, political and religious dominance to maintain their power, especially the disdain and subjugation of the feminine, including the natural world and indigenous cultures. "In the Industrial Revolution . . . a similar dramatic transition took place. These weren't just changes in the small details of people's lives. The whole basis of society was transformed, including people's relationship with one another and with Earth."[13] As people were dominated, they became subjects of overlords; as land and waters were dominated, they became commodified as objects, or, to be more politically correct now, as "resources" or "capital" to be managed, used and appropriated for financial gain. The "sensuous

11. "The land" is a term I will use to describe the waters, lands, living beings, biosystems, elements that support life on this planet.

12. Weller, *Wild Edge*, 50.

13. Macy, "The Great Turning," 2–6.

intimacy with the wind, rivers, rainfall, and birdsong"[14] became a threat to the agenda of empire that sought to control subjects' lives, including their natural working and living relationship with the land.

> At the dawn of the Western tradition of thought, modern sciences, driven by the urgent need to rely on 'irreducible and stubborn facts' in order to face the threat coming from the ecclesial authority, started stripping nature of all those elements that could not be observed by measuring instruments and did not fit the picture of bits of matter wandering through an empty universe of mechanic relations.[15]

Systemic disconnection from the rest of the natural world continues today. Capitalism is based on extraction and use of impersonal 'resources' for financial gain, regardless of consequences. American energy systems and lifestyles remain tied to a fossil fuel, profit-driven, pro-growth agenda, resulting in many threats to our planet's viability to sustain life.

In the early 1960's, Rachel Carson was moved to write the classic *Silent Spring* after years of witnessing the destruction of crops and killing off of birds due to pesticides, the pollution of water with chemical runoff, and the effects on her beloved forests, awakening the American conscience further, and spearheading the environmental movement.

Her writings catapulted public pressure which resulted in the Clean Air Act, the Clean Water Act and the Endangered Species Act, in addition to the creation of regulatory agencies to monitor and regulate industrial activity affecting the environment. The legislation and the related agencies that developed were landmarks of a government taking responsibility to regulate industrial pollution for the benefit of citizens. These policies and agencies are based on an instrumental valuation ethic. Again, instrumental value refers to an ethic of understanding the Earth's organisms and systems as things to be protected (the means) for the benefit of human beings (ends).

Ironically, the environmental laws and regulatory agencies established to regulate industrial interests for the common good ended up continuing the same results of pollution and destruction. The situation has become more dire with the dismantling of government regulatory agencies and the unraveling of vital protections of "natural resources." Mary Woods, environmental attorney, notes that environmental agencies set up to protect natural resources wind up doing the opposite. "Despite a cadre of hardworking and well-intentioned people in many agencies today, perversely, the very system intended to restore nature actually kills nature, while delivering a heavy dose

14. Weller, *Wild Edge of Sorrow*, 49.

15. Muraca, "Relational Values," 22.

of death and despair to innocent citizens."[16] Neither have courts awarded justice for the devastating harms committed against the Earth, indigenous people, people of color, and the poor who suffer most from the ecological consequences of a market-centric worldview. Very little has been done to prevent harm against future generations and biosystems. In fact, government regulatory agencies are authorized by statutes to "issue permits to damage Nature." "Despite its elaborate environmental laws, the United States has wiped out more than half (53%) of its wetlands and nearly all (90%) of its old-growth forests . . . nearly half (44%) of all rivers and streams are unfit for fishing, recreation, and other public uses."[17] This correlation between an increase in destruction following the establishment of policies to prevent such destruction is a clue that something is amiss.

The entrenchment of industrial interests within an instrumental ethic that values the natural world for her "resources" is manifested from a culture based on the illusion of separation. This paradigm is rooted in Newtonian physics, with its isolated, mechanistic, reductionist lens. Among other political norms, this lens shaped the current hyper-capitalist system that seeks endless economic growth, and corporate welfare, at the expense of people and planet. There is no hope that the dominant culture will lead to the changes necessary to alleviate the environmental crisis without a different underlying ethic and worldview based on the interconnectedness of all life. This shift can be witnessed on the margins, in the voices of Indigenous leaders, poets, philosophers, spiritual teachers, and scientists who understand that what happens to one part of a system affects the whole. Life is a web of interrelationships, one affecting the other. *How* we relate in these relationships is what will determine continued cycles of destruction or cycles of life-sustaining reciprocity.

Radical Relationalism—The New Story

> *"The Universe is a communion of subjects not a collection of objects."*
> —Thomas Berry

The dramatic shift from the pre-modern world to industrialization is equal to the emerging shift from post-industrialization to a radical relationalism. The old reductionist Newtonian physics of the 17th century that still inform our culture are based on the human as a separate and independent being in a mechanical and disconnected cosmos, and nature as a lifeless machine.

16. Woods, *Nature's Trust*, 67.

17. Woods, *Nature's Trust*, 7.

The emerging ontology, on the other hand, is based on the interdependence not only between all humans, but between all living beings, the Earth, and the universe. Termed *The Great Turning* by deep ecologist and scholar Joanna Macy, and *The Great Work* by Thomas Berry, this new story integrates a return to our indigenous selves, affirming the ancient spiritual truth that all life forms are interconnected in a web of life—conscious, animate and inspirited. Radical relationalism leads us to consider that all matter is intricately connected, as subjects, not as objects, emphasizing that all beings exist because of the relationships between them, not as isolated lifeless objects. In a quantum world, matter is defined by relationships between and among other corresponding entities, replacing classical physics with a new world that reveals "a world that is more profoundly and mysteriously interconnected place than we ever imagined."[18]

Radical relationalism is supported by 21st century quantum and systems sciences that recognize the whole of life as interconnected, where "organisms can no longer be seen as disconnected entities."[19] These emergent sciences affirm that the web of life and the process of evolution are the result of a highly organized, symbiotic collaboration. David Bohm, credited with advancing quantum theory, noted that, "The notion of a separate organism is clearly an abstraction, as is also its boundary. Underlying all this is unbroken wholeness even though our civilization has developed in such a way as to strongly emphasize the separation into parts."[20] And Albert Einstein, even though he maintained a suspicion of quantum physics, said that "we do not live in a universe with discrete, physical objects separated by dead space. The Universe is *one indivisible, dynamic whole* in which energy and matter are so deeply entangled it is impossible to consider them as independent elements."[21]

Dr. Barbara Muraca, professor of philosophy at University of Oregon, proposes German philosopher Gernot Böhme's term *ecological fabric* to describe this emerging way of viewing nature, not as an object or concept, but as a whole *fabric of being* that includes all of us,

> . . . in which—to use a Whiteheadian expression—a *buzzing world* of activities, interactions, communication, voices, forms, colors is at work. Ecological fabrics are communication fields

18. Ananthaswamy, "Reality Check," 10.
19. Lipton, *Biology of Belief*, 14.
20. Bohm, *Undivided Universe*, 404.
21. Lipton, *Biology of Belief*, 89.

> in which the self-world relation is disassembled in a complex relational field encompassing multiple voices.[22]

In other words, this framework is not about "managing natural resources" well, nor conserving or protecting "nature" out there, but about understanding ourselves as part of nature, a continuous stream of changing, living interrelated beings. We need a larger story such as this to move beyond our narrow, individualistic, race-centric, and species-centric hierarchies.

Radical Relationalism Supporting Restorative Justice

> *"Wrongdoing is more than simply a violation of law; it is a wound in the community, a tear in the web of relationships."*
> —Howard Zehr

Radical relationalism rightly expands restorative justice, as the human/nature relationship is not separate from our communities or ourselves. This approach, which affirms a whole ecology, extends the innate human connection with the rest of the living world, recalling the worldview of Indigenous Peoples. When valuation shifts from instrumental or intrinsic to relational, the "other" is no longer completely external to us. The other can no longer be objectified, and therefore can no longer be commodified. "What has been constructed as 'external nature'—the other of reason and culture—could easily be kept at a distance as an object of scientific observation, use, and exploitation."[23]

Restorative justice is nimble enough, and rooted enough, to expand its branches much further, outside of courtrooms and schools, and into forests and shores and into the hearts of people in relationship with a real place. Its guiding principles of respect, connection and dialogue with the other, along with an unspoken foundation of kinship in the broadest sense of the word, already reflect an underlying relationalism. Restorative justice offers . . .

> . . . a renewed understanding of environmental violations. It does not take the allegations lightly, but allows us to look at them in a different light. Howard Zehr, the grandfather of restorative justice, points out that wrongdoing is more than simply a violation of law; it is "a wound in the community, a tear in the web of relationships." A similar notion could be applied to environmental wrongs, so that they could be looked at as harm

22. Muraca, "Relational Values," 35.

23. Muraca, "Relational Values," 32.

> done to the web of relationships--including the earth at large and vulnerable populations such as future generations.[24]

Restorative justice has found its way into environmental contexts mostly in New Zealand and Australia, expanding relationalism within dialogue processes. For example, The New South Wales Land and Environment Court in New Zealand revises processes to take place within the local harmed jurisdiction, to include interviews with aboriginal councils and other affected stakeholders, and to result in orders to restore harmed ecosystems and provide restitution for victims. Opportunity is also afforded for the defendant to meet with victims in order to listen and to apologize. New Zealand stakeholders have learned that addressing environmental harms presents problems and opportunities to advance relationalism around the important and sometimes intricate issue of identifying all of the victims of environmental harm, and then including those voices in processes and outcomes. The opportunity lies in the need to include the voices of rivers, meadows, forests, and creatures, and the resulting possible shift of consciousness that comes from listening and being changed by this experience. Justice Preston, of the New South Wales court shares a solution:

> Where the environment and non-human biota are the victims, the surrogate victim needs to be able to bring to the restorative process an ecocentric and not anthropocentric perspective. As with future generations, the fact that the environment and non-human biota are not able to vocalise their claims and concerns is not an insuperable problem. A representative can be appointed to speak on their behalf.[25]

Radical Relationalism in Legal Restorative Justice Processes

Changing culture requires shaping the principles and values of a field to align with what is emerging. Restorative justice needs to expand its already aligned values with radical relationalism to apply to all of the natural world, emphasizing the value of *interconnectedness*. Howard Zehr notes that "Although we are connected, we are not the same. Particularity appreciates diversity."[26] This definition invites an expanding view of relationality across a diverse spectrum of human and non-human creatures

24. Motupalli, "Intergenerational Justice," 19–20.
25. Preston, "The Use of Restorative Justice," 8.
26. Zehr, *Little Book*, 35.

and ecosystems. Another hallmark value is *respect* "for all, even those who are different from us."[27]

Restorative justice, shaped by radical relationalism, is oriented to deepen a shift from an *I-It* exchange to an *I-Thou* experience. The hope of such a movement toward restoration of primary relationships between all members of living ecosystems is embodied in a restoration of justice following harm, as well as measures to prevent environmental harm. These values must inform practices within legal environmental cases of harm, extending to include all of the natural world in all phases of the process. These processes can help nurture a new culture based on restoring the human/nature relationship.

In New Zealand, Australia, Canada, and here and there in the United States, restorative justice has begun to expand its branches to address environmental harm. The following norms have been the topic of dialogue, research and writing in terms of how each part of the process presents problems and opportunities within environmental contexts. There are already seeds of radical relationalism emerging from those leading the way. Five areas within the field of restorative justice can serve to redefine traditional norms with expanded inclusion for environmental contexts: *inclusion of all stakeholders, victim-centered process, encountering one another, acknowledging and healing harms,* and *making amends.*

Inclusion of All Stakeholders

Restorative justice processes include all stakeholders to a given harm or grievance, namely the victims, offenders and the community. In environmental conflicts, this would include the harmed community, which could be humans who interact with the environment, as well as frogs, salmon, rivers, oaks, owls, prairies, etc., within the affected watershed. Radical relationalism would prioritize the automatic inclusion of all affected non-human kin and representatives of local Indigenous Peoples as stakeholders.

Victim-Centered Process

All affected victims, whether human or non-human, need to be given voice, protection and priority within environmental cases. Radical relationalism shifts the perspective on other-than-human victims, away from viewing them as "resources," or as "others" separate from humans, to viewing them

27. Zehr, *Little Book*, 36.

as uniquely diverse, yet intimately connected living beings in an interdependent web springing from the same tree of life as us. Indigenous Peoples are also victims in most environmental conflicts or harms, since their land and livelihoods were stolen by colonial powers. Indigenous Peoples should have an automatic voice as a stakeholder regarding environmental matters, particularly when harms affect original tribal land.

The issue has been raised regarding the difficulty of identifying and including the concerns of non-human victims at the table. This is overcome by appointing representatives to speak on behalf of those subjects without voice.[28] Representatives could include locally dedicated environmental group leaders, concerned members of the public, conservationists, or Indigenous People who live close with the land. Representation could also be offered by restorative justice practitioners who have grounded themselves in relationship with their watersheds. One of the practices suggested later in this chapter can be implemented in this context: learning to listen to the Earth and her creatures in order to speak eco-centrically into processes.

Encountering One Another

Applied radical relationalism expands the room for both traditional and environmental processes, and perhaps gets rid of the room altogether. Proceedings should lead to encounters between all stakeholders, or as many as possible within the contested or harmed ecosystem. "Face-to-face" encounters with a tree or a river or salmon may sound stretching, and indeed it should. It is this kind of stretching and immersion that is necessary to plant seeds of radical relationalism. "Nature is often seen as being distinct from humanity and history, simply a backdrop for human events. Encounters with alternative ontological systems can be disruptive to strict categorical distinctions such as those between human/animal or culture/nature."[29] Encounters with a tree or other beings can be transformative, an opening into the cultural fabric of nature to experience life beyond one's own construct. Having wise guides can help facilitate these encounters.

28. Preston, "The Use of Restorative Justice"; Pain, "Restorative Justice for Environment Crime."

29. Reichert, *Transformative Encounters*, 32.

Acknowledging and Healing Harms

Environmental harms and conflicts will require that people include non-humans as well as the relationships between them, in processes of acknowledgment, apology and healing. It is the responsibility of humans, including representatives of government and business, to acknowledge harm and restore relationships to injured ecosystems, including creatures, soil, air, rivers and waterways. The faulty paradigm that leads to objectifying, destroying and harming the natural world must be acknowledged, grieved and healed, making room for the emerging, and ancient, story of interconnection and interdependence.

This acknowledgment is vital to a successful process and to addressing the root causes of much of the crises we face, which is a powerful paradigm-shifting endeavor. Acknowledging harms to nature as a harm to Indigenous Peoples and others who live with deep relationship and kinship with the natural world is a necessary and healing opportunity for addressing the violence of our country's history. Acknowledging harms to nature as harms against ourselves helps realign the human/nature disconnect. Grief processes, which I refer to later, can be part of the healing that is necessary for moving forward.

Making Amends

Making amends is a pivotal action that holds possibility for healing ecosystems and their inhabitants and communities further, taking responsibility for actions that cause harm. While traditional restitution is important, reconciliation and restoring relationships are primary. Sentencing could include apology, stopping a harmful environmental practice that puts water at risk, restoring a destroyed habitat, planting trees, or reorienting a company's bottom-line to prioritize environmental, and therefore human, wellness. Offenders could spend a number of days out in the natural world, connecting with the harmed ecosystem. Restoring people to our true origins as people of the Earth is not only the goal of these processes; it is a primary root strategy for the transformation needed to stop the trajectory toward the looming environmental and climate crises.

Restorative Justice as Cultural Change Practices

Aside from court-based cases of harm, restorative justice can also reimagine its contribution to cultural change by expanding its role from arbiter or mediator of justice to something else--a facilitator of restorative ecology. Outside of the limited number of court-based environmental justice processes, there are examples of individuals and groups in North America who may or may not identify their work as "restorative justice," yet their work very much aligns with the same principles and values, guided by an underlying radical relationalism. I will highlight four of them here, two of which are within the scope of the restorative justice field, and two of which have an indirect connection.

Dr. Elaine Enns has taken new strides into ecological territory, practicing a land-based restorative justice process with groups of indigenous and settler peoples throughout North America, addressing the tragic history of traumatic land conflict. Her 25-year experience with restorative justice has expanded to include the land itself through workshops, writings, and facilitated experiences of reconciliation. She specifically seeks "restorative solidarity" between descendants of settlers/colonizers and Indigenous Peoples, working mostly with faith communities, advocating for white descendants to do their own work of recognizing and honestly constructing their own family narratives of settlement, and also to be open to learning from indigenous communities.

> We need to listen to how indigenous communities are identifying harms, needs, and responsibilities, and investigate our past and present complicity. The just-completed Canadian Truth and Reconciliation process gave us an extraordinary opportunity to do this. Then our churches can covenant to become true "Treaty People," working with First Nations to make things as right as possible. This can include covenants of accountability, restitution, reparation, and (ideally) reconciliation.[30]

Enns's work is based on an innate understanding of the interconnection between people and land, specifically a lived-out history of traumatic conflict based on very different values of land. A white colonizing orientation could be summarized as being rooted in the seeds of instrumentalism--land to be developed and owned and used--whereas an indigenous people's orientation is rooted in the seeds of radical relationalism--land as sacred relationship. This conflict of values led ultimately to the theft of land and subjugation and genocide of Indigenous Peoples that characterize early American history. Enns is offering us not only the opportunity of coming to terms with our complicity in the violence that dispossessed an entire people group, but to open ourselves to alternative ways of living into the future

30. Enns, "Settler Response-ability," 37.

shaped by relations with Indigenous Peoples and their distinctly relational ontologies with the Earth.

Radical Joy for Hard Times is a worldwide community that is based in the United States, dedicated to "bringing meaning, beauty, and value to places that have been damaged by human or natural acts."[31] This is an example of work that is not named as restorative justice, yet is aligned with its values within a radical relationalism paradigm. Radical Joy seeks to restore wounded places through embodied relationship and listening, reconnecting community and repairing harm. "Rad Joy educates, supports, and connects communities around the world to create Earth Exchanges, experiential gatherings in which we visit wounded places, get to know them as they are now, share our stories of what they mean to us, and make a simple, spontaneous work of art there."[32] This initiative is deeply restorative, providing a means for community to develop around renewed relationship with the Earth; this is a beautiful example of work inviting people to *re-member* themselves directly within the ecological fabric of life. As Dr. Muraca points out regarding radical relationalism, "By understanding our own experience we gain access to the understanding of *actual, constitutive relatedness*."[33]

Center for Restorative Practices, located in Santa Rosa, California, offers resources and training based on restorative justice principles. Their mission is to implement "restorative practices and the way of council to the places we work and live."[34] This includes a program specifically with the natural world, focused on "sustainability rooted in right relationships with the world around us."[35] The Center partners with The Association of Nature & Forest Therapy to train practitioners in opening doors for people to enter into relationship with nature, not only for healing and wellness, but to be open "to what happens when people remember that we are a part of nature, not separate from it, and are related to all other beings in fundamental ways."[36] This work is an ideal example of radical relationalism in practice, representing restorative justice as an agent of cultural change and conflict/crisis prevention and transformation.

The Work That Reconnects Network provides a set of resources and activities associated with Joanna Macy. The ethos of restoring and re-membering our primary relationship with the Earth is shared both by

31. Radical Joy for Hard Times, 1–2.
32. Radical Joy for Hard Times, 4–5.
33. Muraca, "Relational Values," 21.
34. Center for Restorative Process website.
35. Center for Restorative Process website.
36. Association for Nature & Forest Therapy website.

restorative justice and Joanna Macy's work during a time she names as "The Great Turning." This turning is the passage that defines the new emerging story governed by radical relationalism which she defines as, "a shift from Industrial Growth Society to life-sustaining civilization." The purpose of this work is to "bring us back into relationship with each other and with the self-healing powers in the web of life, motivating and empowering us to reclaim our lives, our communities, and our planet from corporate and colonial rule."[37] Through writings, online resources, and workshops, Macy and her colleagues offer practices for experiential group processes designed to reconnect people with "our mutual belonging in a relational universe,"[38] awaken us to the injustice of our Industrial Growth Society, and to affirm "that our intention to act for the sake of all beings, and to become allies to all oppressed or marginalized people, can become organizing principles of our lives."[39]

More Suggestions for Restorative Justice with the Earth

The following are ideas for potential restorative practices to help practitioners who want to facilitate environmental conflict processes and/or work toward prevention of continued environmental harm to transform worldview, embody practice, and create processes to reconnect people with the reality of their relatedness with the Earth. These examples are just a few of many other possibilities that could be explored, developed, and integrated into a movement toward restoring justice, which means restoring relationship, between humans and the rest of the natural world. This is prevention work, building a new ecological-cultural framework, "in a buzzing world, amid a democracy of fellow creatures."[40]

> This framework challenges the Western idea of 'nature' as something external to society to be—depending on the dominant paradigm—preserved (nature & wilderness conservation), exploited (eco-efficiency, green economy, weak sustainability), or managed (strong sustainability, wise use). It shifts attention to a radically different understanding of the relation to the 'territory,' with all its inhabitants included in what can be best called a *cosmo-anthropovision*, in which interconnection among different levels of the real

37. Macy, "Foundations of the Work," 25–26.
38. Macy, "Foundations of the Work," 29.
39. Macy, "Foundations of the Work," 33.
40. Muraca, "Relational Values," 35.

(biophysical, human, and supernatural) leads to specific society-nature relations and nature-culture regimes.[41]

Family Constellations Work

Although most people are disconnected from their ancestral history beyond a few generations, we are at the same time deeply affected by the DNA we carry from those who walked even centuries before us.[42] This disconnection from both the people who were our forebears, and to the Earth in which we have been formed over the centuries, is a factor in the continuing destruction of our planetary home.

To access the wisdom needed during a time of planetary emergency, and to address complex conflicts originating in the human domination of the natural world, we need access to our own indigenous knowledge, and learning from Indigenous Peoples in our communities and/or in our places of origin. We are all native to some place, embedded within a certain family of ancestors, both human and non-human, and connected by generations to land, water, and ecosystem. We can reconnect to this wisdom. Addressing and healing our ancestral roots often equates to addressing our complicity in the theft of land and displacement of Native Americans, in slaveholding, and in genocide.

Family and human systems constellation work is specifically geared toward ancestral healing, influenced by indigenous worldviews and traditions. Constellation work involves circle processes where participants are moved from a "noun-oriented" process to a "verb-oriented"[43] process rooted in storytelling, initiating a response from a more innate instinct and embodied connection with people and the natural world, rather than from a reductionist, rational mindset. For many Indigenous Peoples, story is a form of medicine. "Constellation work involves the kind of usage of words, the kind of openness to story as 'medicine.'"[44] Not to be confused with the entrenched "memorized" family story that continues to be acted out, told and retold, but with the stories that, "speak to the heart about healing and the connection of the soul within families" and within communities and with the Earth herself. The importance of this work intersects with the importance of addressing ancestral trauma work within cases of

41. Muraca, "Relational Values," 35.
42. Relethford, *Reflections of Our Past.*
43. Boring, *Connecting to Our Ancestral Past*, 4.
44. Boring, *Connecting to Our Ancestral Past*, 4.

harm, including environmental. "Victims and perpetrators at times share, at a deep soul level, the experience of their shared horror, and subsequent generations may incorporate one or both aspects of that experience."[45] This dynamic includes the land.

Family and human constellations work can be done for individuals, families, and communities, and nature constellation work is intentionally focused on cross-species and cross-group relationships in natural systems. In circles, the people doing the work choose representatives to act as members of their family, their ancestors, and/or as non-human members of the natural world. When people enter roles in a nature constellation, "they experience in their own bodies what membership in the Greater Family means, in a specific context."[46] These experiences have the capacity to heal people, families and communities, and ecosystems.

Grief Work

Restorative justice processes need to include practices that create space for tending to grief, both individually and communally, as an important element of healing wounds and relationships, developing empathy, and preventing conflict. Psychotherapist and writer Francis Weller identifies the loss of our connection with the living earth as one of the most important gateways of expressing grief. Especially during environmental conflicts or when addressing environmental harms, this gateway brings us to "directly experience the soul of the world, the *anima mundi*,"[47] as part of our own. During these times, perhaps our psyches experience not just our own grief, but that of the land or ecosystem herself.

> What if, however, the feelings we have when we pass through these zones of destruction are actually arising from the land itself? What if it is the grief of the forest registering in our bodies and psyches—the sorrow of the redwoods, voles, sorrel, fern, owls, and deer, all those who lost their homes and lives as a result of this plunder of living beings? What if we are not separate from the world at all? It is our spiritual responsibility to acknowledge these losses.[48]

45. Boring, *Connecting to Our Ancestral Past*, 18.
46. Boring, *Connecting to Our Ancestral Past*, 73.
47. Weller, *Wild Edge*, 46.
48. Weller, *Wild Edge*, 47.

Tending to our grief is both an act of restoration and a step toward preventing harm. When grief is repressed or denied, it hides in the collective and individual shadow, but it "doesn't sit there passively waiting to be reclaimed and redeemed; it regresses and becomes more primitive. Consequently, death rattles through our streets daily, in school shootings, suicides, murders, overdoses, gang violence, or through sanctioned sacrifice of war dead."[49] Creating space for grief during emotionally heightened times of conflict, harm and injustice is an important component of restorative processes and conflict prevention. Facilitated processes providing space to connect our grief with the sorrow of the natural world can be powerful and deeply restoring for both human and non-human.

Conversation *With* the Wild

Every leap across paradigms requires some kind of new training or learning, and sometimes unlearning. Personally reconnecting in and with nature is the backbone of preparing for the work of facilitating processes and guiding others. This time in history calls us to remember how to listen to the Earth and to bring about restoration, not only *to* the land, but *with* the land.

> It's not just the land that is broken, but more importantly, our relationship with the land . . . We can't meaningfully proceed with healing, with restoration, without 're-story-ation.' In other words, our relationship with land cannot heal until we hear its stories. But who will tell them?[50]

Our unconscious valuation of the natural world as 'objects' or 'resources' can become apparent in this process, and can change when we encounter them in a new way. Peter Wohlleben tells about his change of heart that influenced his practices as a forester who assessed trees for their market value for many years before his perception was changed. His job working with trees as commodities had distorted the way he saw them. Ultimately, he began to remember his love of nature as a child, and cultivated his relationship to trees, leading him to write *The Hidden Life of Trees: What They Feel, How They Communicate*, a New York Times Bestseller. From his writing, we learn that trees 'talk,' feel, care for their young and the elderly, cooperate, and have memories. He notes, "when the capabilities of vegetative beings become

49. Weller, *Wild Edge*, xviii.

50. Kimmerer, *Braiding Sweetgrass*, 9.

known, and their emotional lives and needs are recognized, then the way we treat plants will gradually change as well."[51]

To have a conversation with a tree or other being, or to imagine a way out of the current crises of disconnection, requires this kind of awareness rooted in experience. Or perhaps it is the other way around. This awareness comes as we learn to converse with a tree. In the process, we cultivate our own native human wholeness. "Trees are sanctuaries. Whoever knows how to speak to them, whoever knows how to listen to them, can learn the truth. They do not preach learning and precepts, they preach, undeterred by particulars, the ancient law of life. Every path leads homeward."[52]

Radical relationalism, and restorative justice, are inherently spiritual frameworks pointing to a unity among all life forms, which stands at the heart of most religions. A small emerging movement of churches popping up across North America is leaving behind traditional church buildings and meeting outside in their watersheds, within the full web of life, in conversation with stars and moon, forest and crops, sea and sky. I am one of the founding members of the Wild Church Network, with a diverse span of congregations within the ecumenical Christian tradition whose congregants include all of the natural world as spiritual practice and community responsibility. The network is a

> growing network of pastors and spiritual leaders, who have made bold moves to launch new expressions of church outside to re-acquaint, re-cover, and re-member our congregations as loving participants of a larger community. In this age of mass extinctions, we feel burdened by the love of Christ to invite people into direct relationship with some of the most vulnerable victims of our destructive culture: the land, waters, and creatures with whom we share our homes.[53]

Some of the churches, including the one I founded, offer acknowledgment and relationship to those community members (human and more-than-human) who have been traumatized by human colonization and destruction. These examples of emerging spiritual ecology offer another form of restorative justice-oriented relationalism.

51. Wohlleben, *Hidden Life of Trees*, 244.
52. Hesse, *Wandering*, 67.
53. www.wildchurchnetwork.com

Where Do We Go from Here?

In the shift from industrial society to living society, reconnection and relationship with the rest of the living world is called forth from a deep understanding that human destiny is radically intertwined with all natural systems and beings. A radical relationalism framework for restorative justice can help us challenge old assumptions about who and what we are in the whole ecology of life. A new story is emerging to help us re-member ourselves back into those core relationships that formed us, bringing with it new language and practices to contextualize them.

In this era, the relevance of any philosophy, practice or institution will be determined by its acknowledgment of our inherent interconnection, not only with one another, but with ecosystems and non-human species. Perhaps what we are witnessing in the world, namely the chaos of society in crisis, is also grounds for hope, as "breakdown is a necessary part of collectively waking up from the painful illusion of separation."[54]

A new story is being born and lived out in the ideas and experiences of ecotheologians, ecopsychologists, ecologists, permaculturists, beekeepers, food sovereignty farmers, poets, writers, along with cultural and spiritual leaders. Restorative justice practitioners who have interest in environmental conflicts and/or concern for the planetary crisis, need ways to come together to share ideas and questions. We need to create or participate in trainings tailored to implementing practices, and imaging new ones, which are rooted in radical relationalism.

The truth is that we are already in a relationship with all-that-is, even if we are not aware of it. So the question becomes, *what kind* of relationship will we choose to have with one another and with the Earth that formed us and keeps re-forming us? In an age of disconnection and destruction, radical relationalism challenges us to re-member ourselves as being intimately related with the natural world, as being part of the same sacred ecology. We are nature. Nature is us. A restorative justice that is aligned this way can create practices that listen to and include all stakeholders—furry and four-legged, swimming and flowing, flying, stationary, slithering, crawling, or walking on two legs—and foster experiences of restitution, reconciliation, and justice for the *healing* and *wholing* of the world.

54. Rich, "Recognizing the Wounds," 4.

Bibliography

Ananthaswamy, Anil. "Reality Check: The Hidden Connections behind Quantum Weirdness." *New Scientist*, April 5, 2017. https://www.newscientist.com/article/mg23431200-200-realitys-comeback-the-hidden-network-that-controls-what-we-see/.

Association for Nature & Forest Therapy. https://www.natureandforesttherapy.org.

Bohm, D., and B. J. Hiley. *The Undivided Universe: An Ontological Interpretation of Quantum Theory.* https://www.scribd.com/doc/33838548/The-Undivided-Universe-An-Ontological-Interpretation-of-Quantum-pdf.

Boring, Francesca Mason. *Connecting to Our Ancestral Past: Healing through Family Constellations, Ceremony, and Ritual.* Berkeley: North Atlantic, 2012.

Calaprice, Alice, ed. *The New Quotable Einstein*. Princeton: Princeton University Press, 2005.

Center for Restorative Process. Santa Rosa, CA. http://www.centerforrestorativeprocess.com/.

Dellinger, Drew. "Change the Worldview, Change the World: New Generations and the Power of Story." *Kosmos Journal for Global Transformation* (Summer 2018). https://www.kosmosjournal.org/kj_article/new-cosmology-and-social-justice/.

Enns, Elaine. "Settler Response-ability." *Geez Magazine* (Fall 2015) 34–37.

———. "Trauma and Memory: Challenges to Settler Solidarity." *Consensus* 37.1, art. 5. https://scholars.wlu.ca/consensus/vol37/iss1/5/.

Ganter, Carl. "Water Crises Are a Top Global Risk." *World Economic Forum* 16 (January 2015). https://www.weforum.org/agenda/2015/01/why-world-water-crises-are-a-top-global-risk/.

Hesse, Hermann. *Wandering: Notes and Sketches.* Translated by James Wright. New York: Farrar, Straus & Giroux, 1972.

Kimmerer, Robin Wall. *Braiding Sweetgrass: Indigenous Wisdom, Scientific Knowledge and the Teachings of Plants.* Minneapolis: Milkweed, 2013.

Lyons, Oren. Turtle Clan of the Seneca Nations of the Iroquois Confederacy. Online video of address to the United Nations in 1977, Geneva. https://www.youtube.com/watch?v=vCIdPK3WaA4.

Macy, Joanna. "Foundations of the Work." Work That Reconnects Network. https://workthatreconnects.org/.

Malkinson, Trevor. "Joanna Macy on the Three Pillars of the Great Turning." *Beams and Struts.* http://www.beamsandstruts.com/bits-a-pieces/item/980-joanna-macy-and-the-three-pillar of-the-great-turning.

Motupalli, Chaitanya. "Intergenerational Justice, Environmental Law, and Restorative Justice." *Washington Journal of Environmental Law and Policy* 8/2 (2018) 333–61. http://digital.law.washington.edu/dspace-law/bitstream/handle/1773.1/1821/8WJELP333.pdf.

Muraca, Barbara. "Relational Values: A Whiteheadian Alternative for Environmental Philosophy and Global Environmental Justice." *Balkan Journal of Philosophy* 8 (2016) 19–38.

National Security Implications of Climate-Related Risks and a Changing Climate. Submitted in response to a request contained in Senate Report 113-211, accompanying H.R. 4870, the Department of Defense Appropriations Bill, 2015.

Pain, Justice Nicola et al. *Restorative Justice for Environmental Crime: An Antipodean Experience*. International Union for Conservation of Nature Academy of Environmental Law Colloquium. Oslo Norway, June 22, 2016. http://www.lec.justice.nsw.gov.au/Documents/Speeches%20and%20Papers/PepperJ/PepperJ%20Restorative%20Justice.pdf.

Popova, Maria. "The Writing of *Silent Spring*: Rachel Carson and the Culture-Shifting Courage to Speak Inconvenient Truth to Power." *Brainpickings*. https://www.brainpickings.org/2017/01/27/rachel-carson-silent-spring-dorothy-freeman/.

Preston, Brian. "The Use of Restorative Justice in Environmental Crime." Paper presented to EPA Victoria Seminar on Restorative Environmental Justice, March 22, 2011.

Radical Joy for Hard Times. http://www.radicaljoyforhardtimes.org.

Reichert, Alexis. "Transformative Encounters: Destabilizing Human/Animal and Nature/Culture Binaries through Cross-Cultural Engagement." In *Constructions of Self and Other in Yoga, Travel, and Tourism: A Journey to Elsewhere*, edited by Lori G. Beaman et al., 29–36. Cham: Springer, 2016.

Relethford, John. *Reflections of Our Past: How Human History Is Revealed in Our Genes*. Boulder, CO: Westview, 2003.

Rich, Jan Peer. "Recognizing the Wounds." *Deep Times*. https://journal.workthatreconnects.org/2018/07/20/recognizing-the-wounds/.

Weller, Francis. *The Wild Edge of Sorrow: Rituals of Renewal and the Sacred Work of Grief*. Berkeley: North Atlantic, 2015.

Wild Church Network. www.wildchurchnetwork.com.

Wohlleben, Peter. *The Hidden Life of Trees*. Vancouver, BC: Greystone, 2016.

Zehr, Howard. *The Little Book of Restorative Justice*. Intercourse, PA: Good Books, 2002.

8

Do We Dare Love the Shooters?

Nine Principles of Firearm Harm Reduction

ETHAN UCKER

> *"They be shooting whether it's dark or not,*
> *I mean the days is pretty dark a lot*
>
> *Down here, it's easier to find a gun than it is*
> *to find a f***ing parking spot."*
>
> —Chance the Rapper

Harm reduction is a compassionate and pragmatic public health framework oriented around an ethics of local community control and self-determination. Successful harm reduction approaches meet people where they are at, offering them strategies to reduce the health and safety risks to which their behaviors expose them, even if they are not interested in stopping those behaviors. Harm reduction interventions seek solutions to social problems that are grounded in the unique insights and experiential wisdom of the people most affected by those problems, while also fostering a sense of trust, inclusion, and representation among them.

This chapter introduces readers to the nine principles animating a hyperlocal infrastructure-building project that adapts and applies a harm reduction framework to illicit gun possession and use. (See Table 8.1 at the end of the chapter.) This project is intended to prevent the premature deaths of young Black and Brown people from poor and working-class urban communities, and to disrupt the ceaseless demonization and criminalization of their politics of survival. It draws on two conjoined strategies to attain these goals: the continued development of safer firearm use education to supplant dangerous and unethical abstinence-only gun education, and the establishment of neighborhood-based safer gun use sites in the midst of communities with high concentrations of illicit gun users on Chicago's South and West Sides.

The criminal regulation of firearm possession in communities where everyone has easy access to guns is a diabolical hazard. Distrust of the police and fear of surveillance throttles conversations and skill-sharing around guns. Young Black and Brown people possess increasingly sophisticated weapons, but they have no legal channels through which to learn about them. The working hypothesis of this firearm harm reduction model is that creating non-judgmental spaces in which illicit gun users can learn about themselves and the guns they carry (in a way that is relevant to their lived experiences, and can de-mystify firearm use rather than stigmatize and criminalize it), will reduce instances of community violence and reduce the number of young Black and Brown people who are living at the edge of fatality—or at least keep them alive longer.

1. The model for safer gun use sites, and for the safer firearm use education conveyed at these sites, is being collectively shaped by the voices, needs, and insights of those who are intimately affected by urban gun violence.

Specifically, this model has emerged through ongoing collaboration with shooters, the gang-involved young Black and Brown people who are actively shooting guns and getting shot at. According to Ethan Viets-VanLear, one of the youth organizers working on this project, the shooters are the ones who, more times than not, are on "both sides of the weapon." Sad to say, it is commonplace for both authors and survivors of gun-related harms to be excluded from debates and decision-making about urban gun violence.

In 2017, a Chicago-based abolitionist collective of organizers and restorative justice practitioners of which I am a part began to think together about what it would look like to treat people who illegally possess and use firearms the way that harm reduction activists treat people who illegally possess and use opioids. During the summers of 2018 and 2019, we organized a series of wisdom exchanges and political education workshops about guns. Drawing on our personal relationships with shooters who represent geographic and gang communities from across the city, (and drawing on our relationships with other youth workers, mentors, attorneys, administrators, and educators to widen the scope of our outreach), we invited them to gather together to share stories, ask honest questions, and have non-judgmental conversations about the role of guns in their lives.

We also arranged individual meetings with those who wanted to contribute, but felt uncomfortable or unsafe discussing this taboo topic in group settings. Everyone who participated received food, transportation (when needed), and an honorarium, except those with whom we met inside prisons and detention centers who could not receive payments. When consent has been given, the words of project participants are quoted directly or summarized in this chapter; in order not to expose them to further incrimination, identifying information has been removed.

Through this ongoing organizing process, criminalized young Black and Brown people are considering the kinds of spaces, resources, and capacity-building processes they would seek out to improve their individual safety, address gun-related conflicts and harms, and make their immediate neighborhoods healthier and more peaceful. What role can guns play in cultivating improved community safety? Can there be safety *with* guns?

2. Firearm harm reduction responds to the predominantly Black and Brown communities enmeshed in the urban gun violence epidemic with the same openheartedness and empathy that is usually reserved for the predominantly white communities enmeshed in the opioid addiction and overdose epidemic.

We were initially compelled to reassess the issue of urban gun violence through the lens of harm reduction because devastating numbers of young Black and Brown people with whom we have relationships were getting shot in the streets, locked up for illegal gun possession, or both. In 2016, the year before we began this project, shootings and homicides in Chicago soared to levels not seen in decades: 4,368 people were shot, 764 were killed; of those murdered, 80% were Black and more than 50% were Black men between the ages of 15 and 34.[1] The first ten months of 2017 produced 3,144 shootings and 569 homicides.[2]

1. Kapustin et al., "Gun Violence in Chicago, 2016," 9–13; Gorner, "Few Answers as Chicago Hit with Worst Violence in Nearly 20 Years."

2. DNA Info, "Chicago Murders."

At the same time, illicit opioids were wreaking havoc at a similarly disproportionate rate on white poor and working-class communities across the country. In 2017, white people accounted for 77.9% of the 47,600 opioid overdose deaths in the U.S.[3] Yet while those white poor and working-class communities are met with de-criminalized needle exchanges and methadone clinics, the Black and Brown poor and working-class neighborhoods being ravaged by illicit guns are met with heightened criminal regulation and police surveillance.

3. Reducing reliance upon processes of criminalization and reducing exposure to the police enables improvements in public health and community safety.

A harm reduction framework acknowledges that, though certain drugs are illegal, people obtain and use them anyway. If you are going to use drugs, this approach suggests, at least be safe. Harm reduction interventions like needle and syringe exchanges are already common practice in the U.S. But in response to the national opioid addiction and overdose epidemic, some municipalities are beginning to extend the principles of harm reduction into what are, in the U.S., largely uncharted political waters. In places like Baltimore, New York City, the Bay Area, and Seattle, broad coalitions of public health advocates, aiming "to reduce harm to drug users and the broader community," are campaigning for the establishment of safe consumption sites (SCSs).[4]

Like needle exchange programs, SCSs distribute sterile injection equipment and naloxone, conduct HIV and hepatitis C testing, offer nurse consultations, low threshold medical services, and emergency overdose response; they also provide referrals to drug treatment, housing resources, legal aid, prenatal care, and mental health services.[5] In addition to these services, SCSs provide an environment in which drug users can actually use (smoke, snort, or inject) their "pre-obtained illicit drugs."[6]

In cities across the world—even if not yet in the U.S.—SCSs have been proven to "measurably improve public health and criminal outcomes."[7] SCS

3. Kaiser Family Foundation, "Opioid Overdose Deaths by Race/Ethnicity"; Hansen and Netherland, "Is the Prescription Opioid Epidemic a White Problem?," 2127–29; Alexander et al., "Trends in Black and White Opioid Mortality," 707–715.

4. Sherman et al., "Safe Drug Consumption Spaces," 1.

5. Kingston and Banta-Green, "Overview of Syringe Exchange Operations," 1–10.

6. Marshall et al., "Condom Use among Injection Drug Users," 121.

7. Sherman et al., "Safe Drug Consumption Spaces," 13.

staff members build drug users' awareness of risk factors inherent in drug use, and invite them to lay claim to safer drug use practices that reduce overdose events and the transmission of blood-borne pathogens.[8] Overall, "people who utilize SCSs take better care of themselves, use their drugs more safely, and have better access to medical (and extramedical), social and drug treatment services compared to [drug users] who do not access SCSs."[9] For as much as SCSs do to reduce individual drug users' high-risk behaviors, they also address health and safety risks at the broader community level by reducing instances of unsupervised public drug use, amounts of improperly discarded injection paraphernalia, and rates of "public disorder" and "local drug-related crime" in their vicinity.[10]

A considerable body of evidence suggests that harm reduction interventions are effective because they decline to criminalize illicit drug use or stigmatize it as immoral. SCSs offer an open door to drug users, an "unhurried" and non-judgmental environment in which to use drugs "without fear of interaction with police."[11]

4. Among the young Black and Brown people most affected by urban gun violence, carrying a firearm is a rational protective strategy.

In spite of heightened law enforcement efforts to curb the flow of illegal firearms into Chicago, guns remain more widely available than ever. Criminalized young Black and Brown people put it bluntly: "Everybody got guns." The once highly centralized, citywide structures of Chicago's gangs have fractured; today, territorial rivalries between hyperlocal cliques are lubricated by ubiquitous and lethal weapons. Shootings—sometimes retaliatory, sometimes accidental, attributed as often to social media insults as to decades-long, multigenerational conflicts—play out with everything from pistols with high-capacity magazines to military-style semi-automatic rifles.[12]

Gun violence is bound up with the material support, protection, and sense of belonging that gangs offer their young members, and with visions of success, politics of survival, and feelings of responsibility rooted in racial capitalism and patriarchal masculinity. The eyes of a young man at the Juvenile Temporary Detention Center light up as he describes the pride he felt when,

8. Hedrich et al., "Drug Consumption Facilities," 306–323.
9. Sherman et al., "Safe Drug Consumption Spaces," 11.
10. Hedrich et al., "Drug consumption facilities," 308–12.
11. Otter, "Safe Consumption Facilities," 2.
12. Nickeas et al., "Some Chicago Gangs Turning to Rifles."

at 15, he was given a gun and sent on a mission to shoot a rival gang member. "It made me feel honored. It reminded me that I put in a lot of hard work. I could finally prove myself as a man. It made me walk with my head higher. I gained more respect, like they looked at me as a leader not a follower."

Gun possession is a logical adaptive response to the omnipresent threat of lethal violence young Black and Brown individuals face due to "the state's failure to keep them safe," the very systems that serve and protect white civil society which do not serve or protect them.[13] Distrust and hatred of the police, for example, is deeply embedded within the collective habitus of their communities, "absorbed into the culture and transmitted [. . .] from generation to generation."[14] The cops are a source of racist violence and brutality, and their presence intensifies, rather than mitigates, feelings of unsafety, dread, and rage.

The sense of safety that guns provide far outweighs potential legal consequences, hence the common refrains, "I'd rather be caught with it than without it," and, "I'd rather be judged by 12 than carried by 6." One 22-year-old reasons it this way: "I strap up every morning—brush my teeth, get dressed, grab my heater. I got to; I can't leave the house without it. Out here it's either shoot or be shot."

5. Between bipartisan criminalization of gun possession and non-profitized abstinence-only gun education, we are hemmed in: attempting to respond to urban gun violence without actually dealing with guns.

Gruesome statistics about urban gun violence are circulated to justify conservative law and order approaches like deploying more police officers in Black and Brown communities and expanding predictive policing. In the ongoing aftermath of mass shootings, these conservative strategies work in concert with the liberal gun control movement, which advocates stricter age restrictions on buying guns and federal sentencing enhancements for criminal offenses that involve firearm possession, sometimes "regardless of whether the gun is ever fired or even brandished."[15] Fueled by bipartisan support, these carceral enforcement mechanisms and policies have produced a "war on guns," which, like its predecessor the War on Drugs, disproportionately

13. Rojas, "Community Accountability as Pedagogical Strategy," 82.

14. Sotero, "A Conceptual Model of Historical Trauma," 96.

15. Denvir, "A Better Gun Control," para. 4.

targets and incarcerates poor and working-class urban communities of color, particularly Black men with felony records.[16]

Compounding the war on guns, non-profit program providers and justice professionals reflexively privilege abstinence-only gun education. Young Black and Brown people who carry guns are shut out of the material benefits of state-supported (meaning government-supported) social services, alternatives to incarceration, restorative justice programs, and youth development initiatives unless they pledge to practice a sanitized version of nonviolence. Whitewashing nonviolence, amputating it from its broader historical context in the U.S., and holding young Black and Brown people who carry weapons to that standard does not honor their lived experiences. A young man explains the dissonance between the message he received in a recent meeting with his case manager and his reality: "I got programmed, growing up in this neighborhood. We can't 'turn the other cheek.'"

6. Though it has been tested in relation to the opioid epidemic, the adaptation of a harm reduction framework to the urban gun violence epidemic is trauma-informed because, in particular Chicago neighborhoods, illicit opioid use and illicit firearm use are comorbid behaviors.

Before mobilizing conceptions of trauma to analyze dynamics within racialized groups of people, it is important to acknowledge that doing so is an odious game. Trauma is invested in individualization: refracted through its lens, socio-political problems are reduced to atomistic units, and rendered analyzable in terms of brain chemistry and individual responsibility. When structural harms are cast as biochemical problems, they are de-politicized. For example, fixating on trauma makes it possible to pathologize a young Black person without attending to the anti-Black histories that shape their behaviors: residential segregation, unremitting police violence, and multigenerational psychic/emotional wounds sustained as a direct result of racial slavery. Trauma enables medicalized diagnoses, and thus makes healing and wellness in marginalized communities the business of specialists with expert knowledge. Dian Million (Tanana Athabascan) noted that "trauma, or intergenerational trauma, cannot capture the infinite meaning of our lives, our histories, or any futurity that is our own. Trauma can only ever be an analytical frame that lends itself, in the long run, to capitalist management."[17]

16. Levin, "Guns and Drugs," 2173–226; Forman Jr., *Locking Up Our Own*.

17. Million, "Spirit and Matter."

"We been getting shot at," explains one young man, recently released after serving time for illegal gun possession. "Our homies been getting killed in the streets all around us. We all got trauma around guns." Gun users are criminalized for harming others, but often, long before they acquire illicit weapons, they have accrued extensive trauma histories of their own. As children, many have repeatedly "witnessed violence and experienced victimization" as a function of growing up in neighborhoods mired in community and police violence.[18] Given the "experience-dependent plasticity" of the developing brain, chronic exposure to trauma during childhood can be "seared" or "built in" to its neural architecture, and predictive of two contrasting stress responses in adolescents and young adults: hyperreactivity and dissociation.[19]

Hyperreactivity is produced when the systems in the brain that are recruited to respond to external stimuli secrete elevated levels of the stress hormone cortisol into the bloodstream, shifting the body into fight-or-flight mode.[20] Repeatedly triggering this defense against threat lowers its threshold of activation; over time, "decreasingly intense external stimuli" can elicit an influx of cortisol and the "generalized anxiety" and "hypervigilance" of fight-or-flight.[21] Induced not just by a traumatic event, but also by "everyday stressors" or reminders of the event, hyperreactivity becomes less an acute state than an "enduring trait."[22]

A dissociative defense to stress, characterized by "emotional nonreactivity" and "withdrawn behavior," is induced by an atypically reduced cortisol profile.[23] To lessen the physiological burden of hyperreactivity, the brain suppresses cortisol levels through the endogenous production and secretion of opioids. Those who become accustomed to "elevated levels of natural opioids" in their brain can experience withdrawal symptoms. Exogenously ingesting opioids allows individuals "to chemically induce a state that mimics" the

18. Aiyer et al., "Exposure to Violence," 1068.

19. Gambino and Holtmaat, "Synapses Let Loose for a Change," 216; Perry and Pollard, "Homeostasis, Stress, Trauma, and Adaptation," 42; Perry et al., "Childhood Trauma," 290.

20. Perry et al., "Childhood Trauma," 278; Lugarinho et al., "Prospects of Studies on Violence," 1329; Peckins et al., "The Longitudinal Impact of Exposure to Violence," 367.

21. Perry et al., "Childhood Trauma," 275–77; Peckins et al., 366.

22. Perry and Pollard, "Homeostasis, Stress, Trauma, and Adaptation," 42; Peckins et al., "The Longitudinal Impact of Exposure to Violence," 367; Lee et al., "Synapse Elimination," 195.

23. Aiyer et al., "Exposure to Violence," 1067–75; Perry and Pollard, "Homeostasis, Stress, Trauma, and Adaptation," 43; Peckins et al., "The Longitudinal Impact of Exposure to Violence," 371.

"soothing, gratifying pleasure" of endogenously orchestrated dissociation.[24] Epidemiologists have found that there is a "probabilistic concurrence" of childhood trauma and opioid use, the latter numbing distressing and painful emotions related to the former.[25]

Hyperreactivity and dissociation can co-occur because they spring from the same etiological source; they are different "enduring neurodevelopmental consequences" of the same trauma history.[26] In the neighborhoods at the center of this project, we observe an admixture of both of these contrasting stress response patterns, and an interaction between them. Many young Black and Brown people move through the world in a sustained state of "hypervigilance and hyperarousal," constantly looking over their shoulders and ducking abruptly down alleys to avoid being seen by rival gang members.[27] In this volatile context, acquiring and carrying a firearm offers a sense of control and a defense against another gun user's unpredictable explosion of "aggressive and violent behavior."[28] Concurrently, illegal gun users also self-medicate with illegal opioids, acquiring and using "dissociating agents" like percocet, codeine-based lean or Actavis, Vicodin, oxycodone, and fentanyl to provide tranquilizing relief from persisting grief, anxiety, anger, and paranoia.[29]

This firearm harm reduction model is not intended to minimize the profound differences between the opioid addiction and overdose epidemic and the urban gun violence epidemic. It is situated within an environment, however, where these urgent public health crises are intertwined.

24. Somer, "Opioid Use Disorder and Dissociation," 511–16.

25. Somer, "Opioid Use Disorder and Dissociation," 513; Van Hasselt et al., "Psychiatrically Hospitalized Dually Diagnosed Adolescent Substance Abusers," 868–74.

26. Aiyer et al., "Exposure to Violence," 1068; Anda et al., "The Enduring Effects of Abuse and Related Adverse Experiences in Childhood," 183.

27. Somer, Eli, "Opioid Use Disorder and Dissociation," 515.

28. Anda et al., "The Enduring Effects of Abuse and Related Adverse Experiences in Childhood," 181.

29. Somer, "Opioid Use Disorder and Dissociation," 515.

7. Instead of advocating that shooters put the guns down, safer firearm use education equips them with the knowledge, skills, and resources they need to make more responsible and mindful choices about the guns they are already, routinely picking up.

Safer firearm use education, explains a 19-year-old from East Garfield Park (a community on Chicago's West Side), is intended to "make knowledge about guns accessible" so that "you know what you capable of, and know the power and responsibility we have with guns." Shooters participating in wisdom exchanges and political education workshops propose that neighborhood-based safer gun use sites offer three different types of safer firearm use education activities.

Candid Conversations

Candid conversations invite young people who have been criminalized for gun use and possession to sit together, to reflect on their relationships to their weapons, the police, and their communities, and to process gun-related conflicts and harms. It means holding space in which they can address the emotional, cognitive, social, behavioral, and physiological costs of being on both sides of the gun by sharing stories of surviving gun violence, as well as (in many cases, for the first time in their lives) stories of being the shooter and authoring harm.

A clear distinction seems obvious: drug users harm themselves and gun users harm others. And yet, when asked the kinds of questions they would be interested in discussing with one another, young people repeatedly blurred this distinction by acknowledging the harm they inflict on themselves when they use guns.

> What feeling do you get after you pull the trigger? What was your experience pulling a gun on someone and how have you handled the things you felt inside afterward? What feelings of guilt, regret, shame, fear, dread, or horror did you experience during or after the incident? Does anyone else have trouble sleeping?
>
> What was your relationship to the person you harmed? How has your involvement in a shooting incident changed you, your family, and affected the other relationships in your life?

> A lot of times the media is de-humanizing us, saying we animals. But we do it too, cuz here [in the song lyrics] it says 'grimey savage, that's what we are.' We talking about how we savages, and we sent off, shooting each other—I want to talk about how we out here de-humanizing ourselves.[30]

Their questions also make connections between paranoia and addiction, and explore the ways that, in their communities, illicit gun use is entangled with illicit opioid, marijuana, and benzodiazepine use.

> I gotta look over my shoulder like all the time. If I'm in action mode I get off the xans (take Xanax) before I do a mission. But weed make me feel smooth, smoking weed is when I stop being hype. My question for the group is how y'all feel about drugs, and what they do for you?

Political Education

During one preliminary listening session, a young man on First Offender Gun Probation said, "I'd like to know how did all these guns get into my community. Where are they coming from?" Another wrote, "Did my ancestors have guns? Also I heard there are places in the world where no one has guns, not even the police, so how come there are guns here?" Political education classes offer an opportunity to examine ways that working-class Black and Brown communities have historically built capacity with, and organized, trained, and mobilized around firearms. They push beyond the abstinence-only gun education and whitewashed versions of nonviolence promulgated by many non-profit program providers and justice professionals by studying approaches to nonviolence that do not disavow the prevalence of guns, including past examples in which nonviolent tactics and strategic action have been complemented and sponsored "by gunfire and the threat of gunfire."[31]

State-supported responses de-politicize urban gun violence by employing ahistorical analytical frameworks that allow for only narrow, "individualized accounts" of it.[32] Gun conflicts are approached in terms of law-breaking and crime (to be policed and punished) or in terms of trauma and contagion (to be medicalized and managed). Political education classes,

30. This quote is from a workshop that made use of Bobby Shmurda's 2014 song "Hot N***a." The song's lyrics are being referenced.

31. Cobb, *This Nonviolent Stuff'll Get You Killed*, 2.

32. Rojas, "Community Accountability as Pedagogical Strategy," 96.

on the other hand, engage shooters in the study and research needed to develop a shared political analysis of gun violence that is de-individualized, properly historicized, and that distinguishes between both intra-community gun violence and state-sponsored police violence.

Applied Skill-Building

Skill-building opportunities can include emergency first responder training, know your rights workshops, and firearm safety classes. A young man writes about a fatal shootout in which he was involved:

> [. . .] were runnin they shoot another 3 shots I look back I see my boy hit the pavement screaming HELP ME I stop running I stop to help my boy but Im scared heart poundin palms sweating and hands shaking I see blood on his hand I see him holding his stomach then his leg then his chest hes crying I start to cry I start to hold him hes coughing up blood he tells me dont leave me he starts tryin to gasp for air I look in his eyes I see that hes scared out of his mind I grabbed his hand Im screaming [. . .]

He wonders if his friend would have lived if he had known what to do to improve his chances of survival in the moments before help arrived. Safer firearm use education includes emergency first responder training, provided through our ongoing partnership with Ujimaa Medics, a Black street medic collective in Chicago. The goal is to equip those at greatest risk of exposure to gun-related harm with concrete and time-critical first aid practices, including treating gunshot wounds, securing free airways, implementing bleeding control measures, and administering CPR. This skill-building also aims to provide illicit gun users with a practical sense of how to manage the chaos of a shooting and what to expect in its aftermath.

Safer firearm use education also includes 'know your rights' workshops that disseminate information about the legalities of gun possession, transport, and use, and criteria for Firearm Owners Identification cards and Concealed Carry Licenses.

Workshop participants exchange wisdom with each other as they raise various technical questions about how to operate and care for their guns. "How do I store my piece? I worry about my baby sister finding it whenever it's at the house." "How do I grip it knowing the kickback coming?" Many of them envision hands-on training in firing guns as a way to reduce gun-related harms; they propose that safer gun use sites offer access to a shooting range, target practice, and instruction in the fundamentals of marksmanship. A young man at a juvenile prison, a boxer, suggests that marksmanship instruction would instill in illicit gun users a heightened sense of responsibility for the safety of their community, analogous to the burden on professional boxers who, because they know how to deploy their fists as lethal weapons, have to be circumspect about confrontations with untrained fighters. Recent evidence makes an adjacent argument by linking martial arts training, with its "themes of repetitive movements, controlled behaviors, and respect," to reductions in physical aggression and violent behaviors among children and adolescents, and to improvements in their "self-control," "emotional stability," and "self-awareness."[33]

Moreover, many young Black and Brown people who are surrounded by and illegally carrying guns for protection are already being taught how to shoot them, often by older gang members. One young man explains, "The big homie, he was the chief enforcer of the Vice Lords when I was growing in the game. He taught me about guns and wars more than anyone else." Hands-on firearm use education already exists, but because it is criminalized, it has been driven underground. Is this safe? What about the ways that shooters use and think about guns would change if they had consistent opportunities to learn from certified firearm safety experts?

Instead of training illicit gun users to fire guns, an idea which provokes understandable resistance from a range of professionals, proposed safer gun use site offerings have been adapted to reflect the National Rifle Association's 4-hour certified home firearm safety course, a non-shooting course. Through firearm safety classes, shooters would learn principles of safe handling, cleaning, care, and storage of guns and ammunition, the basics around firearm components, design, mechanics, and assembly, and how to unload different types of actions.

8. Once established, safer gun use sites can be converted into incubators for multigenerational, community-controlled responses to gun conflicts that honestly acknowledge the presence of firearms and are inclusive of those who use them.

Illicit gun users participating in wisdom exchanges and political education workshops are already considering what it means to heal from gun-related harms they have both authored and received. One young man asks, "I would

33. Harwood et al., "Reducing Aggression with Martial Arts," 97–100.

want to know from someone else who has [a victim] that didn't die is they thinking about apologizing and could they ever have accountability?"

The creation of non-coercive safer gun use sites through which shooters can improve their individual wellness and safety without incriminating themselves interrupts a culture that treats them as social pariahs, offers concrete proof that they are not dispensable, and cultivates their investment in making their immediate communities healthier and more peaceful. It prepares them to collaborate with others from their neighborhoods who are also directly impacted by community and police violence (including elders, currently and formerly incarcerated people, mothers, business owners, and religious leaders), in order to determine and organize individual, family, and community accountability processes. These processes, according to project organizer Brandon Daurham, "heal and connect instead of stigmatizing and incarcerating/criminalizing."

Imagine multiple such neighborhood-based spaces networked together into a de-centralized "infrastructure of accountability" through which hyperlocal responses to harm (gun-related and otherwise) and the tactics to organize them, can transcend and be shared across geographic and gang territories.[34]

9. Honoring (rather than overriding) community wisdom and community-determined solutions means pushing beyond professionally, institutionally, and legally circumscribed notions of justice, healing, wellness, accountability and care.

Some of the culturally-specific firearm harm reduction strategies conceptualized by criminalized young Black and Brown people participating in wisdom exchanges and political education workshops are incommensurable with codified theories of change and social science-backed best practices. Negotiating this incommensurability can be uncomfortable for justice professionals—those of us who are in the business of managing other people's conflicts. Justice professionals include practitioners, educators, researchers, consultants, administrators, and advocates from various specialized fields (criminal justice, law, violence prevention, restorative justice, social work, youth development, alternative dispute resolution). These justice professionals are sustained by institutions (non-profits, philanthropic foundations, think tanks, advocacy groups, professional associations, social

34. Rojas, "Community Accountability as Pedagogical Strategy," 96.

welfare agencies, university research centers, crime labs, LLCs, training centers, school districts, courts, community courts, reentry outfits, prisons, police departments), all of which are arrayed across the nation as interlocking industrial complexes.

What are we justice professionals to do when community-determined solutions to social problems do not include us? How do we respond when community-based leaders request that we stay outside, that we decline to enter spaces or not interfere with lives and communities that are not our own? What if the primary problem, following Nils Christie, is not the amount of gun-related conflicts, but rather the metastasizing "abundance of professionals" who are "trained to prevent and solve" them?[35] When all of our socialization has convinced us that the credentialed expert knowledge that we have to offer is eminently valuable, and when we have a professional imperative to serve, provide, and impart that knowledge wherever it is lacking, where do we go when we are asked to leave? How can we go away when we still have a job to do, a career to advance, not to mention when we still need to support ourselves and our loved ones financially? How will we make a living?

These challenging questions are already confronting the police. For those who are shooting and getting shot at to feel safe to gather together, access safer firearm use education, engage in multigenerational collaboration, and build community accountability mechanisms to address gun-related harms, spaces must be created that are insulated from surveillance and criminalization. Ethan Viets-VanLear writes, "We need de-criminalized spaces where we can talk about these issues safely, and come to terms with the guns in our reality." This call to dislodge the police in order to enable possibilities of improved public health and community safety is consistent with evidence amassed by needle exchange programs in the U.S. and SCSs abroad. If, like those other harm reduction interventions, neighborhood-based safer gun use sites are to be "free from police intrusions," as a young woman participating in this project puts it, the Chicago Police Department (CPD) must stand down. At particular times, in and around particular spaces, CPD must agree not to police, and instead to cede authority to the very racialized poor and working-class communities they relentlessly terrorize and destabilize, so that something else can grow.

But this is not just about the cops. If the police must leave so that healing can occur, which justice professionals get to stay? Who decides? Can we, all of us justice professionals, start to prepare ourselves now, together, to pack up and get out?

35. Christie, "Conflicts as Property," 4–13.

Table 8.1. This model adapts and applies a harm reduction approach to illicit gun use which is widely accepted in relation to illicit drug use.

a harm reduction framework applied to **Illegal Drug Use**	a harm reduction framework applied to **Illegal Firearm Use**
Though certain drugs are illegal, people obtain them from illicit markets and use them anyway.	Though firearm possession is illegal, people with felonies often obtain guns from illicit markets and use them anyway.
Possessing and using illegal drugs is a choice; the behavior is also an adaptive strategy to manage neurobiologically in-built stress responses from extensive trauma histories.	Possessing and using illegal guns is a choice; this behavior is also an adaptive strategy to manage neurobiologically in-built stress responses from extensive trauma histories.
This behavior exposes people who inject drugs, and their immediate communities, to health and safety risks—e.g., increased likelihood of blood borne viral infection and overdose.	This behavior exposes people who use guns, and their immediate communities, to health and safety risks—e.g., increased likelihood of lethal violence and incarceration.
Approaches that criminalize public drug use or promote abstinence-only drug education are dangerous and unethical—they exacerbate health and safety risks.	Approaches that criminalize public gun use or promote abstinence-only gun education are dangerous and unethical—they exacerbate health and safety risks.
Instead, selective decriminalization of illicit drug use helps drug-users to access equipment, safer drug use education, and professional supports to reduce the risks of drug-related harms.	Instead, selective decriminalization of illicit gun use helps gun users to access equipment, safer firearm use education, and professional supports to reduce the risks of gun-related harms.
Provide resources so that people who routinely inject drugs can build awareness of risk factors and grow capacities to improve the health and safety of their communities.	Provide resources so that people who routinely carry guns can build awareness of risk factors and grow capacities to improve the health and safety of their communities.

a harm reduction framework applied to **Illegal Drug Use**	a harm reduction framework applied to **Illegal Firearm Use**
Safer drug use education activities and resources conveyed at safe consumption sites:	Safer firearm use education activities and resources conveyed at safer gun use sites:
• Non-judgmental relationships	• Non-judgmental relationships
• Candid conversations	• Candid conversations
• Emergency overdose response	• Emergency first responder training
• HIV and hepatitis C testing	• Political education classes
• Nurse consultations	• Know your rights workshops
• Distribution of sterile injection supplies	• Firearm safety training courses (non-shooting)
• Safer drug use	
• Referrals to healthcare and social services	• Multigenerational individual, family, and community accountability processes and restorative dialogue

Acknowledgments

This project belongs to the young people—Alicia, Alonzo, Alvaro, Angela, Anthony, Brianna, Brittany, Carlos, Charles, Consie, Corey, Cupree, Deandre, Denzel, Deondre, Desean, Donquel, Dre, Fletcher, Frederick, Gio, Jahari, Jalen, Jawan, Jeremy, JoJo, Kenneth, Kevin, Kris, Lavon, Marshawn, Maurice, both Michaels, Omari, Quinton, Rayquan, Romale, Rondale, Shaunice, Stephon, Tashay, Tayler, Tavon, Tim, Travon, Trayvonte, Tyquell, Vic, Zach, and many others—whose insights, voices, stories, and realities are represented here.

Gratitude to those whose collaboration and partnership throughout this organizing process, or whose incisive feedback on earlier versions of this essay, have sharpened and grounded this work: Emmanuel Andre, Bill Ayers, Kathy Bankhead, Dan Berger, Julie Biehl, Mac Carlson, Dan Cooper, Brandon Daurham, Jean Dennison, Bernardine Dohrn, Annie Dwyer, Will Eder, Marlon English, Anthony Floyd, Noni Gaylord-Harden, Shelley Gilchrist, Michael Gomez, Cheryl Graves, Gillian Harkins, Stephen Jackson, Kenisha Jamison, Mariame Kaba, Rebecca Kling, Ted Lewis, Eleuthera Lisch, Dian Million, Nubian, Dan Otter, Chris Patterson, Sherrif Polk, Alphonso Prater, Elena Quintana, Tony Raggs, Ali Rowhani-Rahbar, Fred Seaton, Carl Stauffer, Juan Tauri, David Ucker, Jennifer Viets, Rob Vickery, Ethan Viets-VanLear, Fred Wallace, Piet Walvoord.

Wisdom exchanges and political education workshops during the summers of 2018 and 2019 were made possible by funding from the Institute for Public Safety and Social Justice at Adler University, and by the kindness and administrative support of Misty Brown and Matt Barrington.

This essay's titular question comes from a series of talking circles that Emmanuel Andre and I co-facilitated in 2012 to process the murder of a young Black man on Chicago's North Side.

Finally, Ora Schub was a mentor, teacher, and other-mother to me. She modeled open-heartedness and generosity like no one else I have known, and in doing so she challenged me to push the limits of my empathy. My contributions to this project are dedicated to her memory.

Bibliography

Aiyer, Sophie M. et al. "Exposure to Violence Predicting Cortisol Response During Adolescence and Early Childhood: Understanding Moderating Factors." *Journal of Youth and Adolescence* 43 (2014) 1066–79.

Alexander, Monica J. et al. "Trends in Black and White Opioid Mortality in the United States, 1979–2015." *Epidemiology* 29 (2018) 707–15.

Anda, Robert F. et al. "The Enduring Effects of Abuse and Related Adverse Experiences in Childhood: A Convergence of Evidence from Neurobiology and Epidemiology." *European Archives of Psychiatry and Clinical Neuroscience* 256/3 (2006) 174–86.

Blankenship, Aaron G., and Maria B. Feller. "Mechanisms Underlying Spontaneous Patterned Activity in Developing Neural Circuits." *Nature Reviews Neuroscience* 11/1 (2010) 18–29.

Christie, Nils. "Conflicts as Property." *British Journal of Criminology* 17/1 (1977) 1–15.

Cobb, Charles E., Jr. *This Nonviolent Stuff'll Get You Killed: How Guns Made the Civil Rights Movement Possible.* New York: Basic Books, 2014.

DNA Info. "Chicago Murders." https://www.dnainfo.com/chicago/2017-chicago-murders.

Denvir, Daniel. "A Better Gun Control." *Jacobin* (15 September 2016). https://www.jacobinmag.com/2016/09/gun-control-mass-incarceration-drug-war-nra-shooters.

Expert Advisory Committee on Supervised Injection Site Research. "Vancouver's INSITE Service and Other Supervised Injection Sites: What Has Been Learned from Research?" *Health Canada* (March 2008). https://www.canada.ca/en/health-canada/corporate/about-health-canada/reports-publications/vancouver-insite-service-other-supervised-injection-sites-what-been-learned-research.html.

Forman, James, Jr. *Locking Up Our Own: Crime and Punishment in Black America.* New York: Farrar, Straus & Giroux, 2017.

Gambino, Frédéric, and Anthony Holtmaat. "Synapses Let Loose for a Change: Inhibitory Synapse Pruning throughout Experience-Dependent Cortical Plasticity." *Neuron* 74/2 (2012) 214–17.

Gilmore, Ruth Wilson. "Fatal Couplings of Power and Difference: Notes on Racism and Geography." *Professional Geographer* 54 (2002) 15–24.

Gorner, Jeremy. "Few Answers as Chicago Hit with Worst Violence in Nearly 20 Years." *Chicago Tribune* (30 December 2016).

Hansen, Helena, and Julie Netherland. "Is the Prescription Opioid Epidemic a White Problem?" *American Journal of Public Health* 106/12 (2016) 2127–29.

Harwood, Anna et al. "Reducing Aggression with Martial Arts: A Meta-analysis of Child and Youth Studies." *Aggression and Violent Behavior* 34 (2017) 96–101.

Hedrich, Dagmar et al. "Drug Consumption Facilities in Europe and Beyond." In *Harm Reduction: Evidence, Impacts and Challenges*, edited by Tim Rhodes and Dagmar Hedrich, 305–31. Luxembourg: Publications Office of the European Union, 2010.

Kaiser Family Foundation. "Opioid Overdose Deaths by Race/Ethnicity." https://www.kff.org/other/state-indicator/opioid-overdose-deaths-by-raceethnicity.

Kapustin, Max et al. "Gun Violence in Chicago, 2016." University of Chicago Crime Lab (January 2017). http://urbanlabs.uchicago.edu/attachments/store/2435a5d4658e2ca19f4f225b810ce0dbdb9231cbdb8d702e784087469ee3/UChicagoCrimeLab+Gun+Violence+in+Chicago+2016.pdf

Kingston, Susan, and Caleb Banta-Green. "Overview of Syringe Exchange Operations in Washington State." University of Washington Alcohol and Drug Abuse Institute (September 2015) 1–13.

Lee, Hanmi et al. "Synapse Elimination and Learning Rules Co-regulated by MHC Class I H2-Db." *Nature* 509 (8 May 2014) 195–200.

Levin, Bejamin. "Guns and Drugs." *Fordham Law Review* 84/5 (2016) 2173–226.

Lugarinho, Leonardo Planel et al. "Prospects of Studies on Violence, Adolescence, and Cortisol: A Systematic Literature Review." *Ciência & Saúde Coletiva* 22/4 (2017) 1321–32.

Marshall, B. D. L. et al. "Condom Use among Injection Drug Users Accessing a Supervised Injecting Facility." *Sexually Transmitted Infections* 85 (2009) 121–26.

Million, Dian. "Spirit and Matter: Resurgence as Rising and (Re)Creation as Ethos." *Symposium: Indigenous Resurgence in an Age of Reconciliation*. University of Victoria (18 March 2017).

Nickeas, Peter et al. "Some Chicago Gangs Turning to Rifles for Added Firepower, Police Say." *Chicago Tribune* (24 February 2017).

Otter, Dan. "Safe Consumption Facilities: Evidence and Models." King County Heroin and Opiate Addiction Task Force (2016). https://www.kingcounty.gov/~/media/depts/community-human-services/behavioral-health/documents/herointf/Safe_Consumption_Facilities_Evidence_Models.ashx?la=en.

Peckins, Melissa K. et al. "The Longitudinal Impact of Exposure to Violence on Cortisol Reactivity in Adolescents." *Journal of Adolescent Health* 51/4 (2012) 366–72.

Perry, Bruce D. et al. "Childhood Trauma, the Neurobiology of Adaptation, and 'Use-Dependent' Development of the Brain: How 'States' Become 'Traits.'" *Infant Mental Health Journal* 16/4 (1995) 271–91.

Perry, Bruce D. and Ronnie Pollard. "Homeostasis, Stress, Trauma, and Adaptation: A Neurodevelopmental View of Childhood Trauma." *Child and Adolescent Psychiatric Clinics of North America* 7 (1998) 33–51.

Rojas, Clarissa. "In Our Hands: Community Accountability as Pedagogical Strategy." *Social Justice* 37/4 (2011–2012) 76–100.

Sherman, Susan, et. al. "Safe Drug Consumption Spaces: A Strategy for Baltimore City." *The Abell Foundation* 29/7 (2017) 1–15.

Smith, Andrea. "Introduction." In *The Revolution Will not Be Funded: Beyond the Non-Profit Industrial Complex*, edited by INCITE! Women of Color Against Violence, 1–18. Cambridge, MA: South End, 2007.

Somer, Eli. "Opioid Use Disorder and Dissociation." In *Dissociation and the Dissociative Disorders: DSM-V and Beyond*, edited by Paul F. Dell and John A. O'Neil, 511–18. New York: Routledge, 2009.

Sotero, Michelle M. "A Conceptual Model of Historical Trauma: Implications for Public Health Practice and Research." *Journal of Health Disparities Research and Practice* 1 (2006) 93–108.

Van Hasselt, Vincent B. et al. "Maltreatment in Psychiatrically Hospitalized Dually Diagnosed Adolescent Substance Abusers." *Journal of the American Academy of Child & Adolescent Psychiatry* 31 (1992) 868–74.

9

Burundi Peace Committees

A Model for Reducing Electoral Violence

Mulanda Juma

Introduction

Burundi has long suffered from violence, especially ethnic-related killings between Hutu and Tutsi. This situation has happened both under dictatorial and democratic dispensations. Transforming destructive relationships between different ethnic groups and preventing ethnic violence is thus fundamental to peace and development at both communal and national levels. This work plays a critical role in preventing electoral violence as it was recently observed in Burundi.

Since 1994, Local Peace Committees (PCs) were created by the Mission for Peace and Reconciliation Under the Cross (MIPAREC) to address this societal need. These committees deal with ethnic violence to prevent the recurrence of the past violence and help the society to move on. Burundi is not the only country where PCs have been used for this same purpose. In Kenya, it was found that during the post-electoral violence of 2007 where over 1000 people were killed, districts that had PCs experienced less violence in comparison to other districts.[1] This further emphasized the importance of building local peacebuilding capacities before violence erupts. In the case of South Africa, PCs were formed in 1992–1994 to facilitate the transition from apartheid to a democratic regime. Regarding Burundi, there are over 400 PC initiatives. PCs are considered as a model of grassroots

1. Wachira et al., *Citizens in Action*.

organization initiated by and made up of volunteers from diverse social and ethnic groups of Burundi, namely Hutu, Tutsi and Twa, displaced persons, demobilized soldiers, freed political prisoners, residents and traditional chiefs. These people are either victims or survivors of violence, or interested community members passionate about building peaceful environments in their communities. They are guided by shared community values, and committed to peaceful coexistence in their localities through dialogue, reconciliation, healing of memories, unity, peaceful management of conflicts, mediation, solidarity, mutual assistance, early warning responses, promotion of gender, and reconstruction.

Ethnic Violence Before the Coming of Democracy in Burundi

The population of Burundi is divided between Hutu, Tutsi and Twa. Since attaining independence from Belgium in 1962, many episodes of ethnic violence took place between Hutu and Tutsi. For example, the insurrection of 1972 resulted in the death of between 2000 and 3000 Tutsis. The consequence was the massacre of between 1,000,000 to 200,000 Hutus In 1988 as many as 500 Tutsi and 20,000 Hutu died in ethnic violence. In 1993, the first Hutu president, Melchior Ndadaye, was elected. After 100 days in office he was murdered by Tutsi army. Subsequently, the war broke out. Between 1993 and 2005 more than 300,000 Tutsi, Hutu and Twa perished. According to Gahungu Peace Committee member in Kibimba, "People were killed not because of what they did but because of who they were." The violence resulted in widespread mistrust and a sense of insecurity with Hutu feeling unsafe in the face of Tutsi and vice-versa. To end the violence, the Arusha peace agreement was signed on August 28, 2000. Parties to the conflict agreed to share power in a democratic process between Hutu and Tutsi but also to two presidential term limits. Elected on the basis of this agreement in 2005 and the constitution crafted thereafter, the government of President Pierre Nkurunziza fostered levels of stability never experienced in the landlocked country for many years. However, this stability was short lived due to a controversial third term for President Nkurunziza in 2015 which became a bone of contention.

Understanding the Election-Related Violence of 2015–2016

In 1993, the first liberal democratic elections were held and led to the election of President Melchior Ndadaye. It was hoped that the advent of democracy would put an end to the long history of violence which characterized the country since independence. But like in many countries in the Great Lakes region of Africa, principles of democracy have been largely overlooked. This has given way to election-related violence. The price paid by civilians is very high. The killing of the first Hutu President plunged the country into a vicious civil war. Hutu extremists massacred thousands of Tutsi civilians. The Tutsi-dominated army responded by killing hundreds of thousands of Hutu civilians. Years of instability followed until 1996, when President Pierre Buyoya, a Tusti, took power for the second time through a coup d'Etat. In August 2000, a peace-deal, agreed to by all but two of Burundi's political groups including the *Front National de Liberation* (FNL), laid out a timetable for the restoration of peace and democracy. After several more years, a cease-fire was signed in 2003 between Buyoya's government and the largest Hutu rebel group—*Conseil National pour la Démocratie et le Développement-Front pour la Défense de la Démocratie* (CNDD-FDD), the current ruling party. In 2005, another Hutu rebel group, the Front for National Liberation (FNL), finally agreed to lay down arms. Elections held in 2005 brought into power the populist government of the CNDD-FDD under the leadership of Pierre Nkurunziza.

While the absence of examples where democracy go to war with each other has become one of the key selling points of democracy in modern days, democracies are going to war with themselves. Burundi is a typical example. Since President Pierre Nkurunziza announced his bid for a third term in 2015 Burundi went to war with itself.

President Nkurunziza was first democratically elected by the parliament (indirect vote) in 2005. In 2010, he was re-elected for the second term by universal direct suffrage. After his two terms in office, the nation looked forward to the first ever peaceful hand over from an elected president to another. This golden opportunity and historical moment was missed. Instead of preparing for a peaceful transfer of power, the first signs of violence began to take place a few years before the end of the second and final term which was due to end in 2015. As is common in the Great Lakes region when political violence is to come, in August 2014, a dozen bodies were found floating in the River Rweru shared between Rwanda and Burundi. Both governments rejected the responsibility for the killings. The hope for a peaceful regime change began to fade away and the fear of being hunted by the past began once again.

On May 5, 2015, six of the seven Judges of the Constitutional Court of Burundi decided that the incumbent President Nkurunziza, could run for a third term through direct universal suffrage. The decision of the High Court was not unanimous. Judges who objected were threatened. For example, fearing for his life Mr Sylvère Nimpagaritse, the Vice-President of the Constitutional Court who opposed the decision of the Constitutional Court sought refuge in Rwanda. For those who supported the decision, the first term was 'a special one' because the President was elected by the Parliament. The bone of contention was the interpretation of the Article 302 of the constitution. It stipulates: "As an exception, the first President of the Country in the post-transition phase is elected by a majority of two thirds of the National Assembly and Senate members sitting together."[2]

The decision by the Constitutional Court strengthened the government position to stay in power beyond the two term limits. Using Article 302 of the constitution as evidence, the government argued that during the first election in 2005, the President was elected indirectly by the Parliament and not by direct universal suffrage required by the Constitution in Article 96. This Article provides that "The President of the Republic is elected by universal direct suffrage for a mandate of a five-year mandate renewable once."[3]

The opposition contended that the third term for the current President was a violation of Article 96 of the Constitution and the 2000 Arusha Peace Agreement. Unlike the Constitution, the Arusha Agreement clearly limits the Presidential terms to two and does not offer any special term. This conflict in the interpretation of the Constitution became a loophole which later led to political violence. I agree with Acemoglu and Robinson that "weak or ineffective institutions perpetuate a system doomed to fail." This is true not only for Burundi but also the Democratic Republic of Congo and many other countries in the Great Lakes region of Africa.

As anticipated, a new deadly violent conflict broke out in May 2015 after President Nkurunziza was elected for a controversial third term. Unlike the previous conflicts, the levels of violence have been far less than might have been expected. Between May 2015 and May 2016, the United Nations (UN) reported that 1133 people were killed from both Hutu and Tutsi ethnic groups. Among those killed there were 999 members of the opposition, civil society and civilians opposed to the third term as well as other

2. Author's translation.

3. Author's translation.

innocent people and 134 police and civilians supporting the government. In addition to the killings, in the same period 250,000 people were displaced. Above indicators show that the ethnic factor does not seem to be strong. This is a major shift because historically all major conflicts, including the post-1993 elections in Burundi had a strong ethnic dimension. A number of factors explain this small number of victims and limited ethnicity factor. Among them, the role played by peace committees long before the violence broke out and during the ongoing conflict.

Peace Committees in Burundi

Peace Committees (PCs) in Burundi are local initiatives born out of the first peace efforts launched in 1994 in Kibimba Commune by Rev. David Niyonzima, then Legal Representative of Quakers church. The initiative received a boost with the involvement of Susan Seitz from the United States of America. Susan was a nurse by profession who came to Kibimba during the height of violence following the killings of President Ndadaye. During the course of her work at Kibimba hospital, she facilitated the process of bringing all parties to the conflict in Kibimba Commune around the table. Her peace initiative received the support of Mathias Ndimurwanko, then Head of the Camp of displaced persons made up of Tutsi. The idea was also welcomed by other community leaders including those from Quakers Church, such as Rev. David Niyonzima, Aloys Ningabira, Domitien Sabongerwa and Rev Elie Nahimana. Interestingly, the peace initiative also received the support of local military Commander, Oscar Nimpagaritse, nicknamed later "Mahoro" (meaning peace) due to his peacebuilding efforts.

The reason to work for peace in Kibimba was due to the need to reconcile Hutu and Tutsi communities and to create an environment where these different ethnic groups could live together in peace and harmony. This was at the time when Hutu lived in bush as internally displaced persons (IDPs) some under the protection of Hutu militia, and Tutsi lived in displaced camps guarded by Tutsi army. According to MIPAREC the following situation prevailed:

> During the time when Tutsi lived in displaced camps in Gitega, no Hutu was considered innocent. Local or foreign from the community, every Hutu was meant to be killed. Many killings took place even in broad daylight and in the presence of public with the army as accomplice. During the same period, Tutsi who went to the field to get some food suffered the same fate.[4]

4. MIPAREC, "Report of Peace Committees," 14.

For a start, access to either Tutsi or Hutu used to be facilitated by peace activists from the same ethnic group. A meeting of the above leaders and representatives of Hutu and Tutsi communities took place out of which they decided to create a community forum for peace on December 6, 1994. The process was filled with mistrust and it took too many rounds of informal negotiations to reach a point of bringing the leaders together. The forum born out of this process was named "Kibimba Peace Committee." Thus, "the centre of Kibimba became a place of refuge instead of a place of chaos."[5]

Elsewhere while mourning his murdered son, the father of President Ndadaye stood for peace and opposed any form of revenge and violence. Upon hearing that his son was killed, Ndadaye Senior told communities in Nyabihanga, the birthplace of President Ndadaye, that "Revenge has never been a way which leads to peace but forgiveness has always been. That way [violence] was not the best support he needed to counsel him or honour his son and his family. The population should refrain from shedding more blood because [the blood] of his son was enough."[6] Subsequent to his advice, the population in Nyabihanga locality always sought peaceful ways of dealing with conflicts between Hutu and Tutsi. Instead of mobilizing for violence, villagers chose to mobilize for peace. These peacemakers managed to advocate against divisive ideologies which led to conflict in other parts of the country. Sindimwo, member of the PC in Nyabihanga, said that "the population of that zone remained united though there were serious provocations coming from the army and Tutsi visiting the village from elsewhere."[7] Ultimately peacemakers created the Nyabihanga Peace Committee.

There are 400 PCs spread across the country, established between 1994–2015 in 11 provinces out of 16 in the country and supported by MIPAREC. By 2015, a sample of 12 PCs has more than 8000 members from different ethnic groups. Participants themselves form a Steering Committee of 12 to 18 members elected democratically for a period varying between 3 to 5 years. Gender is taken into consideration in forming the leadership team. They are also registered by the government as local peacebuilding and development initiatives. They hold regular meetings where they discuss about the situation prevailing in local communities; continue reconciliation efforts and other peacebuilding and development efforts. Members are provided with basic training lasting up to five days on conflict analysis, conflict transformation and non-violence. The curriculum is called "*Ntazibana Zidakubitana Amahembe*" meaning *knocking*

5. Nakuwundi, "Healing in Burundi," 124.

6. Ndadaye Senior, MIPAREC, "Report of Peace Committees."

7. Sindimwo, MIPAREC, "Report of Peace Committees."

horns. Both the training and the diversity within PCs contribute to transformation within the group. Such transformation goes beyond the group and brings change in the communities. After training and before starting reconciliation sessions, issues of violence and conflict affecting communities are identified. Subsequently, reconciliation sessions are launched. Reconciliation meetings result in many cases of storytelling over killings and destruction of property, forgiveness with the aim of reaching reconciliation and preventing the repetition of violence.

PCs have resolved many conflicts. From 2005 to 2015, the following PCs have resolved 711 conflicts mainly between Hutu and Tutsi: Kayogoro, Makamba, Nyaza-Lac, Itaba, Butanganzwa, Butezi, Ruyigi, Gitega, Nyabihanga, Mutaho, Rutegama and Shombo. Conflicts resolved were killings, land disputes, family disputes and witchcraft issues.

Table 9.1: Number of conflicts resolved between 2005 and 2015 by eleven PCs[8]

Number of peace committees	Total of conflicts dealt by the peace committees	Conflicts resolved	Conflicts partly resolved	Pending conflict or being dealt with	Unresolved conflicts
11	711	337	109	195	70

Discussions and Trainings

PCs in Burundi were initiated in 1994 to deal with the ethnic violence between Hutu and Tutsi, and to prevent the recurrence of such violence which disfigured the face of communities and the country. Toward this end, PCs employ many approaches of conflict transformation and violence prevention. Generally, the process starts with training by using the "*Ntazibana zidakubitana Amahembe*" curriculum. This training on nonviolence, conflict transformation and reconciliation plays an important role as the first step toward reconciliation. Among other reasons, training brings participants from different ethnic groups and backgrounds. The experience from Makamba shows that one of their trainings included not only Hutu and Tutsi, but also administrators, local chiefs and soldiers. Because of diversity and safety which the forum offers, different perspectives,

8. MIPAREC, "Report of Peace Committees."

which could not be shared in other settings, are heard, as the respondent from Shombo said. The fact that participants share their perspectives, they are able to learn from one another. Such an opportunity could hardly be found in other settings because of the high level of mistrust between Hutu and Tutsi during the time of conflict.

Training became a breeding ground for PCs, another starting point for the journey to reconciliation for many. The beginning of these trainings presented some challenges. The experience of the 12 participants from Ruhororo shows that the process of conflict transformation is complex and the 'road' is not smooth. During the war, on their way to the training from their village, Hutu and Tutsi participants from Ruhororo did not trust each other. Consequently, they could not share seats on the same bus. Change came about on the third and last day of the training. As trust grew, they decided to form a PC in their village. When the 2015 electoral violence broke out in Burundi, Ruhororo youth did not join armed groups. PC in Ruhororo mobilized young people and shielded them away by involving them in peace-related activities which were already ongoing. Thus, peacebuilding activities played a useful role in preventing electoral violence in that community. This experience demonstrates that even the most destructive relations can be turned into constructive relationships. The first step is to build trust.

With the establishment of PCs comes an opportunity for reconciliation sessions. Between 2005 and 2015, 11 PCs addressed 156 violent conflicts. Some conflicts involved heinous acts of violence. Two of these cases failed as presented in Table I (above). Failure was partly due to unhealed psychological wounds and lack of trust. Healing is central to peacebuilding and breaking the cycle of violence. A lot of work goes into preparation of reconciliation sessions, including individual counseling and home visitation by members of PCs in order to create friendships and to build trust before starting the process. A transformed nation is aware that "if you do not share your healing with the wounded, the wounded will share their wounds with you." As a matter of fact, people move from being instruments of violence to being instruments of violence prevention.

Reconciliation contributes to change not only at personal level but also at community and national levels. Examples abound. The introduction of PCs in Burundian schools affected by ethnic conflicts also added value to violence prevention. At Marumane Primary School in Rutegama, for example, Hutu and Tutsi children are able to play together. Upon seeing the change, parents also became peacemakers in the community. Elsewhere in Gitega, victims (Tutsi) visited offenders (Hutu) in Gitega prison. This had far reaching implications for prevention of revenge. Although initially offenders refused the meeting, through advocacy, they finally accepted to welcome their accusers. When victims arrived with food, offenders refused to eat it because they suspected it was poisoned. Because victims forgave them, some of them were released. After their release, they gave up on revenge.

The change also affected soldiers. During armed conflicts, soldiers and their military bases played a critical role in escalating ethnic violence. Through training on peacemaking, some soldiers were transformed. For example, in Kabungere, transformed soldiers became forces for peace. Through advocacy, some military bases were relocated or transformed. For example, when a Tutsi soldier raped a Hutu girl, a PC in Nyarurambi successfully advocated for the removal of the military base from the community. The administrator's intervention led to the relocation of the military base.

Change came by other means as well. Members of PCs spread the message through successful storytelling, sports events, inter-ethnic marriages, and by turning destructive expressions into jokes. For example, "You hid me that you hate me and I also hid you that I know it." While this expression during the war was used to prepare for revenge and killings, it was turned into a joke for peace. Another example, referring to someone as Hutu or Tutsi does not hurt people like it did before. Unlike in Rwanda were people are not allowed to talk about ethnicity, in Burundi people openly talk about it. Such expressions were used to cause ethnic violence during war time but over the time became harmless. Besides, many people were reconciled through income-generating activities. For example, reconciliation between Hutu and Tutsi women happened through the production of mats in Kibimba, the birthplace of PCs. Reconciliation was also promoted via community development, as seen in the building of houses for victims. It is true that the significance of reconciliation "is not only an end of violence or conflict, but also the construction of a new relationship among parties."[9] In many communities across the country favorable conditions for the reintegration of various social groups were created because of reconciliation.

The work of PCs does not only focus on Hutu-Tutsi ethnic conflict. It also deals with other issues, such as land disputes. For example, in Makamba and Nyanza-Lac, PCs mediated over multiple layers of land disputes between Hutu, Tutsi and Twa. Niyonzima is right in saying that "in restoring relationships the whole village must be involved."[10] The strength of these approaches rests in the involvement of people from different backgrounds including ex-combatants. Women in particular play a critical role. They

9. Lederach, *Building Peace*, 51.

10. Niyonzima, "Healing, Forgiveness and Reconciliation," 123.

provide leadership on truth, justice and love. Love is especially important, because "not loving is hating and hating is killing."

From Kibimba in 1994, PCs spread to 11 out of the 16 provinces of the country. Change brought about by PCs reached the national level. Through this national network, they set up an early warning system. The system was particularly very useful when election-related violence broke out in 2015. For example, in 2015, Ntakirutimana prevented ethnic killings in his Gitega community by using rumor control mechanism. He dispelled rumors that there was a Hutu businessman who hide machetes in his store in order to kill Tutsi. After investigation by Gitega PC, the information was found to be false. Thus, many lives were spared. The work of PCs to collect security information helps people to stay safe by avoiding dangerous areas and acting before violence erupts.

Members of PCs vow "*plus jamais* ça" (*never again*) should ethnic violence consume the Burundian society. The conclusion by Hoffman is true for Burundi: "The capacity that the country has acquired can help measure the successful conflict prevention of the country."[11] Since election-related violence broke out in 2015, the levels of violence are far less than they would have been expected, and the ethnic factor is weak despite calls from political leaders for people to see the conflict as an ethnic one. Now, conflict is relatively obvious and separation between Hutu or Tutsi and the problem is clear than before. As Rwasa, a former Hutu rebel leader, argues, the problem today is not ethnicity but rather a political one.[12] This change did not come overnight or by itself. PCs played an important role in transforming destructive ethnic relationships long before the violence broke out. This drew the attention of members of Parliament. In 2015, PCs in Burundi shared their experiences with members of the Burundian Parliament.[13] As Regina, PC member from Ruyigi once said: "During our meeting, members of Parliament wondered, how did you do it? This was because they were amazed by the transformation brought about by Peace Committees' work across the land." According to Juvenal, a PC member from Ruyigi also, how it happens is that "when I get peace in my heart after reconciliation, I share with people from my ethnic group. The victim also does the same." Sinza, another PC member from Ruyigi, provided the following example, "at school, children from reconciled people play together and seat together." Playing together and seating together is better for electoral violence prevention.

11. Hoffman, *Methods for Evaluating Conflict Prevention.*

12. Jeune Afrique, "Burundi: Rwasa ou l'art de la survie."

13. Four recorded personal comments.

Conclusion

There are currently 400 PCs modeled by MIPAREC in Burundi. They aim to transform conflict and prevent the recurrence of ethnic violence. With this role, they have directly and indirectly contributed to preventing ethnic-related killings in the wake of the current conflict caused by the controversial third term of President Nkurunziza in 2015. Experience shows that PCs have successfully resolved many ethnic-related cases they dealt with between 1994 and 2015, and transformed many destructive relationships between Hutu and Tutsi. Mobilized around the message of "*plus jamais* ça," they have also promoted peace in numerous communities through various strategies, including reconciliation sessions and income generating activities, community development projects, and advocacy. While not being the only key factor, this effort has contributed to the prevention of electoral violence. Hence, compared to 1993 post-election violence, the levels of killings were less in 2015 electoral-related violence and surprisingly lower than in all past major ethnic conflicts in the post-independence history of Burundi.

Bibliography

Hoffman, Evan. *Methods for Evaluating Conflict Prevention*. Metchosin, BC: The Canadian Institute of Applied Negotiations, 2014.

Jeune Afrique. "Burundi: Rwasa ou l'art de la survie." http://www.jeuneafrique.com/mag/296311/politique/burundi-rwasa-lart-de-survie/

Lederach, John Paul. *Building Peace: Sustainable Reconciliation in Divided Societies*. Washington, DC: United States Institute of Peace Press, 1997.

MIPAREC. "Report of Peace Committees." Paper presented at Great Lakes Peacebuilding Institute (GLPI), Gitega, Burundi, 2015.

Nakuwundi, Philippe. "Healing in Burundi." In *Seeking Peace in Africa: Stories from African Peacemakers*, edited by Donald Miller et al., 124–27. Geneva: Cascadia, 2007.

Niyonzima, David. "Healing, Forgiveness and Reconciliation." In *Seeking Peace in Africa: Stories from African Peacemakers*, edited by D. E. Miller et al., 115–23. Geneva: Cascadia, 2007.

Wachira, George et al. *Citizens in Action: Making Peace in the Post-election Crisis in Kenya—2008*. Nairobi: Nairobi Peace Initiative-Africa, 2010.

10

Are We Serving Victims Well?

Considerations on Victim Engagement in Current Restorative Justice Movement Trends

TED LEWIS AND MARK UMBREIT

AS THE RESTORATIVE JUSTICE movement has grown in the North American context over the past four decades, a perennial question continues to surface for both practitioners and stakeholders: Are victim-survivors of crimes and harms being served as well as possible? At the midpoint of this timeframe, in the late 1990s, Howard Zehr and a team of others were prompted to conduct "The Listening Project" to assess how victims were being engaged in the United States through restorative practices. Having already heard some major critiques from victim service workers, the project specifically tuned into those representatives in the criminal justice world to hear first-hand how restorative justice was both perceived and implemented with respect to victim engagement. After an initial phase of interviewing 120 victims and victim advocates, a 2-day meeting allowed victims and victim service personnel to name primary areas of concern.

> Overall, participant victims expressed feelings of injustice, disrespect, exclusion, lack of empathy, and irrelevance as a result of the restorative justice process. There was a sense that although victim input and collaboration are touted as central to restorative justice practices, the voices of victims were not heard during the process.[1]

1. Mika et al., "A Listening Project."

This qualitative research project confirmed initial speculations that restorative justice practices, after two decades of growth, had migrated toward *offender-centric services*, even when the language of victim-orientation or victim-centeredness was present in program literature. According to the authors of this study, the critiques can be summarized as follows:

- **Lack of Inclusion:** restorative justice programs were being implemented without consulting victim service agencies
- **Lack of Supports:** programs had more 'talk' than 'walk' regarding actual supports and follow-ups for victims
- **Lack of Sensitivity:** language in initial communications to victims lacked sensitivity to the needs and empowerment of victims
- **Lack of Flexibility:** dialogue models and services were too limited to constructively serve all referred victims

New recommendations to address these deficiencies included a 10-task action plan that promised more responsiveness to the needs of victims and the concerns of victim advocates.[2] Associated with this plan was the "10 Signposts for Victim Involvement" which are posted at the end of this article. These signposts serve to counterbalance the potential neglect of inclusion, supports, sensitivity, etc., stressing, as worded in the eighth signpost, how "victim opportunities for involvement are maximized."[3]

Canadian studies have also shown how these same trends have not been unique to the United States, revealing inadequate preparation for victims, pressures for victims to be involved, and insensitivity regarding the timing of a victim's involvement.[4] Arlene Gaudreault has described restorative justice as a "disaggregated model" which manifests itself with considerable inconsistency.[5] Consequently, services which have been extended to victims are often difficult to evaluate, given the unevenness of casework. "Despite the high level of satisfaction among victims indicated by the research, particularly studies that focused on mediation, we have to be cautious still and refrain from overstating the benefits of restorative justice."[6] Gaudreault raises an important question. If there are major limits in restorative justice programming that fail to serve victims well, and perhaps even do occasional harm to them, how are we to understand the substantial documentation of high rates of satisfaction

2. Mika et al., "Listening to Victims," 32–38.
3. Zehr and Achilles, "Victim Advocate."
4. Wemmers and Canuto, "Victims' Experiences."
5. Gaudreault, *Limits of Restorative Justice.*
6. Gaudreault, *Limits of Restorative Justice.*

among victims who go through restorative dialogue processes? Several studies by Mark Umbreit have shown that more than 90% of victims in victim offender mediation or conferencing expressed satisfaction with the process of meeting the offender, and would do it again.[7]

One way to understand this tension is to identify how victim satisfaction may in fact be directly related to factors involving best practices that take victim sensitivity and preparation very seriously. There is no major contradiction between the negative critiques mentioned above and the positive outcomes for victims who participated in programs that were sensitive to the needs of victims. Most of the studies conducted by Umbreit and colleagues have evaluated victim offender mediation programs which implemented best practices; today, many of these practices would be referred to as *trauma-informed restorative practices*, emphasizing the priority of victim safety, victim choice to voluntarily agree to participate or exit at any time, and in-person preparation before face-to-face meetings with the offenders.[8] It appears that the primary failures of restorative justice with respect to victim engagement is voiced by the many victims and victim advocates who were *not* included and empowered in potential processes.

But even when this seeming contradiction can be reframed in a way that makes good sense, the anecdotal evidence of North American restorative justice programming, in our current times, persists in showing how victim engagement is lagging in tragic ways. Here are three examples that I (Ted Lewis) became aware of in 2016. An urban restorative justice program for youth offenders that once invited victims to participate in dialogue, has now dropped victim contacts from routine procedures because it is too time-costly. A restorative conference program, after years of operation, assessed victim participation to fall under 25%, and stakeholders were not able to identify the factors that sustained low participation. A mediation-based program was inviting victims to joint dialogue meetings with minimal preparation, and after mediation meetings with offending parties (which included written reparation agreements), no communications were maintained with victim parties after the dialogue sessions. And so, two decades since the Listening Project was documented, the perennial question continues to ring loudly in restorative programs that appear to be offender-centric: Are we serving victims of crimes and harms as well as possible?

While the Listening Project provided a necessary bellwether to reveal the state of victim engagement in the year 2000, we are now at a similar juncture

7. Umbreit and Bradshaw, "Victim Satisfaction"; Umbreit et al., "The Impact of Victim Offender Mediation."

8. Umbreit and Bradshaw, "Victim Satisfaction"; Umbreit et al., "The Impact of Victim Offender Mediation"; Umbreit and Armour, "Restorative justice and dialogue."

point to assess the state of the restorative justice movement. Indeed, *movement theory* itself is having a new impact on how leaders and practitioners in restorative justice are defining and even redefining the core foundations and practices. Issues of race, social conditions, trauma, historical harm, and community systems are taking center stage in the restorative world. As the Introduction to this book indicates, the movement is shifting from restorative justice as *social service* to restorative justice as an agent of *social transformation*. Are we about helping clients or are we about social change?

What this means is that the older chronic challenge of serving victims (within a programmatic context) is now overlaid with a wider set of questions that stem from viewing restorative justice as a transformative movement. These questions can certainly be welcomed, as change in the realm of ideas can spur positive growth in the realm of application. But there are also new challenges in our current scene which, when discussed in conjunction with the classic failure to serve victims well, lead us to echo our primary question: Are we serving victims of crimes and harms as well as possible?

Meanwhile, broader applications far beyond the realm of criminal justice are informing new conceptions of restorative justice. This is certainly seen in models that focus on prevention and community-building, hence the popular growth of circle processes in nearly all realms of restorative work. In short, the shift from simply helping 'clients' in need to promoting large-scale transformation in society is raising new opportunities as well as new challenges. This is in addition to the long-standing challenge presented by the dominant offender-centric programming throughout North America. The remainder of this paper will explore what those opportunities and challenges are with respect to victim engagement.

New Shifts and New Questions

While the restorative justice movement is itself a major paradigmatic shift away from conventional Euro-based forms of addressing conflicts and crimes, there are a number of smaller or sub-paradigmatic shifts that can be observed within the more recent evolution of the restorative movement. In other words (to extend the classic example of shifting paradigms), the Copernican revolution has already been set in motion to offset the Earth-centered view of the world, but in the wake of this revolution, other smaller shifts continue to unfold in more recent years. Here are several that can be identified.

1. Shift from addressing incidents to addressing environments. Fields of conflict transformation and community development have widened the scope of restorative work to address root-causes and sustainable solutions in order to effectively *prevent* future harms and crimes. The hybriding of restorative justice and the field of social work is one example which shows this greater attention to broader social conditions.

2. Shift from helping individuals to helping communities. As a restorative view of crime (and the resolution of crime) has highlighted *webs of relationality*, restorative processes have engaged larger circles of participants who play vital roles in sustaining positive outcomes. The rise of "community justice" in neighborhood contexts is one expression of this. Indigenous concepts such as *ubuntu* from the Zulu tradition serve to sharpen this vision. Restorative models have been designed to help entire communities impacted by oppression or violence.

3. Shift from criminal realm to all realms of human relationships. Widening applications of restorative practices in prisons, schools, workplaces, faith communities, race relations, etc., along with restorative forums and networks for addressing community concerns have all demonstrated that *justice* applies to *the righting of all relationships in all realms of human interaction.*

4. Shift from intervention response to interventions *and* prevention. Concerns for healthy communities and relational networks have expanded dialogue models into the realms of prevention and community-building. Intervention models themselves have been increasingly recognized as having preventative merit; at the same time, these models are critiqued when they fail to address root causes and holistic reintegration. Restorative work in prisons and re-entry, for example, combines healing work with prevention of future harms.

5. Shift from mediation-based models to circle-based models. Circle processes, moving easily between prevention and intervention contexts, have demonstrated an adaptive capacity to promote the values associated with social environment, community, relationships, and prevention. They also teach skills that allow participants to replicate the model in other life settings. At the same time, mediation and conference models have been recognized for their own distinctive strengths which compensate for the limits of circle processes.

6. Shift from the 'narrow present' to the 'deep past.' Increased awareness regarding trauma issues and historical harm have revised ways in which offenders are held accountable and victims are supported. This includes the recognition of victimization in the lives (and ancestral histories) of offending people, and thus the need for healing. Customized models for addressing sexual assaults and domestic violence also include depth-work. Trans-generational trauma initiatives are opening doors for whole communities to address historical harms and to seek reparations.

7. Shift from professional partnership to people-empowerment. Restorative practitioners, while promoting client-empowerment from the earliest years of practice, have largely depended upon strong partnerships with professionals in government positions. With greater supports to empower the people most involved, reliance (and even trust) in professional institutions has diminished. Restorative stakeholders, especially among people of color, are finding new ways to empower prevention and intervention work that is increasingly dependent on community-based and grassroots efforts.

8. Shift from limited victim identities to broad victim identities. Whereas restorative language initially reserved victim identification with people who were deemed 'victims' in a criminal case referral, victimization language now covers everyone in any harming situation, including offenders, as having either backstories of traumatic victimization or direct impacts from a particular incident. This can extend through an entire community of people who may share a common legacy of historical harm. New efforts include the earth's natural environment as being victimized by human activities.

Altogether, these eight shifts within the past couple of decades in the restorative justice movement demonstrate healthy growth and expansion. It goes without saying that they all share an *intersectionality* whereby they cannot be separated out from each other. At the broadest level, they indicate the larger shift from restorative justice as programming for individuals to restorative justice as a comprehensive framework for addressing any and all levels of harm and conflict in communal settings. At the same time, these shifts demonstrate that the primary work of restorative justice has not been co-opted by the main justice system. Indeed, the very expansion of restorative work beyond the realm of criminal justice has allowed the movement to maintain a high degree of autonomy from institutional systems of justice, social work and education. But even with this growing autonomy, major sectors of the restorative justice movement are integrating these very systems with ancient wisdom and community ownership.

The Language of Labeling Victims

One ongoing trend that coincides with the shift in victim identities involves a *shift in language*. Attention to terminology and its effects has been a defining feature of the movement; from the earliest years on, there have always been lively discussions about the need to replace old language with improved language. For example, the word 'reconciliation' was dropped from most of the original Victim Offender Reconciliation Programs (VORPs) of the 1980s since the concept of reconciliation appeared to be too prescriptive. More recently, the very terms 'victim' and 'offender' have come under scrutiny. For many in today's restorative world, the fact that this article even uses both terms freely is problematic. Not only do these words reflect a carry-over from the old paradigm, but they serve to limit a person's identity in ways that could inhibit their journey toward wholeness. At the same time, practitioners have wrestled over using phrases that are cumbersome for common usage, such as "the one who did the harming" and "the one who was harmed." This topic simply highlights how there is a very real tension that exists between older and newer framings during a time of sub-paradigmatic shifts.

As Carl Stauffer rightly asks, "How do we find a new language that does not restrict us to the criminal legal labels of 'victim' and 'offender' that present an artificial bifurcation and a political polarization between people who are harmed and who have harmed?"[9] Jonathan Stith recognized this same "criminalizing binary 'offender-victim' framework that continues to characterize restorative justice practice within restorative practices in education.[10] Not only does this framing help to perpetuate the school-to-prison pipeline, he notes, but it also serves to maintain greater disparities for students of color. Judge Carol Perry of the Navajo Nation emphasized the interdependent "fluidity of healing for everyone involved" whereby when offenders are working to repair themselves, everyone helping them is able to get better, too.[11] All of these examples break down the dichotomy between harming and harmed persons. We could not agree more on the importance of this shift from traditional western thinking. But we are raising an important question in this context. What are the long-term implications of removing or replacing the term 'victim' for people who have been more severely impacted or traumatized by violent crimes? Will shifts in language eventually strengthen or diminish direct services, say, to

9. Stauffer, "Epilogue," 167 below.

10. Stith, "Bigger Than an RJ Circle," 76 above.

11. Stauffer and Shah, "Introduction," xxiii above.

individuals whose lives have been *impacted* ("un-peaced" according to the Latin root *pac*) by a major crime?

A related challenge to the language we use for harming and harmed persons is the rising attention given to offenders and communities as victimized persons or groups. Again, broadening victimized identities has been a positive development during the past decade. The documentary film *Healing Justice*, for instance, opens the window toward the way incarcerated men and women have a true need to be healed from their own backstories of victimization while taking responsibility for their own harming choices.[12] We call to mind the common adage, "Hurt people hurt people." The deeper question is that as restorative practitioners increasingly innovate language to address these broader dimensions of victimization, (and sometimes with a counterproductive hypersensitivity), how well will those who traditionally have been called 'victims' be served? Will they continue to receive services informed by sensitive best-practices that have stood the test of time over the past four decades? Another way to pose this question is as follows. Will the increasing attention to social transformation and community well-being result in reduced attention or improved attention to restorative services for those who are harmed by conflicts and crimes? This framing, obviously, is not implying that both cannot happen together. Not only can they operate in parallel; they can thrive interdependently. At stake, however, is whether or not recent shifts toward larger, transformative aspects of restorative justice will diminish the traditional commitment of services that are tailored for victims of harm or crime.

Combining New Perspectives with Old Commitments

It is our belief that restorative justice practitioners, while embracing opportunities created by new trends toward transformative and liberatory expressions of restorative justice, need to simultaneously reconnect and recommit to the founding principles of the movement from the last century that were so clearly grounded in serving victims well and inviting their active participation in the justice process through various restorative and community justice initiatives. This statement needs to be qualified within the growing universe of restorative practices. We are mostly voicing our concern within the limited realm of criminal justice in the North American context. More specifically, we are referencing the context of restorative *dialogue-based services* available to both offending and victimized parties. The positive opportunity here, to draw together now both the old and the new, is that the very

12. *Healing Justice*, World Trust film, 2018.

insights gained within the last decade regarding trauma, historical harm, community supports, root causes, and even prevention, can all contribute to a wider, more holistic set of services that are rooted in the original commitment of the restorative justice movement to assist those who have been victimized by acts of violation.

This recommitment to original principles, therefore, needs to be anchored in a deep understanding and use of trauma-informed restorative practices. One of the emerging lessons from restorative dialogue practitioners is that in asking both offending and victimized parties to prepare for the benefits of joint, dyadic conversation with each other, both parties share much in common with each other. Both have experienced a type of disorientation and disempowerment as a result of an impactful incident leading up to an arrest. Life is no longer normal for either of them. Both certainly have distrust on many levels, and in this vulnerability, they naturally have their guards up. Trauma stems from the incident itself, but may very well reverberate more loudly from earlier traumatic experiences. All of this is compounded when someone comes from a community that bears the marks of deeper, historical trauma. The effects of trauma include 1) estrangement/sense of isolation, 2) feelings of powerlessness or helplessness, 3) changes in one's view of oneself and the world, 4) devastating fear, loss of safety or trust, and 5) feelings of shame, blame, guilt and stigma.[13] In brief, by looking through the lens of trauma, restorative services will necessarily become more humane and holistic.

This perspective on the commonalities between victim and offender experiences is already an important step in countering the bifurcation that was noted earlier. A sensitive and holistic engagement of offending and victimized persons, in the effort to help them reclaim aspects of their own humanity and see their common humanity in the other person, will help them both take the calculated risk of restorative dyadic encounter. As both parties meet with facilitators in initial sessions, they also experience a similar invitation to *find strength in going down the path of chosen vulnerability*. All of this has to do with the creation of a safe container in which hard but healing conversations can happen. Core principles of trauma-informed care with victims of crime help to ensure the safety of this space. Elements supporting this include:

- Safety: applying "do no harm" to ensure physical and emotional safety

13. Beyer and Blake, "Trauma-informed Care," PPT slide.

- Trustworthiness: modeling supportive, empathetic, and clear communication
- Choice: prioritizing victim choice and control over participating or exiting
- Collaboration: sharing power with the person who was victimized
- Empowerment: practicing a strength-based perspective rather than focusing on the deficits of a victim survivor[14]

New Recommendations for Victim Engagement

Our guiding question can now be modified: *How* can we serve victims of crime well as we move forward in our North American context? On one hand, new measures need to be taken to counterbalance the offender-centric models of restorative dialogue which are mostly rooted in institutional agencies. This issue, as indicated by the Listening Project, is far too perennial if victim service stakeholders (let alone, actual victims of crime) continue to feel alienated. On the other hand, a set of shifting trends within the restorative justice movement provide new opportunities for growth, but also some challenges with respect to our capacity to serve victim-survivors in the midst of serving victimized offenders and communities. What follows now are some recommendations that can help address both sets of challenges while integrating the learnings of recent trends in the movement. These will be split into two main categories, the first pertaining to victims of crimes, and the second related to other realms of harming and victimization. The latter listing is not meant to be comprehensive but only representative of some areas of wider restorative work.

As Related to Victims of Crime

1. Greater attention to serving victims on their *own* terms, hence:

   - More authentic and sensitive initial communications
   - More flexibility in support and listening services
   - More preparation opportunities that present options
   - More invitation for victims to tell their story in other settings
   - More response to victims of crimes with unidentified offenders

14. Adapted from Beyer and Blake, "Trauma-informed Care," PPT slide.

2. Greater use of *other* victim voices in dialogue processes:

- Victim surrogates (with similar crime experience)
- Victim substitutes (with personal impact story)
- Community members (representing impacted communities)
- Victim-shuttle option (relay of impact statements and reparation requests)
- Use of letters or pre-recorded videos for safer encounter

3. Greater use of multi-method approaches to cases:

- Conference before broader Circle sequence
- Blended Circle-Conference model
- Parallel processes for both victim and offender
- Support Circles for victims only
- Post-process communications and supports

4. Greater collaboration with victim service workers:

- Include them in front-end program design
- Include them in guiding case timing factors
- Integrate their volunteerism with restorative options
- Provide brochures on restorative services
- Invite victim-initiated case opportunities

5. Great attention to conditions and community:

- Effort to address root conditions causing crimes
- Effort to include community members in processes
- Effort to link up victim supports with community resources
- Effort to address secondary-victimization
- Effort to provide meaningful community service

As Related to Other Realms of Harming and Victimization

1. Re: Bullying and Harassment: use of *parallel processes* for serving offending and victimized parties as the default model; inclusion and

empowerment of other people (bystanders, friends, family members, etc.); preparation meetings with facilitators are routine; joint-dialogue can sometimes happen *after* signs of improvement and healing; follow-up plans, as in schools, involve a school staff check-in person who oversees progress.

2. Re: Large-scale Trauma on Communities (such as hate crimes, ethical breaches, sudden critical incidents, deaths, etc.): create a team-approach to map out successive, concentric healing and resolution processes; multi-model approach using both conferencing and circling, moving from smaller groupings to larger groupings; methods for informing wider numbers in the community, including forums; longer-term follow-ups and closure meetings forecasted.
3. Re: Incarcerated Offenders (both prison and jails): provide restorative justice learning and dialogue opportunities in both group and individual settings; use of victim surrogates to participate in prison-based circle meetings; open up capacities with state approvals for safe exchange of communications between offenders and victims of similar or same cases; support offender healing opportunities regarding their back-stories of victimization; ensure continuity of restorative supports from prison to re-entry settings.
4. Communities and Law Enforcement: create frameworks that initially introduce restorative dialogue models for community-building; use pilot groups to build up trust and strengthen relationships, and then broaden participation to include others; find respected stakeholders in both community and police realms to share facilitator roles; when resolving grievances and building peace, major on finding common ground in everyone's experiences.
5. Marginalized or Oppressed Communities: provide restorative dialogue models for people with protective-class status who have experienced discrimination of their human rights; support the intersectionality of human and social experiences, also of incidents and past histories; empower leaders representing these groups to facilitate processes; provide community-building strategies through prevention-based dialogue opportunities as a base for having intervention-ready dialogue.

In closing, the first set of recommendations related to victims of crime add up to a recommitment to the original restorative principles as articulated in the movement's early years and summarized well in the Ten Signposts for Victim Involvement (see below). At the same time these recommendations reflect a wider menu of options that require a flexible and communal approach as informed by more recent trends in the movement. The best of the Old and the best of the New need to hold hands together. Including the second set of recommendations for wider settings of harm and impact simply reinforces the *communal and relational nature of all restorative work*. Restorative justice is *not* primarily a service-based model for bringing victimized and offending parties together in the same room for dialogue. It is, rather, a holistic approach to justice that helps victimized and offending people *move forward in life*, whether or not they come together. In this light, an adaptive and flexible approach to restorative justice can find innovative ways for working with *all* persons who have harmed or been harmed, precisely because there are many other conversation partners who can suitable participate in processes that combine healing and accountability.

A good example of where this broadening impulse can rise forth is in a community's commitment to serve victims of crimes where no offender was arrested or apprehended. Many property crimes, for example, occur in situations where offending parties are never caught. Could not a restorative community create specific services and funding to serve people who were victimized, but whose cases never enter the legal realm because their information simply went no further than a police or sheriff's department? A progressive community would find a way to serve 'offenderless' victims no less than other victims who are 'in' the system.

This same commitment can be applied to victim-survivors of past crimes who truly need greater time in their life journeys before they are ready for healing dialogue. The vast majority of victims of severe and traumatizing crimes will not have opportunity to ever meet with the offending person(s) in their specific case, either by choice or by circumstances that distance the offender from reachability. Again, other conversation partners, such as surrogate victims, surrogate offenders, and caring community members, can all be called upon for post-incident opportunities for deep healing. I (Ted Lewis) had the opportunity to facilitate a nine-month process where two people, independent of their respective histories, requested participation in a restorative conference within one month of each other. One was a perpetrator of rape against a young teen girl; the other was a victim survivor of childhood rape. After eight months of preparation, they came together, each with a support person, for a conference that lasted six hours. They each experienced a therapeutic breakthrough that had not been possible through individual counseling. This is simply one example of how restorative dialogue, with its adaptive qualities, can honor the profound, dyadic opportunity to help people move forward in life.

The main concern of this article, altogether, is for victims who do enter a system of justice, be it traditional or restorative, and are not served as well as they deserve to be served. No doubt, limited people resources among victim service agencies are part of this under-serving pattern. This, in part, was the vacuum in which restorative programming could grow over the years since its beginnings in the modern world. Forty years of restorative justice dialogue work in North America has certainly established that victims who participate in well-prepared and well-guided conversations with offenders indicate high satisfaction in the justice they experience. Nevertheless, the state of offender-centric restorative programming in North America has severely limited both the quantity and quality of services to victims of crime. As practitioners attempt to remedy the nature of these services, the newer challenge will be to keep restorative work for victims toward the center of the radar screen as the movement increasingly broadens its vision toward the transformation of social life and institutions. This balanced approach fits well with what Carl Stauffer and Sonya Shah pointed out in the Introduction to this anthology. The main goal is not to become either a reformer or a revolutionary. "The focus of the restorative justice movement is to hold in tension both interpersonal and institutional change while at the same time moving towards a cultural shift or societal transformation of how justice is understood and practiced for the future."[15] It is in this tension that we will renew our commitment to serving victims of crime as well as possible.

The Ten Signposts of Victim Involvement[16]

We are working toward appropriate victim involvement (in restorative justice) when:

1. Victims and victim advocates are represented on the governing bodies and initial planning committees.
2. Efforts to involve victims originate from a desire to assist in their recovery/reconstruction. Benefits to the offender are not the primary motive of the program for victim involvement. Victims should be free from the burden of rehabilitation or assisting offenders (unless they choose to do so).
3. The safety of the victim is a fundamental element of program design.
4. Victims are presented with clear understandings of their roles, including potential benefits and risks to themselves and offenders.
5. Confidentiality is provided within clear guidelines.
6. Victims are provided as much information as possible about the case, the offense, and the offender.

15. Stauffer and Shah, "Introduction," xxvii above.
16. Zehr and Achilles, "Ten Signposts for Victims Involvement."

7. Victims are able to identify and present their needs, and are provided options and choices.
8. Victim opportunities for involvement are maximized.
9. Program design provides for referrals for additional support and assistance.
10. To the extent possible, program services are made available to victims even when their offender has not been arrested.

Bibliography

Beyer, L. L., and Mary Blake. "Trauma-informed Care: Building Partnerships and Peer Supports in Supportive Housing Settings" [PowerPoint slides]. Presentation at Services in Supportive Housing Annual Grantee Meeting. Washington, DC (2010). http://www.samhsa-ssh-meeting.net/assets/documents/trauma_informed_care.pdf.

Bradshaw, W., and Mark Umbreit. "Assessing Satisfaction with Victim Services: The Development and Use of the Victim Satisfaction with Offender Dialogue Scale." *International Review of Victimology* 10 (2003) 71–83.

Butler, Shakti, producer. *Healing Justice*. World Trust film, 2018.

Gaudreault, Arlène. *The Limits of Restorative Justice*. Proceedings of the Symposium of the École nationale de la magistrature, Paris. Paris: Dalloz, 2005.

Lewis, Ted, and Carl Stuaffer, eds. *Listening to the Movement: Essays on New Growth and New Challenges in Restorative Justice*. Eugene, OR: Cascade Books, 2021.

Mika, Harry, and Mary Achilles, Ellen Halbert, Lorraine Stutzman Amstutz, Howard Zehr. "A Listening Project: Taking Victims and Their Advocates Seriously." Restorative Justice (2001) http://restorativejustice.org/am-site/media/listening-project-final-report.pdf.

Mika, Harry, and Mary Achilles, Ellen Halbert, Lorraine Stutzman Amstutz, Howard Zehr. "Listening to Victims: A Critique of Restorative Justice Policy and Practice in the United States." *Federal Probation* 68/1 (2004) 32–38.

Umbreit, Mark, and W. Bradshaw. "Victim Satisfaction with Juvenile Offender Dialogue: Results from a Four-site Study." *Child and Adolescent Social Work* (2004).

Umbreit, Mark, R. B. Coates, and Betty Vos. "The Impact of Victim Offender Mediation: Three Decades of Practice and Research." *Conflict Resolution Journal* (2004).

Umbreit, Mark S., and Marilyn Peterson Armour. "Restorative Justice and Dialogue: Impact, Opportunities, and Challenges in the Global Community." *Washington University Journal of Law and Policy* 65 (2011).

Wemmers, Jo-Anne, and Marisa Canuto. "Victims' Experiences with Expectations and Perceptions of Restorative Justice: A Critical Review of the Literature." International Centre for Comparative Criminology Université de Montréal. March 2002 rr 2001-9e. Policy Centre for Victim Issues. Research and Statistics Division.

Zehr, Howard, and Mary Achilles. "Victim Advocate for the Commonwealth of Pennsylvania" (1999). Also *OVA Newsletter*, Mary Achilles, *Victim Advocate* 4/1 (2000).

Epilogue

Restorative Justice—A Movement in the Making?

Carl Stauffer

As we come to the close of this anthology, it is not hard to imagine our readers asking a number of urgent questions along the way, like how do we guide, nurture, and grow the restorative justice movement? Or, how do we transform the vision of restorative justice as a movement into reality? In this final section I will offer a few observations about systems change, ask a few practical questions, and describe a few indicators of what a restorative justice movement might look like. As movement makers, we most likely will not have the end goal in mind, but we are called out to continually seek, in the words of Dr. Glenda Eoyang, the "next wise move" in this vital work of justice transformation."

Generally, social movement theory points to a number of critical factors that drive successful social movements. These revolve around the following elements: the readiness to seize *political opportunity*, the ability to *mobilize resources* (both human and material), and the creation of a *framing message* (a social narrative) with populist appeal. Based on these three pillars of measurement it seems that restorative justice could be defined as a burgeoning social movement.

Political Opportunity. The United States, and indeed the world, are in a convulsive political moment in history. The status quo institutions of the modern nation-state, such as justice systems, education, economy, and government, are being contested and deconstructed at the core. Competing movements with deep strains of anti-establishment rhetoric (whether from the right or the left) are calling for radical change. The restorative justice movement and its call to reconfigure our perceptions, relationships, and structures of criminal, social, and cultural justice is stepping into this gap with particular relevance.

Resource Mobilization. For the first time, prominent justice donors are asking questions about long-term resourcing and the systemic impacts of their funding. More than in any other time in history, the restorative justice field is experiencing a burst of energy in new theorizing, research, and legislative policy development across a broad swath of professional disciplines and sectors of practice.

Framing Message. Never before have we seen such a keen interest in restorative justice coming from practitioners, educators, politicians, activists, community organizers, the media, and religious leaders. New applications and the accompanying social narrative discourses are being constructed for whole-schools change, trauma-informed approaches to change, nonviolent mobilization, racial justice advocacy, community organizing and development, environmental policy, and war-to-peace transitions and reconstruction.

All of the above descriptors point us in the direction of a "critical mass" or "tipping point" moment in time where a comprehensive cultural shift is likely to occur.[1] Social transformation at this scale requires that we make a systemic diagnosis of the situation and its context, that we develop social capital networks and structures to enable the continual flow of "feedback loops" for reflective practice, and that we find personal identification and passion for the work to progress unhindered in the future. Quantum physics and the new sciences on emergent adaptive systems (EAS) are helping us understand the dynamics of social movements. Dr. Glenda Eoyang and her work with *Human Systems Dynamics* (HSD)[2] advises all who are looking to undergo, guide, and/or channel effective systems transformation to consider three pivotal elements in the process of change. The following questions comprising the CDE model (Conditions Difference Exchange)[3] can help us chart a way forward to strengthen the restorative justice movement.

1. Gladwell, *The Tipping Point*.
2. Eoyang, *Conditions*.
3. Eoyang, *Conditions*.

1. Reflect on, question, and change the Containers (cultural and structural) that hold the system. ***Sample questions might be:***

- How do we move beyond the punitive worldview so prevalent in our society and guide a critical mass attitudinal shift in the direction of a restorative worldview for the future?
- How do we continue to mobilize the application of restorative justice away from solely being defined by the criminal legal system and instead having impact in every sector of society including governance, business, education, family, religion, media, and the arts and culture with which we all interact?
- How do we imagine a structural vehicle for the expansion and multiplication of restorative justice at a collective societal level that is not constrained by only the nonprofit model of organizational functioning?

2. Reflect on, question, and change the perceived Differences that are being defined and reinforced in the system. ***Sample questions might be:***

- How do we find a new language that does not restrict us to the criminal legal labels of "victim" and "offender" that present an artificial bifurcation and a political polarization between people who are harmed and who have harmed?
- How do we identify, educate and advocate for change where racialized systems of governance, education, and justice have led to mass incarceration and racial disproportionality?
- How do we find ways to build coalitions between the western and non-western (indigenous) understandings of worldview, justice, and even the way we name our practices (restorative justice or peacemaking circles) for the purposes of working for a unified sense of the "common good" in society?

3. Reflect on, question, and change the Exchanges (tangible and intangible reciprocities) that are embedded and taken for granted in the system. ***Sample questions might be:***

- How do communities take back the process of solving and transforming their own social conflicts and harms that have been stolen by the State and its apparatuses of surveillance and control?
- How do we resist the tendency to become dependent on the State for our needs of protection, safety, and security, and instead nurture the informal networks of support that will sustain healthy relationships, healing and well-being?
- How do we break the funding-industrial-complex that insists on short 1 to 3-year project grant cycles which belie sustainability and instead challenge the donor community to support long-term and maximum impact funding mechanisms that consider growth in terms of 5–10 years or decadal thinking—20 years plus?

Eoyang suggests that at the reflective core of any emergent Complex-Adaptive System (CAS) we need to be continually asking ourselves what is the next "wise" move? To do this we need to engage in an iterative, *adaptive action* learning cycle that asks three critical questions presented below in Figure 1: What? So What? Now What?

[**CAP**]**Table 1:** Adaptive Action Model[4][/CAP]

What?	**So What?**	**Now What?**
What are current patterns? What do you observe? What surprises you? What happened before? What are people saying? What is the research? What . . .	So what are the tensions? So what is important? So what options do we have? So what does success look like now? So what . . .	Now what will we do? Now what will we communicate? Now what will we measure? Now what will we look for next? Now what . . .

4. HSD Institute, 2015.

In order for restorative justice as a social movement to aspire to become an authentic, vibrant social *justice* movement, there are at least six distinctive characteristics that would need to be embodied:

1. Integrating the populations most affected by injustice (the harmed and the harm-doers, family connections and community networks), and amplifying their voices and participatory liberation in the process.
2. Resisting widespread, 'quick-fix' and/or politically compromised legislation that can often drive institutional co-option and forced uniformity.
3. Insisting on centering and engaging racial and ethnic justice and healing historical harms of colonization and violent oppression in this country and across the world.
4. Determining to make application to transforming personal, social and structural violence and all intersecting relationships that make up the web of human justice.
5. Committing to de-institutionalization, to decentralized organizational structures, and to "bottom-up" justice expressions and processes.
6. Exemplifying shared and emancipatory leadership models and functions.

Holding all these important elements together in tandem with each other will be essential if restorative justice is to transform into a genuine social justice movement and remain durable and sustainable for the long-term future.

Bibliography

Eoyang, Glenda. "Conditions for Self-Organizing in Human Systems." PhD diss., The Union Institute and University, Cincinnati, OH, 2001. http://www.hsdinstitute.org/resources/cde-model-dissertation.html also, What is HSD? At http://www.hsdinstitute.org/what-is-hsd.html

Gladwell, Malcolm. *The Tipping Point: How Little Things Can Make a Big Difference*. Boston: Little, Brown, 2000.

HSD Institute. 2015. "Adaptive Action." https://www.hsdinstitute.org/resources/adaptive-action.html.

Contributors

(listed in order of writings in this book)

Fania E. Davis, a leading national voice on race and restorative justice, is a lifelong social justice activist, a civil rights trial attorney and author with a PhD in Indigenous Knowledge. The murder of two close childhood friends in the 1963 Birmingham church bombing crystallized within Fania a passionate commitment to social transformation. Co-founder and formerly director of Restorative Justice for Oakland Youth, her numerous honors include the Maloney Award for excellence in Youth Restorative Justice, the Tikkun (Repair the World) Award, the Ella Jo Baker Human Rights Award, and the Ebony POWER 100 award. *The Los Angeles Times* named her a New Civil Rights Leader of the 21st Century. Fania's latest publication is *The Little Book of Race and Restorative Justice: Black Lives, Healing and U.S. Social Transformation.*

Carl Stauffer, PhD, is associate professor of Justice at the Center for Justice & Peacebuilding at Eastern Mennonite University. He also serves as co-director of the Zehr Institute for RJ, and academic director of the Caux Scholars Program in Switzerland. Carl earned his PhD from the University of Kwa-Zulu Natal in South Africa. During his sixteen years there, Carl provided RJ services for the South African Truth and Reconciliation Commission and co-founded two peacebuilding institutes in Zambia and Burundi. He has conducted RJ training and consultation in thirty-seven countries on six continents. Carl's research focuses on RJ as a social movement, and the use of indigenous and community justice practices as alternatives to mainstream transitional justice.

Sonya Shah initiated the Ahimsa Collective in 2016. The Ahimsa Collective works to respond to harm in ways that foster wholeness for everyone. She is also an associate professor at the California Institute of Integral Studies. Central to her core values are nurturing community and collectivity, healing and compassion, love and transforming harm. She is a Buddhist, a first-generation immigrant from the Northwestern part of India, and feels most at home in nature. She has two amazing children who remind her what it means to be in love all of the time and currently resides in northern California.

Rose Elizondo brings healing, relationship building, accountability, and transformation to the restorative justice movement. As an organizer, she informs, inspires, and incubates communities to create alternatives to punitive legal systems by facilitating inquiry into the indigenous roots of justice. As a 2017 Soros Fellow, she revitalized healing practices of peacemaking with Navajo community leaders. In 2005, with men in San Quentin prison, Rose co-founded the Restorative Justice Interfaith Roundtable to practice accountability and responsibility. She co-founded the North Oakland Restorative Justice Council, which supports survivors of crime and implements grassroots community restorative justice. Her intergenerational trauma work with Native and Indigenous communities uses truth, reconciliation and reparations processes. Rose incorporates healing, art, murals, dance, and gardening to envision community values and create cultural shifts.

Jovida Ross, the eldest daughter of a solo mom, has always known that the personal is political. Her hope for change led her to work with groups like The Women's Building of San Francisco and Community United Against Violence. Jovida benefited from multiple healing modalities to work with intergenerational trauma, including restorative justice, yoga, and somatic experiencing; she now teaches yoga. As director of programs at Movement Strategy Center, she co-founded The Transitions Initiative which gathers movement leaders to explore how embodied wisdom can generate untapped possibility, potential, and power in their work toward social, economic, and ecological justice. Jovida now works with Real Food Real Stories, drawing on food and stories as practices for seeding cultures towards a caring, regenerative, and just tomorrow.

Mika Dashman is an attorney, mediator and a zealous advocate for restorative justice. She is the founding director of Restorative Justice Initiative, a citywide, multi-sector network of practitioners, advocates and community members seeking to increase support for, and access to, restorative justice approaches for all New Yorkers. Her restorative justice teachers include: Lauren Abramson, Kay Pranis, Dominic Barter, Eric Butler, Ray Deal, and Sara Whitehorse. Prior to beginning her work in alternative dispute resolution,

Mika spent more than six years providing direct legal services to indigent individuals at several New York City non-profits, including Housing Works, Inc., where she also worked on all aspects of the agency's civil rights impact docket. Mika received her JD from the City University of New York School of Law in 2005 and her BA from Sarah Lawrence College.

David Dean is the Associate Director of White Awake where he has taught racial and economic justice-based political education courses for over 4000 participants. He is passionate about supporting activists to build the powerful, multiracial alliances our social movements need to win. In recent years he has also served as an advocate for restorative discipline in schools and researched truth and reconciliation processes for Restorative Justice for Oakland Youth (RJOY). He is currently writing a book that offers white folks critical understanding about how their ancestors were socialized to become "white" and encourages them to connect to a legacy of cross-racial organizing for the well-being of all. To learn more about his work visit davidbfdean.com.

Mikhail Lyubansky is a teaching associate professor in the Department of Psychology at the University of Illinois, Urbana-Champaign, where among other courses, he teaches Psychology of Race and Ethnicity and courses on restorative justice. Since 2009, Mikhail has been bringing his almost two decades of experience in teaching and writing about racial justice to studying conflict and restorative responses to conflict, especially Restorative Circles, a restorative practice developed in Brazil. In addition to multiple book chapters and peer-reviewed articles, Mikhail is the co-author of *Building a Diaspora: Russian Jews in Israel, Germany, and the USA*, and recently co-edited *Toward a Socially Responsible Psychology for a Global Age*. He also regularly explores racial justice and restorative justice themes in his *Psychology Today* blog *Between the Lines*.

Anna Lemler is a nonprofit manager and racial equity professional with a background in youth development, community organizing, restorative justice, and program and policy design. Anna is currently the Network Manager for the Government Alliance on Race and Equity (GARE), an initiative through Race Forward to advance racial equity utilizing a national network. Previously, Anna worked as the Racial Equity Analyst for Washtenaw County, Michigan, and in leadership with Trail Blazers Camps and iMentor. Anna is a restorative justice practitioner and currently manages the Michigan Juvenile Justice Youth Advisory Board, a group of young people impacted by the criminal justice system to leverage their voices in policy-making. Anna is an organizer with The People's Institute for Survival and Beyond, and earned her MSW from the University of Michigan.

Julie Shackford-Bradley is the co-founder and Coordinator for the Restorative Justice Center at UC Berkeley. She has fifteen years of experience teaching in Global Studies and Peace and Conflict Studies, with a research focus on traditional and community-based justice in international and local contexts. She is a trained mediator and RJ practitioner. With the RJ Center, she conducts trainings and circles on campus and in the local community, supervises research projects regarding campus and community-based issues pertaining to conflict, justice, and reconciliation, and facilitates internship programs and other collaborations with San Francisco Bay Area Restorative Justice organizations. Her specific RJ interests include applications of restorative processes for SVSH (Sexual Violence and Sexual Harassment), equity and inclusion and racial healing.

Katherine (Kat) Culberg (RN, PHN), a Euro-American woman, is a registered nurse who quickly developed a passion for public health and social justice with a focus on urban adolescent girls and boys. She has been active in developing and managing school-based health centers in Oakland as well as providing direct service to youth as a school nurse. After years of feeling that traditional models were limited, she embraced restorative justice work in prisons and jails, which led to a position with Restorative Justice for Oakland Youth as programs director. She is co-founder of Circles for Social Change, an organization that consults, trains, and provides individuals and organizations in restorative justice processes, particularly in relation to racial justice and healing through insight, accountability, and action of other white people.

Jill Strauss, PhD, teaches Conflict Resolution and Communications in the Speech, Communications and Theater Arts Department at Borough of Manhattan Community College (CUNY). Her research involves Restorative Practices and the visual interpretation of narrative and difficult histories. She completed her PhD at Ulster University in Northern Ireland in 2010, where she designed an innovative fieldwork project integrating storytelling and visual art for empathy and validation as one way to address a history of mutual humiliation and historical conflict. Jill is co-editor of *Slavery's Descendants: Shared Legacies of Race and Reconciliation* along with other articles and book chapters.

Daniel Rhodes is director of the undergraduate Social Work program at UNC-Greensboro. He received his PhD in Cultural Studies with a graduate certificate in Women and Gender Studies from the UNC-Greensboro in 2008. Before this, he obtained his master's in Social Work from

UNC-Chapel Hill in 1996 and is a Licensed Clinical Social Worker. Daniel has been engaged in community-based work for over twenty years, working in mental health, therapeutic foster care, working with immigrant and refugee populations, and has been a clinical supervisor. He is trained in Dialectical Behavioral Therapy (DBT), a form of cognitive-behavioral therapy that uses mindfulness to deal with issues related to trauma. Daniel is also a restorative justice practitioner and engages and trains students and communities in Peacemaking Circles.

Kathy Evans is associate professor of Education at Eastern Mennonite University, teaching courses in educational psychology, special education, and restorative justice in education. With a PhD in Educational Psychology from the University of Tennessee, her teaching and scholarship focus on ways in which educators participate in creating more just and equitable educational opportunities for all students, including those with disability labels, those who exhibit challenging behavior, and those who are marginalized for a variety of reasons, including race, ethnicity, language, sexual orientation, and gender identity. She is the co-author of *The Little Book of Restorative Justice in Education* and has published articles and book chapters related to restorative justice and school discipline practices, focusing on the ways in which restorative justice is applied to educational contexts.

Brenda Morrison is Simon Fraser University's director of the Centre for Restorative Justice, and an associate professor in the School of Criminology. She is a social psychologist with teaching, research and field experience in outdoor education, governance, and justice. She completed her PhD at the Australian National University, where she also worked as a post-doc at the Centre for Restorative Justice. Internationally, Brenda has presented papers at the House of Lords and UNESCO. Nationally, she is a research partner with PREVNet (Promoting Relationships Eliminating Violence Network), Children's Rights Academic Network, and serves on the Board of Smart Justice Canada. In British Columbia, she has served on working group summits for a Justice System for the 21st Century. In her home community, she is an active board member for the North Shore Restorative Justice Society.

Dorothy Vaandering, PhD, is an associate professor at the Faculty of Education, Memorial University, Newfoundland, and in Labrador was a K-6 educator for twenty years. She draws on life, teaching, and research experience to explore the implementation and sustainability of restorative justice in education. She works to connect theory and practice in her current role as researcher and teacher-educator developing innovative, transformative professional learning grounded in the principles of restorative justice. Most recently she is gripped by the realities of colonization past and present, working to understand reconciliation as a settler-Canadian. She is the (co) author of a variety of publications including *The Little Book of Restorative Justice in Education*. Dorothy is the director of Relationships First: Restorative Justice Education Research & Resource Consortium in NL.

Jonathan Stith is the national organizer with Black Organizing for Leadership and Dignity (BOLD), where he trains Black organizers in innovative organizing and transformative leadership practices. As former national director of the Alliance for Educational Justice, he led the Alliance's efforts to shift federal education policy away from discriminatory discipline and guided the launch of AEJ's National Police Free School Campaign to challenge police presence after the #AssaultAtSpringValley. He has over twenty years of experience organizing with youth and community organizations for education justice. Jonathan is a father of three children, an avid soccer player, gardener and Cabralista.

Valerie Luna Serrels is a life-learner and listener into those spaces between the visible and invisible. She is the founder and guide of Shenandoah Valley Church of the Wild, co-founder of the Wild Church Network, a graduate of the Earth & Soul—the School for Celtic Consciousness, a spiritual director, and Reiki practitioner. She also works with a touring theater company on projects related to social justice and developing programs that bring together spirituality and the arts. Valerie has a MA in Conflict Transformation and Peacebuilding, specializing in restorative justice, applying this to the human relationship with the Earth and all her creatures. She enjoys books, her cats, the wonder of the outdoors, deep conversations with others, and especially time with her five amazing adult children, grandson, and husband in the Shenandoah Valley of Virginia.

ethan ucker is an organizer, restorative justice practitioner, and popular educator. He has worked extensively in prisons, detention centers, high schools, and group homes across Chicago to hold space for creativity and accountability. Through this work, ethan has built multigenerational webs of responsibility, trust, collaboration, and critique with criminalized young people, elders, formerly incarcerated adults, and with other organizers, youth workers, and educators. He co-organizes alongside those whose privileged identities overlap with his own to devise cooperative strategies to address racial and gender-based harms. ethan is the co-founder of Circles & Ciphers, a restorative justice and prison abolitionist organization led by and for young people of color who are impacted by violence. He is also the co-director of Stick Talk.

Mulanda Jimmy Juma is from the Democratic Republic of Congo. He is a holder of a doctoral degree in Politics, Human Rights and Sustainability from Scuola Superiore Sant'Anna, Italy. He also holds a master's degree in Peace Studies from the University of KwaZulu-Natal, South Africa and another Master in Electoral Policy and Administration from Scuola Superiore Sant'Anna, Italy. Dr Juma is a research fellow, Department of Systematic Theology, University of the Free State, Bloemfontein, South Africa. He is the former coordinator of Peace Studies and senior lecturer in Applied Ethics at St. Augustine College of South Africa, Johannesburg. Currently, Dr. Juma is the country director of the Mennonite Central Committee in the Democratic Republic of Congo and Angola.

Mark Umbreit, PhD, is a professor and founding director of the Center for Restorative Justice & Peacemaking at the University of Minnesota, the first academic-based center for restorative justice. He is an internationally recognized practitioner and scholar with more than forty years of experience as a dialogue facilitator, circle keeper, trainer, teacher, researcher, and author of eleven books and more than two hundred other publications in the fields of restorative justice, peacebuilding, dialogue, spirituality, and forgiveness. Since 1990, Mark has provided consultations and conducted training seminars in 29 twenty-nine countries worldwide, and nearly every state in the U.S. He has been recognized as among the fifty most notable and influential social workers in American history, based on his global impact as a practitioner and scholar.

Ted Lewis is a restorative justice trainer and consultant with the Center for Restorative Justice & Peacemaking, University of Minnesota, which is now based in Duluth. Ted was introduced to restorative justice on Pine Ridge Reservation in the early 1990s through Mennonite Central Committee workers. Since then, he has worked in the fields of restorative justice and conflict resolution as a practitioner, trainer, program manager, director, teacher, writer, and consultant. His area of specialty is designing resources and trainings for Victim Offender Conferencing. He also teaches restorative justice courses at the college level. Since 2004, Ted has led workshops and reconciliation services for faith communities, and recently founded the Restorative Church project and website. Living near Lake Superior, he is continually grateful for the gifts offered by this amazing lake through all seasons of the year.

www.ingramcontent.com/pod-product-compliance
Lightning Source LLC
Chambersburg PA
CBHW030305100426
42812CB00002B/579

* 9 7 8 1 5 3 2 6 4 7 4 2 0 *